D0196823

THE KGB BAR READER

THE
KGB BAR
READER

EDITED BY
KEN FOSTER

QUILL
WILLIAM MORROW
NEW YORK

Copyright © 1998 by Ken Foster

Additional copyright notices appear on pages 319–21, which serve as an
extension of this copyright page.

All rights reserved. No part of this book may be reproduced or utilized in
any form or by any means, electronic or mechanical, including
photocopying, recording, or by any information storage or retrieval system,
without permission in writing from the Publisher. Inquiries should be
addressed to Permissions Department, William Morrow and Company, Inc.,
1350 Avenue of the Americas, New York, N.Y. 10019.

It is the policy of William Morrow and Company, and its imprints and
affiliates, recognizing the importance of preserving what has been written,
to print the books we publish on acid-free paper, and we exert our best
efforts to that end.

Library of Congress Cataloging-in-Publication Data

The KGB bar reader / edited by Ken Foster.—1st ed.
   p.   cm.
  ISBN 0-688-16408-0
  1 American literature—New York (State)—New York. 2. American
literature—20th century. I. Foster, Ken.
PS549.N5K44 1998
810.8'097471'09045—dc21   98-20799
                                    CIP

Printed in the United States of America

First Edition

1 2 3 4 5 6 7 8 9 10

BOOK DESIGN BY SUSAN HOOD

www.williammorrow.com

ACKNOWLEDGMENTS

Thanks to Dirk Standen, Fran Gordon, and Daphne Beal, my partners along the way.

Thanks also to Tom Mallon, Deb Garrison, Alice Quinn, and Lois Rosenthal.

And to the cooperative agents at Brandt and Brandt, Georges Borchardt, the Wylie Agency, International Creative Management, the Virginia Barber Agency, and the Melanie Jackson Agency.

And particularly to Ann Treistman, Sharyn Rosenblum, and Kathleen Cromwell, who suggested an anthology when the speakers blew out.

CONTENTS

INTRODUCTION   *ix*

Jacqueline Woodson FIRE   *1*

Steven Rinehart MAKE ME   *6*

Christine Schutt SICKISH   *21*

Michael Cunningham MISTER BROTHER   *33*

Kathryn Harrison TICK   *38*

Matthew Sharpe A CAR   *47*

Lydia Davis OLD MOTHER AND THE GROUCH   *59*

Elissa Schappell NOVICE BITCH   *70*

Ben Schrank THE GOOD CHANCE CHICKEN   *91*

Sheila Kohler CRACKS   *100*

Lucy Grealy DANCING A SAD THOUGHT 109

Helen Schulman P.S. 120

Ken Foster INDELIBLE 132

Jennifer Egan XO 140

Diane Lefer A GOOD GERMAN 154

A. M. Homes HIS CONFESSION 166

Maggie Estep THE PATIENT 182

Elizabeth Gilbert BUCKLE BUNNIES 188

Jan Meissner PLACEDO JUNCTION 197

Joanna Greenfield HYENA 206

Junot Díaz YSRAEL 220

Tom Paine ME & MICHELANGELO 231

Daphne Beal AZURE 245

Randall Kenan NOW WHY COME THAT IS? 255

David Means TAHORAH 274

Rick Moody DEMONOLOGY 285

Meghan Daum VARIATIONS ON GRIEF 296

Luc Sante THE UNKNOWN SOLDIER 311

CONTRIBUTORS 315

INTRODUCTION

The KGB Bar occupies the second floor of a tenement building at 85 East Fourth Street in Manhattan. A small room with an old wooden bar and red walls covered with Soviet memorabilia, it may have been the meeting place of the Ukrainian Club or a cover for the American Communist party, though the details of its past are a little sketchy—just like everyone else's. Nestled quietly between an Italian restaurant and the New York Theatre Workshop, and across from La Mama's theater complex, the KGB Bar is set off from the world in a way that makes it easy for some people to miss it if they don't know what they're looking for, or if someone has forgotten again to turn on the neon sign at the top of the stairs.

I got lost there myself in the late summer of 1994. New to Manhattan and already disappointed, I saw a flyer on a bulletin board in Columbia University's School of the Arts and stole it so that no one else would see it. The flyer was a copy of an article that had appeared in *The New York Times*, describing a reading that had taken place at a small bar called KGB. Handwritten across the top of the page was a request for a volunteer literary events coordinator. It offered no pay but the opportunity to meet people. I called the number listed and met with founder Denis Woychuk and his KGB partner, novelist Melvin Jules Bukiet. Their mandate was fairly simple: Do whatever you want, as long as it works.

So in October 1994, the original reading series at KGB began with Elizabeth Wurtzel reading from *Prozac Nation* and Lawrence David reading an essay about writing a novel during his stay in a mental hospital. By the following January, Tom Mallon had offered his advice on putting together an evening of fiction from *GQ* and Deb Garrison had agreed to introduce the work of three young writers whose work had appeared in *The New Yorker*. The crowds by this point were already out of control—people sitting on laps, on tables, in the windows, standing in the doorway, on the landing, and down the stairs. "Can we sit out on the fire escape?" somebody asked. (The answer was no.) I had to clear the crowd to pull A. M. Homes to the podium for her first appearance. Looking out at the masses gathered, out at the red walls covered with portraits and photographs of Soviet leaders, A.M. muttered, "I feel like Emma Goldman," as she stood behind the podium, preparing to hush the crowd with her story—without a mike, because the room is just small enough, the budget that small too, and the crowd comes ready to really listen.

What could the appeal be of working on a project like this for free?

I had come to New York reluctantly. I'd been in New Orleans, living off unemployment and accident insurance. In the morning, I'd walk to the Latter Library on St. Charles Avenue and then take the streetcar into the French Quarter with my reading for the day. At night, I went to bed early, because my apartment had no furniture and sometimes no electricity, or sometimes electricity but no light bulbs. Shortly after arriving in New Orleans, I'd read at an open-mike night at Kaldi's and met a group of people who held Sunday evening salons to share stories and ideas, or ideas of stories, most of which would never be written, or at least not yet. I'd had a year of terrible luck, and New Orleans seemed the lowest place I could go—geographically and otherwise; it was impossible to fall any further and I felt safe there. I had applied to graduate schools for writing, but had convinced myself that I wouldn't get in, and if I did, I wasn't going. My Sunday night friends knew better and told me so. Upon learning of my acceptance to Columbia, I was gone as soon as I was able to pack, but skeptically, knowing I could always go back once it seemed there was nothing left to stay for.

New York City seemed easy compared to everything that had come before it. An old teacher vacated a rent-controlled apartment just as I arrived, the city was full of newly opened espresso bars looking for an experienced *barista,* and my student loan required only my signature. But the politics and overcrowded classrooms at Columbia seemed only to reinforce the idea that writers can be nothing other than self-centered and competitive. I'd come to New York to be at the center of things; I was looking for a reason to stay.

Early on, I had made a list of younger writers I admired, writers I was curious about, thinking that if I was interested, other people would be too. I had made the list thinking it would be great if, someday, one or two of them agreed to appear at KGB. To my surprise, when I called them, most agreed to read without my needing to persuade them, and the series quickly moved from being monthly to twice monthly to weekly. They appeared in pairs and trios, on theme nights and nights keyed to particular publications, and on nights of debuts, introducing writers we hadn't previously heard of. One night that first February, when I arrived late and had to fight my way through the overflow crowd that lined the stairs, I remembered suddenly an old article in *Interview* featuring these same writers, photographed holding their books proudly in front of themselves. These were the people I wanted to be.

There are stories around stories. There's a lot you can learn if you listen—to other people's stories, to what concerns them, and how they choose to tell it. And there are stories of alliances formed, of writers discovering something in common, of new talent finding publication, of stories that, remarkably, never found a home and others that did. And a tradition, begun early on by A. M. Homes, of authors arriving to read from a recent publication but surprising the audience and themselves by pulling out something untried and new. There isn't room in this book to include everyone, and many people were eliminated by their publishers' inability to allow their work to be reprinted. Some represent the beginning of a writer's career (both Junot Díaz and Joanna Greenfield met with editors following their KGB readings); other pieces show writers doing the unexpected, writing nonfiction when we expect them to write fiction; only a few of these pieces have been published previously in book form, and many appear in print here for the first time. Each of the pieces gathered here stuck in my memory long after I'd heard it read. So this is the essence of four years at KGB, distilled on the page.

What have I learned through all this listening? That writing is an act of curiosity, of generosity, rather than one of selfishness. That, contrary to what we've been taught, there may be just one universal story: Someone loses something. And that the best writers reveal something about themselves that a smarter person would choose to hide.

—KEN FOSTER

THE KGB BAR READER

FIRE

One

My mother would threaten to lose her mind. It scared us, even Ronnie, and nothing scared Ronnie. But my mother standing in the center of our front yard (yes, there were neighbors draped from the windows, at the top of stoops, girls who were my friends playing jacks and hopscotch right there in front of our yard) swearing loudly, pulling at her hair—*Yes, yes, right here in the middle of this block—I swear to you all I'll stand right here and lose my mind.* Even Ronnie ran, peering from behind pulled shades, out at our mother, silently begging God.

You piss all over yourself, Ronnie said. *You lose control.*

Yes, even Ronnie, hidden in the far back of our apartment whispering, "What's she doing now? What's happening?" And me and Richard, shushing her with our hands, peeked wide-eyed past that blind afraid that any moment we'd see the trickle running down our mother's legs, right there in the middle of our yard with every single body in our world watching.

Two

When I was eight, we had a fire, an immense desolation two days before Christmas. We were one of those lost frozen families one reads about in tabloids, and yes, that was us on the cover of the *Daily News* huddled into the folds of a ragged blanket a neighbor had brought to our rescue, staring up tearfully as our building disappeared under its own cover of smoke, flame, and water. My mother, pulling us into her thin arms, screamed for mercy and collapsed. Even in our despair, we were embarrassed more by her fainting than the fire that had resulted in us running pajamaed but barefoot from our building. The youngest, our long-lashed baby brother Richard, carried a stuffed monkey under his arm. In the photo (it is still in my possession although we have lost Richard) he is clutching this animal to his chest as he gazes tearfully upward, his beautiful lashes glinting.

This was my first life—eaten by fire. Dolls, dresses, school photographs, knives, forks, rugs, letters, baby bottles and pictures, gone. Later, as our mother picked through the water-soaked remains of this life, I stood silently in the center of what had once been the bedroom I shared with Ronnie, and cried. My mother held me, believing I was grieving for all we had lost but my tears were tears of relief, that these eight years were over. It was time to move on.

Three

The fire annihilated Richard—from the inside out the way fires are prone to destroy. Sometimes a boy just disappears. Standing right in front of you but . . . disappeared. It's strange how it worked with Richard. One minute he'd be laughing like any five-year-old—that hiccup laugh with nothing but joy behind it and the next moment, he'd be silent and still as death. *Richard, Richard,* Ronnie would yell. *Earth calling.* But Richard was gone. Out of there. As though there was no other time. And no other way to be.

Four

After years and years of us, my mother finally did go mad. But it was not as Ronnie had said. There was no pissing, no screaming into the night, no hair being yanked out in violent tufts. It was much simpler. One Sunday, after we had returned from the Kingdom Hall—we were Jehovah's Witnesses so even though the tabloid had said we'd lost all of our toys that Christmas, this wasn't true. We had never celebrated Christmas or any holiday, had no toys, not even a tree. But for months after the fire, gifts from strangers poured in and it was as though we were meant to make up for all of the gift-giving holidays we had never celebrated—our mother sat down in a rocker (yet another gift from a stranger) and cried herself to sleep. We tiptoed around her. When she awoke, the sky was the color of slate with an orange sun still sinking in the distance. We were sitting in the kitchen and I had been staring at this sky, having recently discovered its immensity. One evening, on my way to the store for my mother, I looked up and realized that this thing called a sky was what we had been taught to believe was Heaven and realized the idea of sky and Heaven being one and the same was absolutely ridiculous. I had grown sullen with the understanding that I had been lied to. Now, sitting in our kitchen watching this sky, I became vaguely aware of being yelled at. Ronnie, her beautiful face curled around some rage, was saying it was my turn, had been for quite some time. We were playing chess. I was new at this game and Ronnie had been teaching me the rules. But from the angle of it all— my court was bare save for a few pawns, a king, a queen, and one rook—I had the suspicion she was cheating. It was at this point, as I turned away from the sky into the wind of my older sister's rage, that our mother made her way slowly into the kitchen, studied the three of us silently, then dropping into a heap against the wall, cried steadily for seven days.

It was Ronnie who lifted our mother from the floor and let her lean upon her narrow shoulder up to her bedroom. It was Ronnie who tucked our mother into bed, while Richard and I looked on. Ronnie who brought our mother decaffeinated coffee laced with honey for seven days. It was Ronnie who stayed up at night listening to our mother's stories about places where her life went wrong—Ronnie who would recount these stories to me in the months to follow and years later, I would retell them to a therapist—editing until I became the hero. And it was Ronnie who took a bucket filled with warm soapy water and a washcloth and swabbed our mother's thin, naked body, then rubbed oil into the aging folds of her while our mother murmured stories and Richard and I looked away, plugging our ears with our fingers.

Ronnie was fourteen. The year was 1975. Her favorite song was Abba's "Fernando" and she would sing the lyrics over and over, watching herself mouth the words in the bathroom mirror. She covered her walls with posters of the group members, who were pale and blonde and immensely unattractive, bought blue eye shadow and pink lipstick that against her dark skin gave her an ashen frail appearance. She bought clogs, a long peasant skirt and a ribbon to tie around her hair, which was longer than anyone's in our family—almost to the middle of her back, wild and black as a dream. We were beginning to lose her.

Five

For a short while, our mother returned to us. She found a job as a secretary for a construction company. Each morning, she made a breakfast of soft scrambled eggs, toast, and jam, watching us eat while she drank instant coffee standing. She had an outfit she began to refer to as her uniform—a ruffled white blouse, black skirt, and wide gold belt. She would pull her hair back into an afro puff then, using Dixie Peach and a fine-tooth comb, would slick the delicate front hairs down against her forehead. The effect of this was beauty, simple—beauty like a fist into flesh—sharp, painful, breathtaking. Our mother was nervous about leaving us in the care of Ronnie whose eyes had taken on a glazed look. Each morning, our mother would warn us to come straight home from school, make us show her the keys strung with yarn around our necks, then place a kiss upon our cheeks and leave. At night, we would sit in the light of three dim bulbs—since the fire, our mother didn't believe in using bulbs higher than forty watts—and study the Bible. We knew everything there was to know about Jesus' crucifixion, adultery, Judas' betrayal of Christ, Lazarus rising, fire and brimstone, manna from heaven, parting seas, and Salome. We knew this world wasn't long for itself, that God had a plan. We had straight backs and clear visions. Something was coming and we would be ready for it. We were a good family. Fatherless but good. Of different fathers but good. Ronnie's father had been part Indian. Richard's father had been a dancer who our mother later discovered preferred the company of men. Richard moved like a dancer and at times like a queer and was prone to fits of crying and stompings of the feet. My own father had been an actor but could not find work. As a result, he had turned to dancing naked for bachelorette parties. Our mother met him at a friend's party, fell in love with the way he moved. They dated for about two months before my mother discovered her pregnancy. He disappeared soon afterward. Our mother swore she saw his face years later, in the crowd scene of *Cotton Comes to Harlem*.

Six

One morning we were awakened by the smell of smoke. Our mother, standing in the doorway, was dancing in circles, a flaming brown paper bag pulled over her head. Richard and I watched, bleary-eyed as Ronnie ran toward her. But at the sound of these footsteps, our mother backed away. Now there was no longer any paper bag but blue flame and her beautiful hair disappearing. This vision, against the light of dawn, was amazing. In the air around us, there was the smell of skin and hair burning and Richard screaming. But I was silent, fascinated. This is madness, I was thinking. This is the thing we had been promised. *This is madness,* I was thinking. *Our inheritance.*

Seven

We were sent to live with a Mrs. Janna Donovan—a devastatingly pale shock of a woman with large bony hands—in Brookline, Massachusetts. This, we knew, was an accident. *Someone's cruel joke,* Ronnie said.
    We huddled into each other, Ronnie, Richard, and I.
    And we were black.
    And we could not blend into the day or night.

Eight

But we waited. Our mother would be returned to us. Somehow we knew this. And while we waited, our silent brother Richard struck match after match in the darkness. And Ronnie, moving like someone old and broken, secretly stashed away brown paper bags.

MAKE ME

On the sixth day of her hunger strike Lydia Martinez entered my dreams and immediately died there. She died so convincingly that I awoke and for a few moments could not imagine her alive again. I had to force it. I forced it and then I saw her, behind a Bunsen burner, her pretty face framed inside her black hair and lit by the lapping blue flame. I felt better, much better, but as much as I tried I could not fall asleep again. Lydia was not just any girl; besides being the brightest, she was my One and Only—the one and only student I was allowed to think about in that way I thought about her.

"Do you know what day it is?" I asked Pearl the next morning in the teachers' lounge, over a cigarette. Pearl was my ex-girlfriend—an English teacher. Through an arrangement the two of us shared, she was allowed to think about Gabriel, her One and Only. Gabriel was Lydia's former boyfriend and the reason for the girl's hunger strike. Think only, Pearl and I had agreed; that way no one gets hurt. At least that was the way it had started.

Pearl blew smoke out her nostrils. "How could I not know?" she said. "She stage-whispers it to him every day in homeroom: 'I'm on Day Five, Gabriel,' she says. 'Day Six today.' She's got him worried to death."

"He didn't seem particularly worried in Earth Science this morning,"

I said. "But just for the record, it's Day Seven. Seven days since you drove the boy home."

Pearl blew a mouthful of smoke at the dirty window that overlooked two granite benches donated by the Class of '78. The windows in the teachers' lounge were never cleaned. The janitors refused, the teachers refused. No one else was allowed inside.

Then Pearl looked at me with tears balanced in the corners of her eyes, a device she had always used to great effect. "Chris, I'm just barely making it," she said. "Sometimes I think I'm not going to make it. I know it's not the smart thing to do, but I'm just barely hanging on. A skin-of-the-teeth kind of thing. Do you know what I mean?"

"Oh, Pearl." My voice was more tender than I wanted it to be. "Don't be dramatic. He's just a boy. Think about it."

"That's the trouble—it's all I think about." She laughed, and the laugh dislodged the tears.

"Anyway," she said, "it's not like I expect you to know what I'm talking about." She sniffed out another laugh and then sighed. "I'm really very sorry I said that."

"Forget it," I said.

There was a pause, and after a moment I filled it. "If nothing else, consider Lydia."

She snorted. "I don't give two shits about Lydia and her stupid hunger strikes. She'll quit just like the other times. She always eats eventually."

"No," I said, "she never just quits. Gabriel always comes back to her, then she eats. That's not the same as quitting."

"She'll quit this time. I'll bet you anything she's eating by Friday."

I didn't say anything for a moment, then I rubbed my eyes hard. "I'm having trouble sleeping," I said.

"Again?" Pearl mashed the nose of her cigarette in the center of the ashtray. It stayed there, bent and broken, its pink end in the air.

"Why do they humor her?" she said. "They should yank her out of school when she pulls this stuff. It's only for the attention. They should just yank her out for her own good."

Outside the dirty window some stray papers blew across the grass. A girl shrieked and a bad muffler blatted into the distance.

"Who's they?" I said.

*   *   *

I had only kissed Lydia, and I had only done it once. It happened last week on Parents' Night. Lydia's father—of all people—sought me out at the front lab station, where I explaining the periodic table to a single mom whose child was nowhere to be found. He drew up behind me and out of the corner of my eye I could see him shifting his weight from foot to foot. Lydia hung back in the doorway and watched us, her tiny chin low to her chest. From that distance the pupils of her eyes, lost inside dark irises, seemed enormous.

"What is this about?" he asked when the woman had left. He waved a paper in front of my eyes.

I took the paper from him and read it. It took two passes before I recognized it.

"Advanced lab takes some extra equipment," I said, handing it back. "It's just a deposit. If nothing is broken it's all refunded at the end of the semester."

He examined the paper doubtfully. Lydia turned her face away from the room.

"Just in time for Christmas," I added. By then the vice-principal had noticed the scene developing from his office across the hall, where he was entertaining a man in a business suit. He glanced at Lydia and then frowned at me. The man in the suit spoke to him but the vice-principal continued frowning through the doorway.

"I pay this already," Lydia's father said, staring at the paper. He looked panicked. "Already pay."

The vice-principal circled around the man in the suit to be closer. "Great," I said, taking the sheet. "Thank you."

Lydia's father nodded uncertainly and turned to leave. He was almost at the door and then he stiffened and took Lydia by the arm and pulled her back to me. She was pale. Her black hair fell into her face, as if she were hiding behind it. The vice-principal escaped from the man in the suit and stood right in the doorway next to my poster of the Curies. He stood with his nose slightly in the air, sniffing scandal.

"This," Lydia's father said. "This is my daughter."

I nodded at him. My hands went in and out of my pockets.

"You know her," he said. He was starting to look angry.

"Yes," I said. Madame Curie and the vice-principal stared at me.

"She is paid."

"Yes, of course, Mr. Martinez," I said. "My mistake." When I said his name, Lydia's father nodded at me and let go of her arm. The fabric of her sleeve remained puckered where he had gripped her. He walked out the door and Lydia followed behind, brushing past the vice-principal, who had been collared once again by the businessman. She never looked up.

At half past nine I snapped the locks shut on my briefcase and closed the door to the classroom behind me. Pearl had left long ago, and I walked across the varsity diamond to the teachers' parking lot. When I reached it Lydia was sitting on the trunk of my car with her feet on the bumper. Her hands were pressed between her knees and her hair fell on either side of her face.

"Gabriel went off with her," she said, not looking up. "Why didn't you stop them?"

"It's nothing," I said. "There's nothing to worry about." I was too tired and too disappointed to think about Pearl anymore. She and I had played out our big scene just a few days before. My feelings and faults, so recently exhumed, lingered about me like an unpleasant odor. I put my briefcase down and sat on the trunk next to Lydia. I thought of five or six things to say but instead I leaned over, moved her hair, and kissed her. She didn't raise her head and I almost missed her pretty mouth. I felt the soft, slick tip of her tongue, just for an instant, but for the most part she gave me nothing. I kept my face next to hers for a moment, and then I straightened up.

"It's all so disappointing," she said. She pulled her knees up to her chin.

I felt my face heat up stupidly. "What is?" I said.

"Everything," she said. "Just everything."

"Well, you don't have to worry, I won't do that again."

She finally raised her head, but I couldn't see her eyes in the shadows. She didn't say anything for a moment while she looked at me. Then she turned away. "See what I mean?" she said.

On the way home we stopped for an ice cream. She barely touched her cone; I left a block from her house with it dripping down around her fist. That, as far as I knew, was the last time she ate.

On Day Eight in Earth Science Gabriel was napping in the last row when the two AV drones, twin brothers with twin eyeglasses, wheeled in the TV and VCR. Gabriel's head lay sideways on his arms, a mass of soft black curls. As soon as the video started he jerked his head up and wiped the back of his hand across his lips. It was a film about cellular mitosis. When they showed a rabbit being inseminated and then dissected, he leapt to his feet.

"You mean they killed it?" he cried. "What is this, Mr. Bergman, some kind of bunny snuff film?"

"Gabriel," I said. I was always tempted to stop there, at just the recitation of his name, but he was one of those people who was affirmed by his name being spoken aloud, just the ways others are diminished. It was like food to him, and I didn't like seeing him fed in my class.

I stopped the film. "Gabriel, the term is sacrifice, not kill. We've been over this."

"Kill is kill, Mr. Bergman," he said. "Dead is dead."

"This is about life beginning," I said. "I really think that if you'd just sit down and watch you'd be interested."

"I don't know," he said doubtfully. "There's the whole eye-for-an-eye thing . . ."

"Sit down, Gabriel."

Gabriel sat down, somehow larger and more beautiful than before. I started the film. When the egg finally divided—the chromosomes cleaving and rushing to their opposite poles—the class twisted in their seats to look back at him. He was asleep, his head on his arms. The remainder of the film seemed interminable.

"Pearl," I told her that night at her kitchen table, "you're crossing the line. I don't know what else to say to you. Think of Tess of the Whatshernames, think of Sister Goddamn Carrie."

But it was too late; just then I realized that she had already gone through with it. She was glowing but trying to hide it.

"Wrong sex, to begin with," she said. She fingered her strand of faux pearls, her trademark. She didn't realize the pearls rode too far up the nape of her neck and emphasized her slightly hunched shoulders and sallow coloring. I had told her once that she reminded me of Garbo, but not the reason why.

"Let me show you something," she said. "You aren't going to believe this." She crossed her yellow kitchen and brought back a tin canister. Inside was white sugar, polluted with what looked to be tiny brown crumbs.

"He puts sugar on absolutely everything. Toast—covered with butter, covered with sugar. Can you believe it?" She licked her finger and poked it into the canister. She held it up in front of her, coated. "Not a single cavity in his entire head. Teeth of steel." After a moment she wiped the finger on the tablecloth.

"Lydia Martinez fainted in Kaplan's class," I said in a calm voice.

She stood up quickly and ran water over her hands. "I'm not going to feel guilty. It has nothing to do with me." She rubbed her hands on a dishtowel.

"I had a dream she was dead. I mean a nightmare. I haven't slept since."

"You told me this already."

"I called her house. Her parents pretended not to understand English. They put her little brother on, and he called me a whore lover and hung up."

She examined her pearls absently. "They thought you were selling something. Did you say who you were?"

"When she came to, she asked them what day it was. Kaplan told her Tuesday. He didn't know what she meant."

"God, would you listen to yourself," she said. "Why don't you just admit how badly you want to sleep with the girl and get it over with?"

My hand gripped the tablecloth. "Don't make fun of me."

"Jesus," she said. "I didn't say you had to do it. I just said that you should admit it. It would be good for you."

I stood up. The tablecloth was crumpled where I had grasped it. "You're not exactly the expert on what would be good for me, are you?"

Pearl rolled her eyes. "Then why did you come over here? To show me what a tough time you're having?"

"To help you, although now I can't remember why." I picked up her sugar canister and dumped it on the table. "Maybe it was so you could tell me the fascinating sugar anecdote. Got any spiral notebooks to show me? Gym socks to hold under my nose?"

She said something, but I was already moving toward the door. The screen slapped shut behind me, followed quickly by the slam of the interior door.

I drove past Lydia's house on the way home.

* * *

By Day Eleven Lydia didn't seem thin as much as translucent. Her skin was mother-of-pearl. Her face was serenity itself: her glance at the wall clock, her gaze at the classroom door, her entire aspect, watching me, serenity. I explained quantum theory to the class the way it had been explained to me. I understood the loathing in their eyes.

After class I locked the door and turned out the lights. The feeble afternoon sunlight that slanted through the window seemed deadened by the looming blackboards. I sat on the edge of a desk and laid my fingers gently on the bones of Lydia's hand.

"Did you understand that?" I asked. "Do I make any sense?"

"No," she said. "It's kind of like Mass, except without God, without any feelings."

I put pressure on her hand. "Lydia, you're losing muscle by now. You're losing calcium. Look at the periodic table. That's not just rocks and metal, that's you."

"Jesus fasted for forty days and forty nights."

I shook my head. "If he really did that he was looking to make a big splash." I could feel her tiny Catholic pulse quicken in the back of her hand.

"Have you ever fasted?" she asked.

"No."

"It reminds you that we're all just tubes, you know. In and out. I know that sounds disgusting, but it's funny; when you don't eat, nothing sounds disgusting the way it usually does. Everything seems so clean."

"It's an illusion," I said. "I can explain the chemistry behind it."

"I know you can, but not now, okay?"

"Okay," I said.

"It's like this," she said. "I lived for Gabriel and now he's gone. Why should I keep going if what I lived for is gone?"

I lifted my hand. "You say that because you like the way it sounds."

"You see?" she said. "I try to tell you but you don't believe me." Then she took my hand back and her grip was strong. "It's not that I want to think about him; I don't want to think about him. I just want someone to think about me." She raised her hand and put the ends of my fingers against her lips. My arm hung heavy and limp between us.

"You know," she whispered, "you could make me want to stop." I could feel the breath from each syllable on my fingertips. "Why don't you just make me?"

"I dreamt that you died," I said. "I haven't slept since. Isn't that enough?"

But it wasn't. She sighed her disappointed sigh and looked at the clock above the door. She stood up, dropping my hand. I stood up to follow her but she was already gone; after all, it was Friday afternoon and the week was over for the likes of me.

That night on the phone Pearl spoke with the kitchen tap running in the background.

"What is this?" I said. "It sounds like you're being gassed."

She laughed too loudly. "What a clever thing to say. You're such a wit."

"He's there, isn't he?" I said. "And you're afraid he'll hear? Where is he, on the couch?"

"No. Guess again."

"I don't have to guess again. He's on the couch, watching television. You're pretending to like it. 'What is this show about?' you ask him. 'Now, who is he, I forget who she is.' You ask him every five seconds if he wants something to drink. You make the mistake of talking during some murder or explosion and he tells you to fuck off why don't you."

The water rushed louder. "You listen to me," she said.

I waited, but all I heard was the water. "I'm listening."

"Be quiet a second." Her hand went over the receiver. When the water noise came back I could hear her breath.

"I have to go," she whispered.

Before I could answer the water stopped. Pearl's voice lightened artificially. "Okay, Chris, I'll see you on Monday. I'll be sure to bring that book."

"*Fuck*," I yelled into the mouthpiece. "*Fuck!*" It was loud enough for him to hear; loud enough if she hadn't covered the earpiece on the way to the cradle.

Earth Science, bonehead science, science for simpletons. Monday, Day Fourteen, and Gabriel sat in the front row. He yawned twice; once for real and once for me. He wasn't wearing socks. He had a seventeen-year-old's silly weekend peach-fuzz beard. He scratched himself. The girl in the next seat watched him with sad but hopeful virginity.

"What I want to know, Mr. Bergman," Gabriel said, "is why animals don't like intercourse. They always scream."

Titters. "Gabriel . . ."

"Cats act like they're being killed."

"I don't know that that's true."

"It is. It's a nightmare. Sometimes they get stuck together." More titters. "No, seriously, they do."

I tried a stern note. "We're not talking about reproduction anymore, Gabriel. That was last week. Pay attention."

"I want to review. I didn't get it all the first time."

I sighed and tried levity. "Neither did I, Gabriel, but life goes on."

"Mr. *Bergman*," he said. "Good one."

"Who knows what phloem is?" I asked, over his head.

Gabriel cleared his throat noisily, and the class laughed out loud at this one. But he was through. He was, after all, exhausted.

Fifty minutes later Pearl stood in the teachers' lounge swirling coffee in a stained Styrofoam cup. There were no stirrers; there hadn't been for weeks. I usually used a Bic.

"Your young man is practically passed out," I said. "Lydia Martinez—"

She put both hands to her ears. "Stop," she said. "It's not even ten o'clock, Chris. Give me a morning's peace, why don't you?"

"—is in the nurse's office. She fainted in Kaplan's class again. He's beside himself. I heard him on the phone to his wife; I think he was crying."

"He's manic-depressive, for Christ's sake. The man weeps when the cafeteria runs out of Tater Tots."

"What about your job?" I said. "What about your career?"

"God," she said. "If you had any kind of heart."

"We had this conversation, remember? Everyone's not like you two, you know."

Her mouth wrinkled. "Oh, yes, I forgot. The chaste virgin. You wouldn't believe the things Gabriel says he's done with her."

"I'm not interested."

"Then why are you so pale all of a sudden?" She put her coffee down and closed her eyes for a second. "Look, I'm sorry, but you started it."

"I told you I haven't been sleeping. I'm starting to see flashing lights out of the corners of my eyes. Whispering voices. I haven't had that since college."

Her eyes flickered with concern, but just barely. "No sleep for two weeks?"

"I don't have the dreams, at least, but I still can't sleep."

"Is this about me? Chris, I gave you chances. I gave you chances until I couldn't give anymore."

"I don't need chances," I said. "I've got more chances than I can cope with right now."

Just then the vice-principal stepped in through the door. We stared at him. He wrinkled his nose and stepped back out. The vice-principal got his coffee from the ladies in the office. He had either wanted to use the teachers' bathroom or wanted to locate the two of us, establish our whereabouts. The expression on his face fit either scenario.

We waited for fifteen seconds, picked up our briefcases, and left in opposite directions for second period.

The vice-principal had been hired the previous fall. Before he arrived there had been both a vice-principal and a dean of students. Soon afterward they canned the dean of students and gave his duties to the new vice-principal. It was obvious that he considered this some kind of promotion and not a screwing like the rest of us did, so from then on everyone figure him to be either an idiot or a zealous bureaucrat and avoided him altogether. The whole thing ended up making him bitter and suspicious and awfully good at his job.

The vice-principal's office walls were lined with books that he had swiped from the library; they still had the cellophane sleeves with decimal codes typed on white strips across the bottoms of the spines. He kept a football on a wooden stand on his desk; it had a leather satchel handle sewn onto the laces. He had been a coach of some kind at his last school and this was a gift from his players, young men who had apparently adored him. The students at our school were constantly stealing it. When they weren't stealing his football with the handle they were writing his name on the paper bottoms of butter pats along with an obscenity and tossing them up to the ceiling of the cafeteria, where they would stick. Every once in a while, without warning, one dropped, like a dead thing, into someone's food.

"Mr. Bergman," he said, leaning back in his gray vinyl chair. "We have a couple of situations. At least two that I know about."

"Two," I said, nodding. This set off the little flashing lights in the periphery of my vision.

"We have an emotionally unbalanced student on our hands and, I believe, a troubled instructor. A very troubled instructor."

"Teacher," I said.

"I beg your pardon?"

"We have teaching certificates, not instructing certificates. I'm not a lifeguard."

"Yes, I'm aware that you're not. I wonder if—"

"I'm sorry," I said quickly. "I haven't been sleeping."

"I beg your pardon?" He had leaned forward in his chair.

"I don't sleep. It's as simple as that. Please continue with what you were saying."

"Fine. I thought I should tell you that the Superintendent of Schools has been enquiring about Lydia Martinez." He said that, the bastard: *enquiring*.

"Well, when she dies he'll probably stop enquiring. Not right away, but eventually."

"You're close to her," he said without a beat. "She's in your sixth period." His face showed no hint of accusation, not really.

"And now you want me to shoot myself in the foot. Isn't that a term you people use? Shoot yourself in the foot?"

"Not really," he said calmly. "I want you to get your girlfriend to talk to her, that's all." He picked up his football, not by the handle but by one blunt end, as if he were fondling a breast. The late afternoon sun suddenly appeared through the window behind him, and I had to lean a bit to the side to avoid getting it full in the face. It struck the vice-principal halfway through the back of his head; his face darkened and his right ear glowed red around the edges.

"To think," he said, staring at his football. "We give them films about VD, about HIV, but we don't mention this danger at all."

"What danger?" He was trying to confuse me; I knew it.

"Tragic," he said.

I closed my eyes, the easier to block out the sun. "All right," I said. "What do you want her to say?"

He looked up at me. There was no triumph in his expression. "Frankly, I don't know."

"Then what would satisfy you?"

"Calories," he said. "An orange, a pear. A carrot stick. The goddamn Apple Brown Betty would do, but I don't recommend it." He smiled at his own joke. He was smart, though, I had to give that to him. She would probably listen to Pearl; more than anyone else, she would listen to Pearl.

"Okay," I said. It sounded inadequate, but I was tired from not sleeping.

"Good," he said. "Kaplan will be happier."

"I beg your pardon?"

He flashed an innocent smile. "Our troubled teacher. I have a feeling this will perk him up."

For a second I was stunned. You're priceless, I thought. Still, long after we're gone you'll be here.

I started to get up to leave, but I sat back down. "Before I go," I said, "what danger were you referring to?"

"Oh, I thought it was obvious." He put the football back on its stand. "Mental illness." He tapped his forehead as emphasis.

"She's not mentally ill. She actually has a point if you listen to her."

"I wasn't referring to her. She'll come around. It's all for the attention, I'm sure." He looked at my face and smiled. "Kaplan," he said, "of course."

"Of course," I repeated. I left him there in his little slant of sunlight, behind his football.

"Fuck him," Pearl said, back in the teachers' lounge. "Why should I?"

"It's the right thing to do," I said. "You owe it to her."

"You need help, Chris. You need real help. Haven't you been paying attention to what's going on here?"

"Don't start. This isn't about me."

"No, of course not," she said. "Never about you."

"I told him you'd do it. I think he suspects something with you and Gabriel."

"Jesus," she said. "Did you bother to ask him why he had to involve you, then? Didn't you wonder about that?"

"Look, like it or not he's actually right. All you have to do is talk to her. She'll listen to you."

"God," she said. She closed her eyes and shook her head. "This is something that should be begged."

My heart pounded and the lights flashed. "You're crazy. I'm doing you the favor. I covered for you."

When Pearl opened her eyes she looked at me calmly. "If I talk to her, I tell her everything," she said.

"Tell her anything," I said. "Tell her I have no heart. Tell her I beat you. Tell her the truth if you have to. Tell her whatever it was you told yourself. Just talk to her. This is me begging."

She sighed and looked out the dirty window. "Where and when?" she said. "Let's get it over with."

Pearl sat in the driver's seat. Lydia sat in the passenger's. I watched them from the bleachers of the varsity diamond as the sun went down behind me. When they were done Pearl drove off and Lydia stood alone under the trees by right field. It had gotten dark fast and the streetlights were already coming on. She stood for a few moments and then walked over to me.

"I feel scraped out," she said. Her glance was feathery; she was fighting hard to concentrate. I wondered if she saw the flashing lights like I did.

"Is she always like that?" she asked.

"Yes," I said. "But maybe not so much anymore."

She sat for a moment. "She told me to tell you something. I don't know if I should."

I shook my head. "I want to know what she told *you*."

"She told me to tell you this first."

"All right. If you want to."

"She said to tell you that she doesn't feel sorry for you anymore."

"She's smart," I said. Some white flashes went off and I had to close my eyes for a second.

"Everyone says you two used to be in love. Were you in love with her?"

"No," I said. "What else did she say?"

"Is it true I got you in trouble? You might lose your job?"

I almost laughed. I could have made that up myself. "Maybe," I said.

"And everything would be okay if I just ate?"

"Yes, it would." I was lying so quickly now, so easily, lying to impress a seventeen-year-old girl. Her martyr, her hero.

"I didn't want to hurt anybody," she said.

"Lydia, I need to know," I said. "Did she say anything else?"

Her lips went tight. "She said that she's never going to give him up."

The flashing lights again. "Anything else?"

"She said I should help you and be with you. That it's important."

My heart sank. Oh, Pearl. Then the streetlight behind me came on, and suddenly Lydia's face was lit and stayed lit, and I could finally see it, the whole of it. Her skin glowed; I wanted to touch it with the back of my fingers. I did.

"Lydia," I said. "You remember what you said to me before, about making you? I could do that. I could just make you."

But then that familiar resigned look crept in, very adult on her seventeen-year-old face, and I was suddenly afraid that I might be too late.

"It sounds all right now," she said, "but what about in a couple of days? You might feel different."

"I won't," I said. "I won't ever feel different."

She looked away, moving her face in front of the street lamp. Blocked now, it scattered its light into the air surrounding her head.

"But *I* might, you see?" she said. She turned back to me. "It's just that I never know how I'll feel after I start eating again." She said. "I might start eating and then it would all seem bad and I'd never want to see you again."

Then for God's sake, don't eat, I wanted to say. I'd rather you disappeared. I'd rather the earth opened and swallowed you whole. I'd rather you were dead.

"What would you do then?" she asked, her eyes suddenly bright and sharp and piercing. She took my hand and squeezed my fingers hard, down near the ends. "What would you do if that happened?"

"What would I do if that happened?" I repeated. I sat for a second. "That's not what's important," I said. "What's most important is that you eat and get better."

She lowered her head, and shadows eclipsed her whole, thin face, as if she had swallowed her disappointment in one gigantic gulp.

"That's what everyone keeps telling me," she said. "And that's exactly why I can't."

She sat there on the bleachers, flashes going off all around her, and I put my arm around her. It hung, limp, off her shoulder. I knew that I wanted to do more than put my arm around her, that I wanted to kiss her right there on the varsity diamond bleachers in front of God and the vice-principal and Madame Curie and everybody, but I didn't right then, I didn't.

SICKISH

The years, she saw, fell heavily as books: the missing husband pinging a racket against the chuff of his hand, her charmed sister at the rental's beach, the raging Jean herself. In a coil of towel, the little boy named Jack was powdered free of sand. She tended to him then—absent, curious, easeful—and he calmed under the warmth of her hand. Now Jack's body was his own and not a thing she felt branched of, her hands growing out of; mother and son, they had even smelled the same once when Jack's teeth were growing in. Now she did not get close enough—did not want to get close enough—to smell him. Jack's skin was given over to the wild fluctuations of his age, which meant it was one day clear and smooth, and the next erupted, and still later newly healed and probably sore. Now the boy smoked.

It was what he asked for first with the smoke of something smoked down clouding around his head: "Did you remember cigarettes?" Yes, yes, her soft assent. "But what I need," Jack said, "are socks." Snack foods, paper, stamps: the listlessly articulated list from every visit grew as the corridors grew or so it seemed to Jean in her drift through the swabbed facility with its smell of Lysol and fish!

"Stamps," Jack said, "are what I really need. I want to write to friends."

Jack said, "I wrote myself here," and he showed Jean what he did every night on the edge of the table, which was a deeply scarred table, full of dates and initials, profanations, codes, and there on the edge, his knifeworked *Jack.* Jack said, "I want people to know I've been here and that I was okay. I had friends. Fuck," he said, "I've made a lot of friends," and so he had. An odd assortment said hello or made motions to speak to Jack each time they bumped past.

Jean said to Jack, "So what do you do with your friends?"

"They're not all friends," he said. "Some of them"—and he pointed to a boy with an old, black face and voluptuously muscled body—"that guy," Jack said, "already has a kid. He's been in jail. And the fat girl bit a girl for trying to comb her hair. I don't talk to that crazy. Nobody does. There were stitches. That's how bad it was."

How bad it was Jean told her sister. Jean called the place the facility, eschewing its bucolic name and using Jack's slang when she was angry. Then she called the facility a dry-out place, a place for rehab on the cheap. A motel it had been or a conference center, the facility had past lives in the same way as did its staff. First name only, confessing only their abuse, the pallid staff wore cushioned shoes and shuffled small steps. Their talk, too, was small and coughed out with erasures from whatever they saw looking back—*not that, not that*—but ahead, the home contract, the dickered pact, the rules to school the house against the wily abuser. "Addiction," the staff said, "we've been there—and been there. Relapse is common with friends still using." The staff twitched matches, frantically serene.

Jean told her sister. "These are the guys helping Jack with his homework. These are the people meant to be his friends."

But Jean's sister, being her sister, and wiser, Jean's sister said, "This is where Jack should be."

The hours at the facility were blocked and named: group, individual, free. "I'm climbing steps," Jack said, smiling. "I'm making progress here, Mother. You'd be proud!"

Jack she was used to the shard of his name since he shortened it. His hair color, too, had changed, was leaden and beaten by the last school's cap, the same he wore through the meeting.

"Jack!" she said.

"What?" he asked.

Mother, son, counselor, here they were again, the weekend group in consultation: *Family* was the name on the schedule.

Who was getting better, she wondered, who was sick?

Jean asked her wiser sister, "Am I?"

"Are you?" she asked back.

Yes, it was all too common a story—Jean knew, she admitted as much—a woman on her own and what she had to do because of the children. Because of them she had to ask the missing husband for what he did not have that yet was needed.

"Look at what I've had to do for money," Jean said, home again, on the couch with the quiet son, Ned. The men she had let wander into the apartment. Think of them! and she did—and didn't he? "Don't you think of them sometimes?"

Ned said, "I was very young, Mother."

It was Jack, years older, who had said he remembered a man who shook her upside down for quarters.

"Oh," Jean moaned as Ned was getting to and scratching some un-reachable places. "Oh, I hope you don't remember," she said. Then, "Yes! that feels good!" she said, and said again, "That feels good!" and Jean let her towel drop in a way that made her wonder: Since there wasn't a man to put lotion on her back, should she ask her son to do it?

Jean, at the facility, said to the counselor, "Ask Jack what he did with my bank card. I bet he didn't tell you." Freely spending with the pur-pose to be caught it seemed, Jack had bought what in the moment moved him, leaving waxy, bunched receipts between the sheets for her to find of what he had signed for with abandon, largely. Felonious boy, that Jack! Skulking the facility, as she had seen him, butting what he passed—doors, walls, wheeled racks hung with visiting coats—Jack scared Jean a little, and she came home tired.

And Ned was tired! Tired from scratching. Tired from the yawn of Sat-urday, from homework, from art class, from girls. From streets and apartments, cigarettes, beers—from more girls. On almost any Sunday, late in the morning and cragged in a gray sheet, the boy slept in his room, which was also gray. Thin light, lingering smoke. Something there was about Ned gray, too: the pale skin of his outstretched leg, blue-black hair in a cuff at his ankle. Only his foot, the heel of it, was full of color—not old pavement to be razored and still not reach the pink of—Ned's foot was young. It invited petting, touching to say, wake up. "Wake up," she said, looking at the covered boy and trying to keep the room in her eyes watery because she did not want to see what was on the bedside table, although Jean saw it clearly: the cigarettes first, the ashy spill around the glasses, orange juice pips on the rim of the old-fashioned. Haywire spirals yanked out of notebooks, Post-its curling on the tops of papers: See me! one of them said. Jean was looking at the screen dead computer. The drawers, too, she saw, but did not open. She knew enough about Ned. She knew he drank and smoked, carried condoms, broken jewelry. She knew he liked to kiss; he liked the girls. Girls, girls, girls, girls. Their voices ribboned out from faces closely pressed against the cradle of the phone—babies still, most often shy. "Is Ned there?" they asked.

"I'm sorry," Jean said—and said—"he's still asleep."

Lifted in the wind, the blinds banged their music on the sill; it was a sound of small breakage—of saucers, of cups—in a rhythm like the rising and falling of a chest, like breathing, a boy's, his. Tiptoed and unsteady, she silenced the phone next to his bed. She put the ringer on off—and why not? The calls were usually for Ned, so let him sleep, she thought, another hour. Let him grow in his twisted sheets! Bent, crooked, an impression of bones he was, a tent of bones, a sudden arm slung above his head and the black tuft of hair there as startling as his sex.

Think of something else, think of the Sunday papers. Consider this fall's color on girls stood back to back, with their skinny arms crossed, as girls crossed them, coyly. The girls who visited Ned stood at the door coyly, toed-in and stooped with baby backpacks on their backs, asking from behind ragged bangs, "Is Ned home?"

"Yes," she had to say, "but still asleep."

And Jack? Jack was now so tipped against the sun—the bright shard of his name again—that just to speak of Jack hurt Jean's eyes; and she did not want to think about the place where she had been or what Jack was doing there or what he would be doing there at night in the facility.

"Not knowing where he sleeps is fine by me," Jean admitted, but only to Ned. To Ned she complained. Now when she sat on the couch, still red from washing off the facility, she said, "Jack makes me believe he has paid for whatever it is we are doing to him. Does that make sense?" She said, "Please, my back."

Ned said, "You never made Jack do this."

Sometimes Ned used a comb on her back. He made tracks and designs with the comb. He wrote his name and asked, "So what did I write then?"

She sat on the couch, tickled by the comb tracking through the lotion, and she said to Ned, "I can't help myself sometimes. When I am in *Family* I say terrible things . . ." And she told the boy what things she had said about a man who was yet the father—and she knew that, yet she would speak. She wanted to tell Ned everything. Now, every weekend, it seemed, she came home parched and queasy, calling out to Ned, "Are you here? Anybody home? Yes? No? Who else?"

Once a girl with rainbow hair lay unbuttoned on Ned's bed. The girl was quick to sit up, and she smiled at Jean, but the distraction of the girl's hair, knotted and skyward from however the girl had been with him, was such that all Jean saw was the girl's hair and those parts erect from tugging. Just look at the girl's stubby nipples! So this was Ned's idea of pretty, Jean thought, and wondered, was the girl disappointed in her? Was she drab to the girl, for that was how she felt.

"Is this your mother?" from the girl in a girl's voice, just a whisper.

"Yes."

This was the mother breaking open gel caps and licking up sleep or the opposite of sleep, extreme wakefulness, speed. This was the mother using scissors between her legs, staying ready, staying hairless, should someone want to lick her.

Something Jean could never bring up at the family consultation in the facility was what she was doing at home, because she was hardly ever sober herself but she was prudent in her daily use of substances. She measured, she counted, she observed fastidious rituals. She soaped and creamed and powdered when the high was at her throat. At night she drank—then only ales, wines, rarely hard liquor. But she drank to ease the restlessness from the petty drugs she took, gouging tinbacks with a pencil to release sealed tablets, over-the-counter nondrowsy—four, six, eight pills a pop—a petty habit, nothing serious, but growing, at the worst growing, at the worst becoming what her father's habit was: Vicodin, Prozac, Valium, Glucotrol, Synthroid, Mevacor, plain old aspirin. Jean's father had offered, saying, "I don't know what it's called, but it's good." No, no, no, Jean had resisted. She wanted most of her habit nonprescription and cheap.

No one noticed what she did.

This was especially true at the facility where Jean had expected to be found as if passing by a screen and seen clear through; but she slipped past and into the facility with her son and her son's counselor, and she was fearless again. Everyone was looking at Jack, asking him, "So what do you do around users?"

Jack said, "I don't."

Everyone agreed his was a good answer, clever.

Avoid some mothers, Jean thought, avoid me; the thought of being worse than the mother she remembered as having was hurtful, but not so hurtful as to keep her from using more expensive substances. The guilt didn't keep her from calling Suzette and speaking in their code, "I need some pantyhose," and welcoming the girl at any time of the night—even introducing Suzette to Ned. "We work together," she had said. A traveling-house of a girl come to them at any hour, a bulk, a shape zippered or buckled, pilot glasses, sneakers, Peruvian hat, Suzette didn't much surprise Ned. He was used to interruption, to the phone at odd hours and hand-delivered gifts, the rustle of things dried, split pods, seeds flying. The flare-up affairs with names Jean might use for weeks—Nora, Mark, David, Marlene—Ned was familiar with this much of the life his mother had in another part of the city.

The city, if only that were to blame, but there was her own father, the one who managed to be sick in the country. Jean's father couldn't remember Jean's address or the names of the boys, saying, "Your oldest will be sixteen before I see him," when Jack was almost eighteen yet already sick the way he was. And Jean was sick, too—and maybe Ned. The baby creases of his neck had smelled of smoke, greasy exudations from the bonfired night, bright drops, coin-size, clear.

"Oh, God," Jean said, and Jean's careful sister asked—and asked often—if Jean was taking anything she shouldn't?

Jean said, "Nothing. Why should I?"

Once Jean let Ned visit Jack, and she was happy for his company, and Jack was made happy, too, just to see his brother. They shivered to be near before they touched and were teasing again, boys again, brothers. The brothers walked together and apart from Jean, waving at their mother with their smoking hands because they could, being here, at the facility. Look at the troughs of sand used for ashtrays! They were mad smokers here at the facility, but what else was there to do, Jack asked, except to smoke and answer questions and earn steps. Every week he reached a new level; now there was talk about a contract.

"The home contract is something we agree on," Jack said, "if I'm to come back to the city and live with you."

He showed Jean a draft. To the question about curfew, he had written, "None."

Jack said, "Shit, Mother, I snuck out all the time."

"So where were you going?" Jean asked; but when he made to speak, she said, "Don't tell me."

She didn't want to read Jack's home contract either and not, as it happened, when Ned was along and all of them sitting at the scarred table with Jack pointing, "See? My name's all over this fucking place."

"Jack, please!" Jean said.

"I've lived without a curfew," Jack said, and every weekend said, "I've changed. I'm on the third step. I want my medal."

At the scarred table with her sons, Jean cried. "There is so much to be sorry about," she said, but her sons were embarrassed, it seemed to her, and sad and scornful of her rustling for a hankie. "Anyone?" she asked. "I'm sorry." She bent her head, snuffling, using a cloth when she found one. "I'm sorry," she said. "I'll be all right."

The story Jean most often told Ned was Jack and what Jack did. She told Ned of the friends his brother had made at the facility, even the fat girl now, the one who had bitten a girl for approaching with a comb, even she, was his friend. Jack said he was popular, the most popular kid. Jean said, "I think he thinks he is running for class president." Jean said, "Where does he think he is."

In *Family* Jack said he wanted to live in L.A. He said he was old enough, he had worked last summer, he had had the responsibility of a job.

"Putting up boxes!" Jean said.

Jack said to the counselor, "Do you understand now? Do you see what I've been saying? Look at her!"

Jean said in passing Ned's room, "I don't want to talk about your brother."

Ned said, "Mother!" Sometimes he said, "It's not your fault," and he offered, "I'll rub your back if you'll rub mine." Sometimes he said, "Why do you listen to Jack?"

Ned said, "I don't know. I don't know the answers to all your questions."

Ned said, "Why should I?" when the question of curfews came up. "Jack didn't."

Sometimes Ned got angry and his hand, long still against her back, withdrew, and he went to his room and turned on his music loudly. The telephone rang; he slammed the door, or he talked to her in the way his brother did, absently: the falt-voiced *yes,* the *what?* that was nasty. The nimble imitative skill Ned showed was common. Jack did it and others of his friends and Ned's friends; she had heard them speaking to their parents in their parents' voices. They hissed new words that meant dumb and ugly. She said, "Talk to me in your own voice, Ned; talk to me so I can understand."

Sometimes Ned did speak earnestly, and when he spoke to her in this voice, she wanted to take him by surprise, to touch him, to kiss his mouth as it moved—and would go on moving, saying, "Mother! Don't!"

Sometimes Ned said, "Will you not, please," but she went on. She wormed her fingers between his toes; she tickled him or worked Q-Tips, painfully, around the curled folds of his ears. "Damn it, Mother, that hurts!" yet he was the one who asked her to do it. "Cut my nails," Ned said, and she cut too close.

She said and she said and she heard herself saying—whining, really—"Please, you are the only one who knows how to scratch."

Hadn't she heard? Jack asked; but no, the sound of a body thrown against a wall was not a sound she had ever heard. The sound of a hand raised against another body, yes, that was familiar to her, and objects ripped, broken, smashed, whipped, snapped, yes; wails over a blaze of language she had heard many times before, and her own voice rising was familiar. Think of that! so that what did Jack know compared to her?

"Plenty," Jack said, and he read from his home contract febrile stories: what he had done and what in the future, once home again, he would contract not to do: No more drugs with lyrical names; those suggestive, glittery tabs of magic, he vowed he would not take—no, not again, never again. He didn't need to be high. He was going to think.

Meetings, yes he agreed to go to them, to find them.

Strategies for avoiding users: avoid users.

Curfew.

Curfew was always an issue.

Every weekend Jean repeated, "Write it down! No later than one o'clock!" when Jack, of course—of course, extreme—said, "No."

He said, "The home contract has to do with trust."

Then she thought of Jack as he appeared in his home contract stories, the ones he wrote so freely, attaching pages to the contract, pulling from his pocket more stories penciled on folded notes with linty seams and so worn in their appearance that she wondered: Had Jack started these stories before the facility? Was he writing these scary stories while they were happening at home?

The starless urban nights he described, kiosks on corners, the shuddering homeless, Jack and his buddies, whoever at the time, even he didn't always remember which friends but that there were several, and they walked the city. They stood in the sheeted stalls on busy streets—all-night markets ablaze in awful light; but the surly cashiers sold them anything: imported beers and cigarettes, for which they pooled their money. Jack had stolen from his mother to buy what he snorted in the stalls of bathrooms. He stole so largely he was caught.

"Look at the pages I've got!" he said and thumbed the home contract.

* * *

In a tub she kept hot, she sweated out the smell of the scrub used at the facility; she soaped; she flexed her toes and admired the polish she still put on, insisting she would yet be playful, as once she had been playful, surely, and perverse and curious and young. On her knees, in one of the early bathrooms, she hung over the tub and watched, as he did, a small rising.

Oh, they had their casual routine. Jean and Ned, the two of them, she thought, living well together and easily, passing even shyly in the hall, sliding against the wall to keep from touching. Observant, quiet, gently agreeing or asking on the way out, "Do you want anything?" This was the way they were together, alone, Jack at the facility and the husband years missing.

Tub-pink and powdered, holding out the lotion, asking, "Will you do my back now, please?" Often asking, "Please, my back?"

"Please, stay home," she called out, but Ned did less and less. And less and less he called, or when he did his voice was muzzy, or else he sounded angry and confused. "What's the number where you are?" Jean asked and heard him speak to someone near, "Whose house is this? Where are we?"

Oh! To have those summers back and time on the rental's beach, a weathered house where sand collected on the windowsills and grass blades thatched the mud room. Country on small, green scale was what she told her sister that she missed. Jean missed the sloppy blossoms that were roses, beach roses, casual pink daubs against the fence and sugared sand. Blown before picked, the beach roses, perfuming the air as a girl would, largely indiscriminate, the beach roses Jean missed and the smell of them and the colors of this country, which was not the country she drove through on her way to the facility. No, that country—why talk of it?

Jack only talked about the city, about his enemies and friends. Cale, Urbinger, Schwartz, were guys out to get him when Jack got back, which was one of the reasons he feared going back and joked of never leaving the facility. Fucking Urbinger claimed Jack had stolen his watch and that he, Jack, owed him.

"Jack," Jean said.

"What?" Jack asked. "What is it?"

*   *   *

The tabs he let melt on his tongue were easy to come by in the parks where he dangled in the stories he was telling—old sleeper—waking to the skaters' whir, the poor's hobbled passing. Gnawed at gnawing rats, bald and balding, tamed up his leg snooting food—that's how still Jack was, watching: island drummers, shufflers in exploded shoes, the man and his python, parading his snake. Venomous keepers, women padlocked like safes—threaded lips, encrusted ears—the faces Jack saw had the slack, caught look of fish. Fishy, guilty, up to no good, they were passing out cards to any hand that would take one, and he did, didn't he? "So much in the city is easy to come by," Jack said, which was what his novel was about. The novel he was writing was called by different titles, all of them familiar to Jean for being, Jack admitted, someone else's. But the story was his. He had lived it. Some of it was attached to the home contract. "The Z-B Club," Jack said, "is real. It happens near the park every night."

The friends Jack described jingled in Jean's ears when she listened to Jack's story: the braid-beads on girls, the strung shells, buttons, bells they wore around their necks, several at a time—yoked, choked—their necklace music, the chafe of jeans when they walked, the chafe of candy-colored lighters: sweet *canabis* smoke! The club lights drift through the seeded air confettied with drugs, with curlicues of edible, mind-bending paper. That stupid Cale got sick—and almost died—but he was rushed to Lenox Hill. "Where I live," Jack said, "is dangerous. That's why I need the home contract. I need some rules to live by."

Jean came home from the facility and soaked in hot water until she was warm again and asked Ned to please put some lotion on her back. "I don't care if it is cold," she said. She wore her bathrobe as a stole, shrugging to where she wanted it. "There," Jean said, "and there."

In the blare of October, on sullen afternoons, Jean watched Jack carve *Jack* along the rim of the scarred table in the dining hall. He was putting his own name everywhere, too, chipping at it while he lured his mute friends with smut. Boys with home-done haircuts and scars, they touched themselves lightly and laughed. She had walked toward this same scene before and seen them and seen Jack, slunk in his indolent stories—all *then, then, then*—gouging the wood with a fork.

Jean was afraid for Jack. Jack was such a baby! Jean was afraid for him when she looked to where he slept in the cinderblocked facility: two floors, picture windows. B movies, fifties sets, people sashed in bloody curtains was what Jean saw looking up to where Jack lived. The facility had once been something else—a health club, a retreat, a motel? There was the empty swimming pool just beyond the patio—another good spot for a death. Here were crazies who would bite a hand that moved to touch them. And such sounds Jean had heard, lonesome and wild, streaking past Jack when he was on the phone to her, and cowled, as she imagined, secretive, shoving off others, saying, "Asshole! I'm talking to my mother!"

"Who is it?" Jean asked.

"No one," he said. "This kid."

The sky cleared to fumy colors, to oranges and pinks; the horizon was precise. She asked Ned, "What do you think about Jack? What did you think about what he said? Did you believe him?" Jean asked, "Can someone mix all those drugs and stand?" She asked, "Do you think Jack's any better?"

Ned said, "How should I know? I wasn't there."

Home from the beach! Remember? The little boys come home! The hair on their heads—matted shocks stuck up in sleep, the crooked parts sanded—was warmly fragrant of weeds and salt and sea. Jean had liked to smell the boys. She had bent to their heads and sniffed, but their shirts! Always their shirts smelled worn and unwashed to her—sour, rusty.

The beach in noon light was hurtful as foil to look at, and she didn't.

The beach in any light. In the white folds of Ned's skin, in the white folds of Jack's, she had fingered baby sweat. Jean had lifted the wisps of hair from off their baby scalps, marked as the moon, with their stitched plates of bone yet visible. How often she had thought to break them.

MISTER BROTHER

Mister Brother is shaving for a date. Mister Brother likes getting ready and he likes having had sex. Everything in between is just business.

"Hey, Twohey," he says. "Better take it easy on the sheets tonight, Mom's out of bleach."

Twohey (that's you, if you're willing to wear the skin for a while) says, "Shut up, you moron."

"Ow," Mister Brother says, expertly stroking his jaw with Schick steel. "Don't call me a moron, you know how upset it gets me."

Mister Brother, seventeen years old, looks dressed even when he's naked. His flesh has a serenely unsurprised quality not common in the male nude since the last of the classical Greek sculptors cut his last torso. Mom and Dad, modest people, terrorized people, are always begging Mister Brother to put something on.

"Shut up," you tell him. "Just shut up."

You, Twohey, I'm sorry to say, are plump and pink as a birthday cake. You are never naked.

"Twohey, m'dear," Mister Brother says, "haven't you got any pressing business, ahem, elsewhere?"

You say, "You bet I do."

And yet you stay where you are, perched on the edge of the bathtub, watching Mister Brother, naked as a gladiator, prepare himself for Saturday night. You can't seem to imagine being anywhere else.

Mister Brother rinses off, inspects his face for specks of stubble. He selects an after-shave from the lineup. To break the scented silence, you offer a wolf whistle.

Mister Brother says, "Honestly, if you don't let up on me, I'm going to start crying. I'm going to just fall apart, and won't that make you happy?"

Mister Brother is a wicked mimic. When you tease him, he tends to answer in your mother's voice, but he performs only her hysterical aspect. He omits her undercurrent of bitter, muscular competence.

You laugh. For a moment your mother, not you, is the fool of the house. Mister Brother smiles into the mirror. You watch as he plucks a stray eyebrow hair from the bridge of his nose. Later, as the future starts springing its surprises and you find yourself acquainted with a drag queen or two, you will note that they do not extend to their toilets quite the level of ecstatic care practiced by Mister Brother before the medicine cabinet mirror.

"Hey, honey, come on now; don't cry. I didn't mean it," you say, in an attempt at your father's stately and mortified manner. Imitation is not, unfortunately, the area in which your main talents lie, and you sound more like Daffy Duck than you do like a rueful middle-aged tax attorney. You try to hold the moment by laughing. You do not mean your laughter to sound high-pitched or whinnying.

Mister Brother plucks another hair, rapt as a neurosurgeon. He says, "Twohey, man." He says nothing more. You understand. Work on that laugh, okay?

"Where are you going?" you ask, hoping to be loved for your selfless interest in the lives of others.

"O-U-T," he says. "Into the night. Don't wait up."

"You going out with Sandy?"

"I am, in fact."

"Sandy's a skank."

Mister Brother preens, undeterred. "And what've you got lined up for tonight, buddy?" he says. "A little *Bonanza*, a little self-abuse?"

"Shut *up*," you say. He is, as usual, dead right, and you're starting to panic. How is it possible that the phrase, "lonely, plump, and petulant" could apply to you? There is another you, lean and knowing, desired, and he's right here, under your skin. All you need is a little help getting him out into the world.

"So, Twohey," Mister Brother says. "How would you feel about shedding your light someplace else for a while? A man needs his privacy, dig?"

"Sayonara," you say, but you can't quite make yourself leave the bathroom. Here, right here, in this small chamber of tile and mirror, with three swan decals floating serenely over the bathtub, is all you hope to know about love and ardor, the whole machinery of the future. Everything else is just your house.

"Twohey, brave little chap, I'm serious, *capish*? Run along, now. On to further adventures."

You nod, and remain. Mister Brother has created a wad of shifting muscles between his shoulder blades. The ropes of his triceps are big enough to throw shadows onto his skin.

You decide to deliver a line devised some time ago, and held in reserve. You say, "Why do you bother with Sandy? Why don't you just date yourself? You know you'll put out, and you can save the price of a movie."

Mister Brother looks at your reflected face in the mirror. He says, "Out, faggot." Now he is imitating no one but himself.

You would prefer to be unaffected by such a cheap shot. It would help if it wasn't true. Given that it is true, you would prefer to have something more in the way of a haughty, crushing response. You would prefer not to be standing here, fat in the fluorescent light, with hippopotamus tears suddenly streaming down your face.

"Christ," Mister Brother says. "Will you just fucking get out of here? Please?"

You will. In another moment, you will. But even now, impaled as you are, you can't quite remove yourself from the presence of your brother's stern and certain beauty.

What can the world possibly do but ruin him? Mister Brother, at seventeen, can have anything he wants, and sees nothing extraordinary about the fact. So what can the world do but marry him (to Carla, not Sandy), find him a job, arrange constellations over his head just the way he likes them and then slowly start shutting down the power? It's one of the oldest stories. There's the beautiful wife who refuses, obdurately, mysteriously, to be as happy as she'd like to be. There's the baby, then another, then (oops, hey, she must be putting pinholes in my condoms) a third. There's the corporate job (money's no joke anymore, not with three kids at home) where charm counts for less and less and where Ossie Ringwald, who played cornet in the high school band, joins the firm three years after Mister Brother does and takes less than two years to become his boss.

All that is waiting, and you and Mister Brother probably know it, somehow, here on this spring night in Pasadena, where the scents of honeysuckle and chaparral are extinguished by Mister Brother's Aramis and Right Guard, and where the souped-up cars of Mister Brother's friends and rivals leave rubber behind on the street. Why else would you love and despise each other so ardently, you who have nothing but blood in common? Looking at that present from this present, it seems possible that you both sense somewhere, beneath the level of language, that some thirty years later he, full of Scotch, pecked bloody by his flock of sorrows, will suffer a spasm of tears and then fall asleep on your sofa with his head in your lap.

That night is now. Here you are, forty-five years old, showing Mister Brother around the new hilltop house you've bought. As Mister Brother walks the premises, Scotch in hand, appreciating this detail or that, you feel suddenly embarrassed by the house. It's too grand. No, it's grand in the wrong way. It's cheesy, Gatsbyesque. The sofa is so . . . faggot Baroque. How had you failed to notice? What made you choose white suede? It had seemed like a brave, reckless disregard of the threat of stains. At this moment, though, it seems possible—it does not seem impossible—that men don't stay around because they can't imagine sitting with you, night after night, on a sofa like this. Maybe that's why you're still alone.

Tonight you sit on the sofa with Mister Brother, who lays his head in your lap. You tell him lots of people go through bad spells in their marriages. You tell him things at work will turn around after the election. Although you still call him by that name, this man is not, strictly speaking, Mister Brother at all. This is a forty-eight-year-old nattily dressed semi-bald guy with a chain around his neck. This is a tax attorney. Here he is and here you are, speaking softly and consolingly as the more powerful constellations begin to show themselves outside your sliding glass doors.

And here you are at fourteen, in this suburban bathroom. You stand another moment with Mister Brother, livid, ashamed, sniveling, and then you finally force yourself to perform the singular act that should, all along, have been so simple. You leave him alone.

"So long, asshole," you say weepily as you exit. "And fuck you too."

If he thought more of you, he'd lash out. He wouldn't continue plucking his eyebrows in the mirror.

You go and lie on your bed, running your fingers over the stylish houndstooth blanket you insisted on; worried, as always, about the stains it covers. You hear Mister Brother downstairs flirting with Mom, shadowboxing with Dad. You hear his Mustang fire up in the driveway. You lie on your bed in the room that will become a guest room, a junk room, a home office, and then the bedroom of a stranger's child. You plan to lose weight and get handsome. You plan to earn in the high five figures before you turn forty. You plan to be somebody other people need to know. These plans will largely, astonishingly, come true.

As Mister Brother roars away, radio blasting, you plan a future in which he respects and admires you. You plan to see him humbled, weeping, penitent. You plan to look pityingly down at him from your own pinnacle of strength and love. These plans will not come true. When the time arrives, reparations will be negotiated between a handsome, lonely man and a much older-looking guy in Dockers and a Bill Blass jacket; an exhausted family man who's had a few too many Scotches. Mister Brother won't come at all. Mister Brother is too fast. Mister Brother is too cool. Mister Brother is off to further adventures, and in his place he's sent a husband and father for you to hold as the city sparkles beyond the blue brightness of your pool and cars pass by on the street blow, leaving snatches of music behind.

TICK

"So, do people get run over by cars and then God, who is invisible, just picks them up from where they are all flat and bloody and he throws them into Heaven?" my daughter asks. "Is that what happens?" She holds out her hands, palms upturned in a gesture of inquiry and impatience.

Sarah's theories of the afterlife are marked by athleticism—sudden changes of spiritual status accomplished by God's bouncing or kicking souls from one world to another. She's a defender of reincarnation, thinks of Heaven as a waiting room, and claims that women are impregnated when God hurls souls of the recently dead into empty female stomachs.

"Is that what you think happens?" I say. Sarah shrugs, drops her hands to her sides.

"I'm asking *you*," she says. "I know what I think."

I go on brushing my daughter's hair. We're standing before the window, looking out on a field bright with wildflowers. Arranged on the windowsill are the hair ornaments that Sarah has selected for the day: a set of pink barrettes, three green elastic ponytail holders, a fake tortoiseshell headband, and two ribbons. In sum, many too many decorations for one small head.

I brush longer than I need to. The tangles are out and the brushing soothes me with its repetitive motion, like sewing or sweeping or fucking, late-night, too-tired-to-fuck fucking.

"Hold still," I say to my daughter.

"I hate this," Sarah says.

"I know," I say. "Everyone does."

I gather the mass of my daughter's hair, pull it back over her shoulders. "Hold still," I say again. It's quixotic to embark on a French braid without having a television to tranquillize my five-year-old daughter, but that's also what makes these braids so beautiful on a small, always moving head: the very impossibility of them. I pick up the first handful of hair and weave in sections from the side, moving down the back of her skull. An undetected snarl halts my progress, and I reach for the hairbrush, which falls from the windowsill. I hold the hair with one hand while I stoop to retrieve the brush.

"Did Daddy make a hole in you with his penis?" Sarah asks.

"No!" I say. "What do you mean?"

"Well, at school they said that babies come from seeds planted in the mother, and that the mother has a egg and that the fathers plant the seeds and that they do it with their penises, so what I mean is, is the penis like the little shovel thing that you use to make a hole before you plant a seed. That's what I mean."

"Oh," I say. "The fathers don't have to make a hole because the mothers have a place for the seed to go in. Everything is all ready for the seed."

"Is it your mouth? Do you swallow it and then it grows in your stomach?"

"No," I say. "It's the place between your legs. The seed goes in the same place that the baby comes out. We talked about this before." We've talked about it a lot, because this summer all we talk about is sex and death, something I'll regard with unexpected nostalgia when we reach the next of humankind's compelling topics: excrement.

As I braid, my fingers encounter something soft and slightly flabby just behind Sarah's right ear. A kernel of corn, I think. Every night in the country we've eaten corn, and the children attack it messily, shearing the bright-yellow buttons off the cob with their sharp little teeth so that half of them drop into their laps and onto the floor. I hold the unfinished braid in my left hand and search through Sarah's hair with my right. I've found corn kernels in the couch and in the beds—even in their shoes. The thing on Sarah's scalp is the size of a large kernel and has a stale, liverish yellow color, but it doesn't brush away. I bend over to look more closely. It's a tick, so engorged that its color has gone from brown to yellow: it has swallowed so much blood that it is pale with intemperance.

I drop the hair I'm holding. Involuntarily, my hand rushes to cover my mouth in a cinematic gesture of shock and revulsion, one I find absurd even in its helplessness. Sarah is engrossed in watching the woodchuck that lives by the compost heap—he's dragging off one of last night's corncobs—so I have a moment to collect myself in the bathroom before I have to gather what I need: tweezers, hydrogen peroxide, cotton balls.

Sarah's hair hangs to her waist and naturally attracts trouble: burrs and gum and pine tar and glue. There's not much that hasn't got stuck in it before. So why am I on my knees on the bath mat, tears dripping into my lap? "Don't be silly!" I would say if it had been Sarah who began to cry. "You're a big girl."

In the cluttered bathroom, toys and toiletries strewn over the floor, my three-year-old son looks up from his clandestine occupations. I can see only one of his eyes behind the big Superman mask he's wearing, its eyeholes cut too far apart to accommodate both of his eyes simultaneously. Seeing that I'm too preoccupied to scold or impede him, he returns with satisfaction to unfolding the towels, all of which he dumps into the damp bathtub.

By the window, Sarah is standing still. Her hair has fallen back over the tick, hiding it, and her face is rapt and beautiful, bathed in clear morning light. I move behind her and, with the tweezers, part her hair to expose the tick.

"Mom!" she wails. I have the tweezers clenched on what looks like the head of the tick and I'm pulling hard, bracing myself with my left hand planted securely against the crown of my daughter's head. But the tick is not letting go; its hold is preternaturally fierce. Just inside the grip of the metal pincers, the bloated bag of the tick's body seeps blood. Sarah's A-positive life wells up around the eight flailing legs of the tick. I pull harder, and the legs stop moving. They stiffen, as if with resolve. I twist it a little, hoping to loosen the animal's jaws or fangs or mandibles—whatever mechanism it has for holding on so tightly. My hand is slick with sweat, the tweezers begin to slip in my fingers.

"Mom! Mom! Mom!" my daughter cries. What could have possessed her mother, she must wonder, to turn a morning braid into this torment?

"I'm sorry, sweetie," I say, my voice unnaturally chipper. "There's something stuck in your hair. I just have to get it out."

Don't pull the body off the head! Don't pull the body off the head! I tell myself. Sarah struggles against my left hand, which still holds her skull tightly, and against my thighs and pelvis, which pin her to the window-sill so she cannot escape. If she gets away, she'll go under the bed or hide in the deep, out of reach corner of the linen closet, the way she does when she gets a scrape and I go after her with the disinfectant. She isn't weirdly, improbably stoic like her little brother, now standing silent in the doorway between bathroom and bedroom, staring at the two of us. Sarah regards most parental interventions as acts of unwarranted aggression.

The tick comes free, and she collapses sobbing on the bed. "I hate you!" she screams, choking on tears.

In the bathroom I dump the toothbrushes from their mug and drop the tick inside. I debate whether to show my daughter the animal and vindicate my behavior or to protect her from the knowledge of the vileness of ticks. Sarah is in one of her frightened periods. She is afraid of things she knows—fire, dogs, spiders, worms, candle smoke, and vaccinations—and of things of which she has heard but of whose horror she cannot quite conceive: earthquakes, vampire bats, and appendicitis. Wherever we go—her grandmother's, the beach, the supermarket, or, as we did one week at the end of winter, Florida—she asks, hesitating distrustfully before disembarking from car or train or bus or plane, "Are there earthquakes here?"

Already Sarah suspects that grown-ups lie to protect her from her fears—when they aren't lying to trick her into obedience—and she considers their answers to her questions darkly, her small eyebrows meeting in fierce appraisal. I decide to show her the tick, but when she looks into the mug she's unimpressed and scowls at me. I have to sit on my daughter to clean the tick bite with peroxide, which foams around the small, bloody place on her scalp. Her heels goes into my crotch with angry force. She calls me a witch and says that I am ugly and *spiteful,* a word I threw at her just last night. Sarah will spend the rest of the morning putting on puppet shows for her little brother. In each production, the witch puppet will be killed by Red Riding Hood: once by fire, twice by drowning, and many times by being plunged to her death from a cliff provided by a staircase behind the theatre.

In another part of the house, I pursue my own drama. The tick lies on its back on the bottom of the blue toothbrush mug. If I discount the mouth and legs, its body's shape and color really are exactly those of a large, stale kernel of corn, a resemblance I find repellent.

Fat with greed, the tick moves its legs with languid strokes of gluttony, as if it were swimming slowly in my child's warm blood. I thought that in removing it I had dealt the tick a mortal wound, because when I squeezed and pulled, a red bead of blood—Sarah's— formed bright on its dull underside. But the blood it lost seems now to have been reabsorbed, sucked back in through the little pore that surrendered it.

Under the tick's back, cloudy stains of toothpaste render its imprisonment in the blue china mug absurdly celestial; and this, along with the delighted, drunken motions of the animal's legs, makes me cruel as well as angry. I flip on the overhead light, a collective three hundred watts that reveal the striations on the tick's body. They look like flattened pleats, places where, accordionlike, its body expanded as its hunger was satisfied. *How will I kill it? How will I torture it?* I think.

On the shelf above the toilet are manicure tools in a red leather case, each implement secured under a tiny girdle of red elastic—a long-ago present from my mother. I select a shiny, stainless-steel wand, a genteel device for nudging back cuticles. When I press the tip of it into the tick, the metal descends into the strangely leathery button of the thing. The tick, motionless, doesn't betray any suffering. I push harder, feeling sick to my stomach. Perhaps I should just drown it in rubbing alcohol, I think. But I'm committed to the idea of punishment. Vengeance makes little sense against a tiny adversary that may not even register its pain, but it is what I want.

We received a set of steak knives as a wedding gift and never used them. Heavy-handled, with blades as narrow as stilettos', the knives are dangerously unbalanced. *I will poke the tip of one of them into the tick,* I think, moving tentatively toward the kitchen, the mug held gingerly out from my side. *I will stick the point of the knife into that place where the blood oozed out before, that sort of tick asshole.* Or I could pull out the legs. Or cut them off with the scalpellike knife. But, I think, standing in the quiet kitchen, those knives aren't in the drawer, are they? No, they're in one of the cryptically marked cartons in the basement. This is our first summer in the country house, and I have yet to move our things into their proper places.

I shake the mug, and the tick bounces around inside like a bean. It draws its legs in tightly against its liverish sides. A tick is not an insect, I recall from high-school invertebrate biology. A tick has eight legs and is related to spiders and crabs. A tick wants blood more than anything, I know, and as I say the words to myself, as I articulate the tick's longing, I understand what I myself want: to make it bleed, to make it surrender what it stole from my child. It's not that I demand this creature's imagined remorse, but what was Sarah's must be returned. A nervous, cool dread uncoils within me.

There's no point in tearing through all those boxes for the steak knives, so I select another kitchen tool, a mysterious implement that resembles an attenuated nutpick. Whatever it is and wherever it came from, I've never had need of it before and won't mind discarding it after this one profane use.

I cut off the first segment of the tick's right foreleg, my determined barbarism making my scalp tighten. I put the pick down, my hand straying unconsciousy to the place above my right ear, touching the spot on my own head where the tick bit Sarah. When I pick up the implement again, I'm not aware of my hand shaking, but the tip of the pick wavers so that it's hard to pin down the rest of the leg and separate it from the body. The tick draws its other limbs into its sides, curls them so tightly that they look like dots on a ladybug. Lying beside its own amputated joints, it betrays no pain or dismay, just the resolve that the other legs will not be so mistreated.

When the phone rings, I almost drop the mug. *"What?"* I say.

"Kathryn?" says my husband, at work in the city.

"Yes," I say. "Hi."

"What's up?"

"Nothing. I found a tick on Sarah."

"Oh," he says, sounding unconcerned. "A big one or a little one?"

"Big."

"Well, that's good, right? It's the little ones that are bad."

"The Lyme ones are little," I concede. "But they're all bad."

My husband tells a tick-related anecdote about his boyhood dog. Understanding that this is intended to relieve my anxiety, I pretend that it does. I tilt the mug back and forth, rolling my wrist so that the tick makes slow circles around the perimeter of the bottom. What is happening inside that tiny, secret brain? Dizziness? Fear? Pain? At least one of these, I hope. I stop swirling the tick in the mug to check to see if it's still moving. It is.

I remember suddenly where I'll find the steak knives. They didn't fit into the last kitchen-miscellany box, so I put them with the books. I slipped the knives between Garrison Keillor and Milan Kundera, a slot where they seemed, during a punch-drunk phase of packing, to make an apt transition—Keillor, Knives, Kundera—dividing the two kinds of humor. In the box is also the unreadably compact, two-volume edition of the Oxford English Dictionary, still in its dark-blue case, which includes a drawer with a magnifying glass.

"So," my husband says. "How's it going? You working on your book?"

"Fine," I say. "Yes," I lie. We talk for a few more minutes, and then I go down to the basement, leaving the cordless phone on the stairs, where I won't remember to find it the next time it rings. I tear open the tape on the carton. The steak knives are there, just where I pictured them. I think for a moment and then slide out the little drawer of the O.E.D.'s case and take the magnifying glass as well.

The tick is using its last leg to cling to the blade of a steak knife, a surface that the magnifying glass reveals to be utterly smooth, lacking any hold for purchase. The tick trembles in the air but magically does not fall. I am pitting myself against a tiny creature of pure instinct, a button programmed for survival, a blot of life unaffected by hope or fear, a fleck of animate energy with an admirable reluctance to die.

We must have rubbing alcohol somewhere, I know we do, but I can't find it, so from the cupboard I get a bottle of white Island rum, a gift from my husband's parents, recently returned from St. Croix. I twist off the sticky lid and pour the heavy liquid out over the tick, and it has a strangely clarifying effect. The rum brings the tick horribly close to my eye, so close that the bloated gut seems planetary in its hugeness.

Yes, huge: there is nothing bigger in the world than this tick stuffed with its minute apparatuses of consumption and digestion.

The surface of the gut consists of gradations of pigment, variances both subtle and extreme. I'm mesmerized by the tick's belly, its topography of shadow and light. The tiny orb becomes, suddenly, a moon. One smudge unmistakably recalls the largest of the lunar landscape's shadows, the Sea of Tranquillity, or whatever it's called—Sea of Longing, of Lonesomeness. All those dim, blue bodies of unwater. When long-dead astronomers peered through their antique, imperfect telescopes, they thought of water: *Mare Undarum,* Sea of Waves. *Mare Serenitatis,* Sea of Fair Weather. But I always get the names wrong. Sea of Loneliness, I think, Sea of Trepidation, of Solemnity. My husband shakes his head. "Why such sad names?" he says.

The rum has dissolved the toothpaste, and the tick floats in a blue the color of a suburban pool. Its one remaining leg curls and uncurls, making a tiny hook, like a beckoning black finger. What passes for its head has gained complexity and even features in the bath of rum. It looks wise and ancient, innocent by virtue of its primitiveness. It looks like the head on a pre-Columbian sculpture squatting under thick museum glass. Like an icon, the tick cares nothing for its incidental, man-made environment. Its kind existed centuries before me and will persist for centuries hence. Ticks evolved to their present state as soon as there was warm-blooded life to support them. And why should they change? In response to what threat? I have taken more than an hour not yet to kill one.

Does it breath? It survives, missing seven legs and submerged in the alcohol. Why is its desire to live so unbeatable?

I consider whether I ought to push the blade into the tick's belly while it lies on its back, aiming for that tiny anus or whatever that little hole is or do what seems less grisly and shove the blade through its back. I swirl the rum in the mug, and the tick turns from its back to its belly. Dorsal, ventral. Decent words of erudition. Civilized words from twelfth-grade science-class dissections of frogs, rats, worms.

I pin the tick belly down. The blade skis off until I lodge it in one of the creases left from its expandable pleats. Surprisingly, pressure does not rupture what's left of the body; instead, an elegant silver stream of bubbles erupts from each of the seven places where I tore a leg off. I push the knife harder, and it goes in at last with a tiny pop. But still no blood. I withdraw the knife's blade and use the handle to press on the tick until a fat, black bubble—of what? intestine?—exudes through the hole I made in the tick's skin. Its exoskeleton.

I am waiting for Sarah's blood to drift into the rum, to waft pinkly over the tiny corpse. The reappearance of my daughter's stolen life will qualify as redemption. That's why I have performed this abomination. But, though I have made ten holes in the tick with the fine point of the blade, and from each of them pressed a tarry bubble, I have not drawn blood. The tick's leg curls and uncurls, each tiny jointed segment beautiful in its persistent perfection. The body is a mess. Pulped. Nothing left to plunder. All of what the tick drank from my daughter is digested, evidently; Sarah's blood has turned to excrement before I could reclaim it.

In the bathroom, I consider the dismembered submarine carnage of tiny, torn legs and what seem like trailing intestines that undulate in the rum. Cloudy now instead of clear, the spirit reveals my cruelty as a dulling process: one of obfuscation. I lift the toilet lid and pour the rum into the water. The pieces of tick sink, sliding slowly down the concave incline of the white bowl. The tick has won.

Matthew Sharpe

A CAR

Dreamlike images appear: a girl in a white dress on a swing, malevolent clowns holding a gigantic key . . .

GIRL'S VOICE: *It was like some kind of bad dream. By the time Dad was finished, I was scared to death of buying a car. It would be obvious this was my first time, but it had to be done. . . . So while everyone else was spending money, I made some. And when Dad announced he was coming along, I didn't stop him. As if I could have. (Now father-daughter car-shopping scenes appear.) After a few of those places, I began to think Dad really knew what he was talking about. Scary, huh? Then I had this idea. Going in, Dad says, "Now don't act too interested. . . ." He was supposed to do the talking, but there were no hassles. Even over the price. So I bought one. Dad goes, "Well, it's a good thing you had me along." The thing about Dad is, he likes to feel useful, and that's cool.*

—TV advertisement for a car

Our daughter's body is a reproach to us. She has recently turned into a little monster of physical fitness and moral rectitude. Which doesn't mean that I don't know there are shifts in a family, and that no one is ever prepared for them. I remember, for example, the entire year when I was ironic. Maybe I hit upon irony because it is the thing that terrifies me most. Irony is like an evil twin that clubs you over the head, gags you, and throws you down the basement stairs and takes your place at the breakfast table with your family. And it says exactly what you would say, only instead of saying, for instance, "I love you," it says " 'I love you.' " I was ironic for a year because that was the period during which I was infatuated with a certain woman in my office. I would like to point out that even during that year, I was loyal to my wife and daughter almost down to the tiniest scruple. It must have been awful for them.

Still, my infatuation ended, and so did my irony. Our family mended and moved on. It's different with Susie, our daughter, who is sixteen years old. We're afraid her current behavior is not merely a mood, but a temperament.

The three of us have had a tradition of eating breakfast together in our pajamas, but lately, Jane and I teeter down the stairs stiff and weary on our skinny legs, rubbing the crust out of our eyes, and Susie is already in some absurd yoga position on the floor of the breakfast nook. One morning we showed up and Susie was kneeling on the clean, bare linoleum floor in her little exercise getup, thighs smooth as plastic. Without ceasing to kneel, she lay back with her legs tucked under her. The back of her head and the nape of her neck were touching the floor. We could see her ribs and the outline of her hard little abdomen under her cotton jersey. She inhaled deeply and said, "You two are like a furnace of foul odors." She said it with such good humor that we didn't know how to take it. The whole thing was very odd. From her position on the floor, all lean and contorted, she had this power over us. Jane and I looked at one another and I could see that it was a bad day for Jane. We turned around and walked slowly up the stairs, no doubt with terrible posture, and we got back into bed and we fell asleep.

She runs ten miles, she swims three miles, she rides her bicycle forty miles, she does her homework, she works at a tanning salon after school and saves her money, she goes out with her nice friends and has a good time engaging in moderate activities. She's going to buy a new car. I want to say to her, "Susie, get a fake ID and have a few drinks. Buy a quart bottle of Wild Turkey and get sick. Borrow my car without asking. Skip school. Smoke pot. Have an affair with a forty-year-old alcoholic woman with a ring in her nose." But Susie runs fifteen miles. She runs thirty miles.

My wife's body fits my own so nicely, our ungainly, saggy bodies, as we lie in bed holding one another and talking. It's a bit of solace against this stinking world. The other night we were discussing Susie's impending purchase of a new car. Jane said, "Can't you take her aside for just fifteen minutes and tell her what kind of a crazy circus she's going to encounter in car sales?" We were lying on our backs, angled slightly to face one another. Her head was resting on my arm and our bodies were in gentle contact all the way down to our ankles. The lights were off but I could see Jane's face as it was illuminated by the streetlamps our town government had put up, and by the small lantern we have in our front yard, both of which are on timers that turn them on an hour after sunset and off an hour before sunrise. Jane's face is not beautiful, but there is nobody's face I would rather look at. Show me the most gorgeous twenty-eight-year-old model for eyeliner or moisturizing creme—my heart might race for a couple of seconds, but don't make me face her for an hour. Familiarity is better than beauty. The extra grooves in Jane's skin, the puffiness around the eyes, the small amount of flesh that has accumulated below her jawline during the twenty years of my having looked at her steadily: these things are a life's work. Jane and I own each other's skin.

"Yes, that's good," I said. "Circus. That's just it. It *is* a circus. But how am I gonna tell her? You now how she is."

"Please. Don't tell me about how she is. I'm her mother. It's worse for the mother. With the father I don't think there's the same humiliation." I could see the echo of the word "humiliation" in the muscles of her face the instant before she smiled in that pained way. "Humiliation" has a particular meaning for us. Rather, it has a particular meaning for me that Jane is aware of. She doesn't know the details of the single event in my life that makes the word resound at the very core of my being—namely, the ending of my infatuation with the young woman—but she understands. This seems to be the gift of women: to know the feeling of an event without knowing the event. Thus Jane can say, "Oh I saw the most wonderful movie on public television the other night," and I'll say, "What was it called?" and she'll say, "I can't remember," and I'll say, "Who was it by?" and she'll say, "I don't know, I think it was Australian," and I'll say, "What was it about?" et cetera. (In this regard, by the way, our daughter, Susie, is more like a man.)

"Okay, now tell me what you mean by circus."

"You know, they're a bunch of clowns, car dealers. They'll deceive her with illusion and falsehood. They're famous for it. The whole enterprise is just going to be another defeat for our family. Could you go with her maybe?"

"You mean accompany her while she shops for the car? First of all, she probably won't let me. Second of all, it's a dreadful prospect, spending a goal-oriented day with that supercilious little American girl."

Jane laughed. "Oh for Christ's sake, we've got to help her."

A car went by on the street in front of our house and we both watched the crucifix-shaped shadow of our window frame move from one side of our bedroom ceiling to the other.

"My arm is asleep," I said, and tried unsuccessfully to wiggle it out from under her heavy head.

"It's funny that you say, 'My arm is asleep.' What you really mean is that your arm, as the result of a trauma, has fallen unconscious. Your arm has fainted. It's been overtaxed. Your arm's getting older, dear."

We laughed. Jane didn't move her head and I didn't move my arm. We fell asleep.

I made a point of getting up early, showering and deodorizing, shaving, and putting on a fresh, crisp shirt and pants before going down to breakfast. As I approached the door to the kitchen, I saw Susie's two tall, clean, golden legs sticking up side by side from behind the table in the breakfast nook, toes pointed. "Morning, sweetheart. I'm all clean and not smelly."

"Look, this is the candle position, Dad. Can you touch your toes?" Her entire weight was balanced on her shoulders and neck and the back of her blond head. I don't know where she got her coloring from since Jane and I are brunettes. She exhaled and rolled forward one vertebra at a time. When her legs were flat out in front of her, she continued to move forward until her fingers were holding the bottoms of her feet and her face was between her knees.

"Susie, are you going to start your car hunt today? I thought we should just talk over your strategy on buying this car."

She didn't answer. Her breathing was steady and slow. It was clear that these idle greetings and questions of her father's were an annoying distraction.

After she had held that same position for a couple of minutes, she unfolded herself and stood up. She went to the cupboard and got a glass, which she held under our refrigerator's automatic ice dispenser, and then she took the carton of orange juice out of the fridge and poured some into the glass. "We should stop buying this stuff," she said. "*Consumer Reports* rated a couple of the new electric juicers really high. I think we ought to invest in one. Most of the nutrients are lost in the concentrating and rehydrating process, not to mention the flavor."

"What do you do, casually flip through *Consumer Reports* in your spare time? Most girls your age are languishing in their rooms listening to Janic Ian over and over, reading *Seventeen* magazine."

"Most girls my age don't read. They also don't save their money or spend it wisely." My daughter talks this way, like Ben Franklin or something.

"So about the car," I said.

"The Japanese cars seem good," she said. "There's that new American car company that seems to have a lot of integrity. I'm looking at the area between compact and midsize. Gotta have passenger side airbag. Gotta have antilock brakes. I'm thinking four-wheel drive for winter safety but I'm not sure the terrain in this area demands it."

"You don't know where you'll be going to college," I said.

"Good point, Dad. Excellent point," she said thoughtfully.

It's pretty rare that she finds something I say worthy of consideration. I could feel myself blush when she said that. I had momentum, so I said, "I just want you to be careful because even though you may know a lot about the cars, the car dealers are tricky and deceitful. A car dealership is like, you know, a circus. You go in there, they throw a lot of jargon at you. They say 'reclining bucket seats' and 'V-six engine' and 'ergonomic design' and 'hard-body steel construction' with big smiles on their faces."

"Dad, give me a little credit for knowing something. Also you're exaggerating the evil in human nature as usual."

"No. You know what? You give *me* a little credit. I'm not paranoid. I have actual experience with car dealers. I've bought cars. I even once knew a car dealer. If you do this all on your own, you're gonna get hurt."

She was silent for a moment. "It sounds like you relish the idea of me getting hurt," she said. "Excuse me. I'm going for a bike ride."

As she walked out the back door, I called after her, "I do not relish the idea of you getting hurt."

I often have this sensation after talking to Susie or Jane that I've left out the most important thing. I can never put my finger on what it is, but I feel that if I were to say it, even once in one conversation, it would make us a winning family instead of the other.

"She resented my input," I said to Jane that night. We were lying in bed again. Inertia epitomizes our marriage. I don't mean that we don't change or that we're frightened of progress. I mean that our last moments of consciousness each night, when we talk and lie together, amount to a dark nest of quiet truth amid all the racket. Our conversations are the opposite of a car.

"Don't say 'input,' " she said. " 'Input' is like 'reclining bucket seats.' "

"You're right," I said. " 'Input' is a dirty word."

Jane smiled and snuggled against my soft, hairy shoulder. "What did you say to her?" she asked.

"I said the thing about car dealers being clowns."

"But what was the point? What were you hoping to persuade her to do?"

"Let me come along and protect her." As soon as I said this, I pictured Susie's body, which is like a coat of armor, and I realized how absurd a thing it was for me to protect her, and so did Jane, and we had a good laugh.

"So I guess she turned you down."

"I guess so."

"Are we just going to let her go through with this by herself?"

I sighed. We were silent for a moment and I could hear the alarm clock ticking on the night table on Jane's side of the bed.

"I mean what are we going to do with her?" Jane said.

"Pack her off to boarding school?"

"I think she really needs the opposite of boarding school."

"What's the opposite of boarding school?"

"Maybe she could climb in bed and sleep with us the way she used to?"

"Maybe we could accidentally push her down the stairs."

Jane gasped and rushed to put her forefinger to her mouth and say, "Shhh," as if suddenly Susie could hear our whispers from down the hall. But I saw that smile breaking out behind her finger.

The following day was a Saturday. At eight-thirty A.M. on my way to the bathroom, I saw that the thermometer outside our bedroom window indicated 65 degrees. In anticipation of Susie's subtly perfumed limbs at breakfast that morning I lost all hope and went back to bed for an hour and a half. Jane and I were feeling so embattled that when I finally did get up, we agreed that I would scout out the breakfast nook. If *she* was still there, I was to grab a box of cereal, some milk, a couple of spoons and bowls, mumble something about "your mother's menopause," and retreat to the bedroom.

"Dad," she said, before I had caught sight of her, "let's go; get a move on; shake a leg. I want to have a car all picked out by five o'clock this afternoon." She had evidently finished with her yoga. She was wearing a new pair of fancy jeans and an off-white short-sleeved silk blouse and a delicate gold necklace and elegant brown pumps: a car-hunting outfit.

"What?" I said. "You want me to go with you?"

"Of course I do, Dad. How would I be able to do this without you?" There it was: Susie's evil twin.

I showered. I put on a polo shirt, khaki pants—the Dad outfit.

As we were walking out the door, Susie threw on a blue blazer, put a Walkman in her pocket, stuck the tiny speakers in her ears, and proceeded to listen to music that only she could hear.

"You gonna wear that thing when we talk to the salesman?"

"What do you think I am?" she said, louder than she needed to.

The first place we went was to the showroom of the American car with integrity. We walked in. No one approached us. All the walls were made of glass. The lighting was subdued. The air smelled processed. The cars were shiny and resting gently on the gray carpet. I felt as if we were in a fancy restaurant that had cars instead of food. I became nauseated. What did she need a car for? She was sixteen, she could ride her bike. I prepared myself to forbid her to buy a car.

Susie marched us over to one of the sales offices. When I caught a glimpse of the salesman sitting behind his desk, I put my hands over my face. In the few moments my face remained covered by my hands, I gave up on Susie; I gave up on her altogether. Then I turned so that my back was to the salesman, dreading that he had seen my face, and I asked Susie to step away from his office for a moment.

Very quickly and monotonously I said, "I've decided to let you handle this by yourself. I think this car company *is* different and they won't take advantage of you. This will be a good experience too, for you to buy a car on your own. If you can do this you'll be ready for adulthood."

"What? Excuse me, Dad, but this is very weird."

"I've thought it over; this is what I want you to do. Here are the keys to my car. I'll take the bus home."

"Thought it over? It seems like you, like, are freaking out on the spur of the moment. You said you were gonna buy the car with me."

"You didn't really want me to."

"Yes." Her face was red. She looked confused. It was all I could do to walk and not run for the door of the showroom.

The salesman, you see, was the husband of that young woman who had caused me to be ironic with my family for an entire year seven years ago. I had known way back that the guy was a car salesman, but it must have slipped my mind. Not only did his wife work in my office; she was my secretary. I cannot put into words how beautiful she was. I thought that any life with her in it would be better than what I had, no matter how high the price.

I wanted to fire her but there were no grounds. For a year I practiced self-restraint. Then, one warm Friday in spring, when everyone else in the company had gone home, she wore a sleeveless blouse into my office to water the plants, and I got down on my knees. She was standing above me and I took her hand and told her I loved her and I asked her if she would go away with me the following weekend. She ran out of the office and never came back.

For several months after that, I came home from work, ate dinner, and went to bed; on the weekends I slept as much as possible and rarely left the house. I did not tell Jane what had happened, but my irony was gone and I'm sure she understood, in that way she understands without knowing. What she did was remarkable. She spent the time in bed with me. If I lay in bed until noon on a Saturday, she lay in bed until noon. If I went to sleep at eight o'clock on a work night, she climbed in next to me and held me in her warm arms. It must have been tough on nine-year-old Susie, her two parents hiding in the bedroom, cohabitating in their defeat.

*   *   *

Jane was not at home when I arrived. I didn't know what to do with myself. I sat at the kitchen table. I saw ahead of me an afternoon of sitting and waiting and I was afraid.

At this point I had the following thought: What would Susie do? The answer was that she would run ten or fifteen miles and then go for a thirty-mile swim. So I actually went up to our bedroom and found a pair of sweatpants and a T-shirt and put them on. On the way down the stairs I felt hopeful. Then, in the driveway, I felt stupid. I was in my pajamas, practically. Then Jane came up the driveway in the station wagon.

She got out of the car and laughed. "Say it isn't so!" She was referring to my jogging attire.

As a kind of preemptive strike, I scrutinized her outfit. She never dresses well. She had on an old pink T-shirt with a worn, frilly hem. It was too small for her. Her jeans were baggy and her tennis shoes, which she had worn to play tennis about twice, were dirty and frayed. Her graying brown hair was stuck up on top of her head with a random assortment of bobby pins and barrettes.

"What happened? Did you get kicked off the car-hunting team?"

I nodded.

"Ooh, you look so cute in your getup." She came over smiling and grabbed my shoulders and kissed me all over the face, making with each kiss an enhanced, artificial kissing noise—*mwa*—as if we were a brand-new couple in our twenties.

"Frankly, you don't look so great at the moment yourself," I said, before it dawned on me that she was not being ironic.

Her face looked pained, and then calm. "So it really smarts that Susie wouldn't let you shop for the car with her, eh?"

"Yeah, that's right," I said, "I guess it really does smart."

Now she squinted, which meant she knew there was a discrepancy between what had happened and what was being said. "Why don't you come inside," she said "and we'll split a beer while we wait for her to come."

There was such assurance in the way she said that, and in the way she hooked my arm with hers and steered us toward the front door, that I was afraid of her. Surely when Susie got home my lie about getting kicked off the car team would be found out. And if I sat across the kitchen table from Jane just waiting for Susie to come home, it was conceivable that *all* my lies would be found out. "I feel disgusting. I'm going to take a shower," I said.

"Do whatever you want."

As I was dressing, I looked out our bedroom window and saw Susie coming up the driveway in a brand-new economy-size hatchback from the American car company. I ran downstairs and out into the driveway. Susie got out of the car. Her face was flushed. I gave her a big hug. "I'm sorry, honey," I whispered before Jane caught up with her.

"Dad, it's fine. It worked out for the best. You'll never believe what happened. Mom," she said to Jane, who was strolling toward us, "you'll never believe what happened."

"What happened?"

Sweat was pouring from my armpits onto my freshly laundered polo shirt.

"So we're in the car taking a test drive, just me and the salesman, right?"

Jane and I nodded eagerly. Here was this beautiful new car in our driveway that Susie had purchased all by herself. Jane was infected by the car and by Susie's radiance. The two of them made their mouths into these big alarming smiles.

"So we're on the highway, right? And I'm driving? Well this guy puts his hand on my knee. The car salesman does. For real." Jane stopped smiling. "And then he starts asking me things and saying things to me. I can't even tell you what they were because I'd be too embarrassed. But he said like five separate gross things to me. I had no idea what to say to him, so I didn't say anything, I just concentrated on getting back to the lot as fast as I could, but I also didn't want to get a ticket or anything.

"And then, check this out. Mom, Dad, when we get back to the lot, I have this brilliant idea. Dad, remember how I had that Walkman in the pocket of my blazer that you were giving me a hard time about? Well, I jump out of the car and show him the Walkman and I, like press one of the buttons like it had been on the whole time and I say, 'Look, mister, I just recorded everything you said to me in that car, and that is totally sexual harassment. Not to mention I'm a minor.' So you know what I made him do? I made him sell me the car for fifteen hundred dollars below list price. I got the Achilles for six and a quarter! Is that awesome or what?"

Susie laughed with sheer joy and jumped up and down, and she wanted her parents to jump up and down with her, but we were too old and out of shape, and her story was actually pretty depressing.

Even though I thought it might still emerge that I had abandoned Susie at the door of the salesman's office, among other things, I feigned happiness, as Jane seemed to be doing, and I said I'd take everyone out for a nice celebration dinner.

Susie went up to her room and Jane and I sat down across from each other at the dreaded table in the breakfast nook.

"What do you make of this?" Jane asked.

I had my hand over my mouth. I shook my head.

"Did you meet this fellow, the pervert?"

I shook my head again.

"You didn't see him."

"I saw him."

"But you didn't meet him."

"Right."

"You didn't really get kicked off the car-hunting team, did you? You resigned, didn't you?"

I thought this was it. I saw everything collapsing. "How did you know?"

"Please," she said. "I understand."

"You do?"

"Well no," she said. "I really don't understand. I believe there's something—" She didn't finish the sentence. She stood up and walked to the window that overlooks our driveway and stared down at Susie's new car. Then she came back to the table. "Whatever else happened, it's clear to me that Susie's story is false," she said. "Let's get ready for dinner."

I tried to take Jane's hand and walk up the stairs with her, but she pulled her hand away and went up by herself.

When I got to the top of the stairs, I heard water running in the bathroom down the hall. Susie was taking a shower, though she had taken one just before we left to buy the car. I have since verified that

Susie did indeed pay six and a quarter for the car, but, like Jane, I don't think it happened the way Susie said it did. Behind the sound of the shower was another sound, a funny noise. I walked down the hall and stood outside the bathroom door and I realized what the noise was. It was Susie sobbing. That means she's not as good a liar as her father is. Surely this fact alone constitutes a victory for our family.

OLD MOTHER AND
THE GROUCH

"Meet the sourpuss," says the Grouch to their friends.

"Oh, shut up," says Old Mother.

The Grouch and Old Mother are playing Scrabble. The Grouch makes a play.

"Ten points," he says. He is disgusted.

He is angry because Old Mother is winning early in the game and because she has drawn all the *S*'s and blanks. He says it is easy to win if you get all the *S*'s and blanks. "I think you marked the backs," he says. She says a blank tile doesn't have a back.

Now he is angry because she has made the word *qua*. He says *qua* is not English. He says they should both make good, familiar words like the words he has made—*bonnet, realm* and *weave*—but instead she sits in her nasty corner making *aw, eh, fa, ess,* and *ax*. She says these are words, too. He says even if they are, there is something mean and petty about using them.

Now the Grouch is angry because Old Mother keeps freezing all the food he likes. He brings home a nice smoked ham and wants a couple of slices for lunch but it is too late—he has already frozen it.

"It's hard as a rock," he says. "And you don't have to freeze it anyway. It's already smoked."

Then, since everything else he wants to eat is also frozen, he thinks he will at least have some of the chocolate ice cream he bought for her the day before. But it's gone. She has eaten it all.

"Is that what you did last night?" he asks. "You stayed up late eating ice cream?"

He is close to the truth, but not entirely correct.

Old Mother cooks dinner for friends of theirs. After the friends have gone home, she tells the Grouch the meal was a failure: the salad dressing had too much salt in it, the chicken was overdone and tasteless, the cherries hard, etc.

She expects him to contradict her, but instead he listens carefully and adds that the noodles, also, were "somehow wrong."

She says, "I'm not a very good cook."

She expects him to assure her that she is, but instead he says, "You should be. Anybody can be a good cook."

Old Mother sits dejected on a stool in the kitchen.

"I just want to teach you something about the rice pot," says the Grouch, by way of introduction, as he stands at the sink with his back to her.

But she does not like this. She does not wish to be his student.

One night Old Mother cooks him a dish of polenta. He remarks that is has spread on the plate like a cow patty. He tastes it and says that it tastes better than it looks. On another night she makes him a brown rice casserole. The Grouch says this does not look very good either. He covers it in salt and pepper, then eats some of it and says it also tastes better than it looks. Not much better, though.

"Since I met you," says the Grouch, "I have eaten more beans than I ever ate in my life. Potatoes and beans. Every night there is nothing but beans, potatoes, and rice."

Old Mother knows this is not strictly true.

"What did you eat before you knew me?" she asks.

"Nothing," says the Grouch. "I ate nothing."

*   *   *

Old Mother likes all chicken parts, including the liver and heart, and the Grouch likes the breasts only. Old Mother likes the skin on and the Grouch likes it off. Old Mother prefers vegetables and bland food. The Grouch prefers meat and strong spices. Old Mother prefers to eat her food slowly and brings it hot to the table. The Grouch prefers to eat quickly and burns his mouth.

"You don't cook the foods I like," the Grouch tells her sometimes.

"You ought to like the foods I cook," she answers.

"Spoil me. Give me what I want, not what you think I should have," he tells her.

That's an idea, thinks Old Mother.

Old Mother wants direct answers from the Grouch. But when she asks, "Are you hungry?" he answers, "It's seven o'clock." And when she asks, "Are you tired?" he answers, "It's ten o'clock." And when she insists, and asks again, "But are you tired?" he says, "I've had a long day."

Old Mother likes two blankets at night, on a cold night, and the Grouch is more comfortable with three. Old Mother thinks the Grouch should be comfortable with two. The Grouch, on the other hand, says, "I think you like to be cold."

Old Mother does not mind running out of supplies and often forgets to shop. The Grouch likes to have more than they need of everything, especially toilet paper and coffee.

On a stormy night the Grouch worries about his cat, shut outdoors by Old Mother.

"Worry about me," says Old Mother.

Old Mother will not have the Grouch's cat in the house at night because it wakes her up scratching at the bedroom door or yowling outside it. If they let it into the bedroom, it rakes up the carpet. If she complains about the cat, he takes offense: he feels she is really complaining about him.

* * *

Friends say they will come to visit, and then they do not come. Out of disappointment, the Grouch and Old Mother lose their tempers and quarrel.

On another day, friends say they will come to visit, and this time the Grouch tells Old Mother he will not be home when they come: they are not friends of his.

A phone call comes from a friend of hers he does not like.

"It's for you, *angel*," he says, leaving the receiver on the kitchen counter.

Old Mother and the Grouch have quarrelled over friends, the West Coasts, the telephone, dinner, what time to go to bed, what time to get up, travel plans, her parents, his work, her work, and his cat, among other subjects. They have not quarrelled, so far, over special sale items, acquisitions for the house, natural landscapes, wild animals, and several other subjects.

A woman dressed all in red is jumping up and down in a tantrum. It is Old Mother, who cannot handle frustration.

If Old Mother talks to a friend out of his earshot, the Grouch thinks she must be saying unkind things about him. He is not right: often, by the time he appears glowering in the doorway, she has gone on to other topics.

One day in June, the Grouch and Old Mother take all their potted plants out onto the deck for the summer. The next week, the Grouch brings them all back in and sets them on the living room floor. Old Mother does not understand what he is doing and is prepared to object, but they have quarrelled and are not speaking to each other, so she can only watch him in silence.

The Grouch is more interested in money than Old Mother and more careful about how he spends it. He reads sale ads and will not buy anything unless it is marked down. "You're not very good with money," he says. She would like to deny it but she can't. She buys a book, secondhand, called "How to Live Within Your Income."

They spend a good deal of time one day drawing up a list of what each of them will do in their household. For instance, she will make their dinner but he will make his own lunch. By the time they are finished, it is time for lunch and Old Mother is hungry. The Grouch has taken some care over a tuna fish salad for himself. Old Mother says it looks good and asks him if she can share it. Annoyed, he points out that now, contrary to the agreement, he had made *their* lunch.

Old Mother could only have wanted a man of the highest ideals but now she finds she can't live up to them; the Grouch could only have wanted the best sort of woman, but she is not the best sort of woman.

Old Mother thinks her temper may improve if she drinks more water. When her temper remains bad, she begins taking a daily walk and eating more fresh fruit.

Old Mother reads an article which says: If one of you is in a bad mood the other should stay out of her way and be as kind as possible until the bad mood passes.

But when she proposes this to the Grouch, he refuses to consider it. He does not trust her: she will claim to be in a bad mood when she is not, and then require him to be kind to her.

Old Mother decides she will dress up as a witch on Halloween, since she is often described as a witch by the Grouch. She owns a pointed black hat, and now she buys more items to make up her costume. She thinks the Grouch will be amused, but he asks her please to remove the rubber nose from the living room.

The Grouch is exasperated. Old Mother has been criticizing him again. He says to her, "You should have married a man who didn't drink or smoke. And who also had no hands or feet. Or arms or legs."

*　　*　　*

The Grouch is exasperated again. Again, Old Mother has been criticizing him. This time he says, "If I changed that, you'd only find something else to criticize. And if I changed that, then something else would be wrong."

Old Mother tells the Grouch she feels ill. She thinks she may soon have to go into the bathroom and be sick. They have been quarrelling, and so the Grouch says nothing. He goes into the bathroom, however, and washes the toilet bowl, then brings a small red towel and lays it on the foot of the bed where she is resting.

Weeks later, Old Mother tells the Grouch that one of the kindest things he ever did for her was to wash the toilet bowl before she was sick. She thinks he will be touched, but instead, he is insulted.

"Can't you agree with me about anything?" asks the Grouch.

Old Mother has to admit it: she almost always disagrees with him. Even if she agrees with most of what he is saying, there will be some small part of it she disagrees with.

When she does agree with him, she suspects her own motives: she may agree with him only so that at some future time she will be able to remind him that she does sometimes agree with him.

Old Mother has her favorite armchair, and the Grouch has his. Sometimes, when the Grouch is not at home, Old Mother sits in his chair, and then she also picks up what he has been reading and reads it herself.

Old Mother is dissatisfied with the way they spend their evenings together and imagines other activities such as taking walks, writng letters, and seeing friends. She proposes these activities to the Grouch, but the Grouch becomes angry. He does not like her to organize anything in his life. Now the way they spend this particular evening is quarrelling over what she has said.

Both the Grouch and Old Mother want to make love, but he wants to make love before the movie, while she wants to make love either during it or after. She agrees to before, but then if before, wants the radio on. He prefers the television and asks her to take her glasses off. She agrees to the television, but prefers to lie with her back to it. Now he can't see it over her shoulder because she is lying on her side. She can't see it because she is facing him and her glasses are off. He asks her to move her shoulder.

Old Mother hears the footsteps of the Grouch in the lower hall as he leaves the living room on his way to bed. She looks around the bedroom to see what will bother him. She removes her feet from his pillow, stands up from his side of the bed, turns off a few lights, takes her slippers out of his way into the room, and shuts a dresser drawer. But she knows she has forgotten something. What he complains about first is the noise of the white mice running in their cage in the next room, and then the wrinkled sheets.

"Maybe I could help with that," says Old Mother sincerely as they are driving in the car, but after what she did the night before she knows he will not want to think of her as a helpful person. The Grouch only snorts.

Old Mother shares a small triumph with the Grouch, hoping he will congratulate her. He remarks that some day she will not bother to feel proud of that sort of thing.

"I slept like a log," he says in the morning. "What about you?"
    Well, most of the night was fine, she explains, but toward morning she slept lightly, trying to keep still in a position that did not hurt her neck. She was trying to keep still so as not to bother him, she adds. Now he is angry.

"How did you sleep?" she asks him on another morning as he comes downstairs late.
    "Not very well," he answers. "I was awake around 1:30. You were still up."
    "No, I wasn't still up at 1:30," she says.
    "12:30, then."

"You were very restless," says the Grouch on yet another morning. "You kept tossing and turning."

"Don't accuse me," says Old Mother.

"I'm not accusing you, I'm just stating the facts. You were very restless."

"All right: the reason I was restless was that you were snoring."

Now the Grouch is angry. "I don't snore."

Old Mother is lying on the bathroom floor reading, her head on a small stack of towels and a pillow, a bath towel covering her, because she has not been able to sleep and doesn't want to disturb the Grouch. She falls asleep there on the bathroom floor, goes back to bed, wakes again, returns to the bathroom, and continues to read. Finally the Grouch, having woken up because she was gone, comes to the door and offers her some earplugs.

The Grouch wants to listen to Fischer-Dieskau singing, accompanied by Brendel at the piano, but to his annoyance he finds that Fischer-Dieskau accompanied by Brendel is also accompanied by Old Mother humming, and he asks her to stop.

Old Mother makes an unpleasant remark about one of their lamps.

The Grouch is sure Old Mother is insulting him. He tries to figure out what she is saying about him, but can't, and so remains silent.

The Grouch is on his way out with heavy boxes on his arms when Old Mother thinks of something else she wants to say.

"Hurry up, I'm holding these," says the Grouch.

Old Mother does not like to hurry when she has something to say. "Put them down for a minute," she tells him.

The Grouch does not like to be delayed or told what to do. "Just hurry up," he says.

In the middle of an argument, the Grouch often looks at Old Mother in disbelief which is either real or feigned: "Wait a minute," he says. "Wait just a minute."

Well into an argument, Old Mother often begins to cry in frustration. Though her frustration and her tears are genuine she also hopes the

Grouch will be moved to pity. The Grouch is never moved to pity, only further exasperated, saying, "Now you start snivelling."

The Grouch often arrives home asking such questions as:

"What is this thing? Are you throwing coffee grounds under this bush? Did you mean to leave the car doors unlocked? Do you know why the garage door is open? What is all that water doing on the lawn? Is there a reason all the lights in the house are on? Why was the hose unscrewed?"

Or he comes downstairs and asks:

"Who broke this? Where are all the bathmats? Is your sewing machine working? When did this happen? Did you see the stain on the kitchen ceiling? Why is there a sponge on the piano?"

Old Mother says, "Don't always criticize me."

The Grouch says, "I'm not criticizing you. I just want certain information."

They often disagree about who is to blame: if he is hurt by her, it is possible that she was harsh in what she said; but it is also possible that her intentions were good and he was too sensitive in his reaction.

For instance, the Grouch may be unusually sensitive to the possibility that a woman is ordering him around. But this is hard to decide, because Old Mother is a woman who tends to order people around.

Old Mother is excited because she has a plan to improve her German. She tells the Grouch she is going to listen to Advanced German tapes while she is out driving in the car.

"That sounds depressing," says the Grouch.

The Grouch is cross about his own work when he comes home and therefore cross with her. He snaps at her: "I can't do everything at once."

She is offended and becomes angry. She demands an apology, wanting him to be sincere and affectionate.

He apologizes, but because he is still cross, he is not sincere and affectionate.

She becomes angrier.

Now he complains: "When I'm upset, you get even more upset."

"I'm going to put on some music," says the Grouch.

Old Mother is immediately nervous.

"Put on something easy," she says.

"I know that whatever I put on, you won't like it," he says.

"Just don't put on Messiaen," she says. "I'm too tired for Messiaen."

The Grouch comes into the living room to apologize for what he has said. Then he feels he must explain why he said it, though Old Mother already knows. But as he explains at some length, what he says makes him angry all over again, and he says one or two more things that provoke her, and they begin arguing again.

Now and then Old Mother wonders just why she and the Grouch have such trouble getting along. Perhaps, given her failures of tact, she needed a man with more confidence. Certainly, at the same time, given his extreme sensitivity, he needed a gentler woman.

They receive many Chinese fortunes. The Grouch finds it correct that her mentality is "alert, practical and analytical," especially concerning his faults. He finds it correct that "The great fault in women is to desire to be like men," but it has not been true, so far, most of the time anyway, that "Someone you care about seeks reconciliation" or that "she always gets what she wants through her charm and personality."

Certainly the Grouch wanted a strong-willed woman, but not one quite as strong-willed as Old Mother.

The Grouch puts on some music. Old Mother starts crying. It is a Haydn piano sonata. He thought she would like it. But when he put it on and smiled at her, she started crying.

Now they are having an argument about Charpentier and Lully: he says he no longer plays Charpentier motets when she is at home because he knows she does not like them.

She says he still plays Lully.

He says it's the Charpentier motets she doesn't like.

She says it's the whole period she doesn't like.

Now she has put her stamps in his stamp box, thinking to be helpful. But the stamps are of many different denominations and have stuck together in the damp weather. They argue about the stamps, and then go on to argue about the argument. She wants to prove he was unfair to her, since her intentions were good. He wants to prove she was not really thinking of him. But because they cannot agree on the sequence in which certain remarks were made, neither one can convince the other.

The Grouch needs attention, but Old Mother pays attention mainly to herself. She needs attention too, of course, and the Grouch would be happy to pay attention to her if the circumstances were different. He will not pay her much attention if she pays him almost none at all.

Old Mother is in the bathroom for an inordinately long time. When she comes out, the Grouch asks her if she is upset with him. This time, however, she was only picking raspberry seeds out of her teeth.

NOVICE BITCH

"Want a treat?" my mother asks, but before I can even open my mouth, she slips a hot-dog-shaped dog yummie between her teeth, bends down, and scoops Waffles up off the kitchen floor. Waffles obediently bites down on the tiny weenie and, for a second, nose to nose, they kiss.

"Well, that's revolting," I say.

My mother raises an eyebrow, and I wait for her to share some inane dog factoid with me, like how a dog's mouth is cleaner than a human's, but she doesn't; instead she sighs. She's the wounded mother persecuted by a selfish, ungrateful daughter. Mildred Pierce of Park Avenue.

"Dogs are easy. They listen. They respond to kindness," my mother says, stroking Waffles as she peruses the day's schedule for the Westminster Dog Show. She won't even look at me.

Waffles is a King Charles spaniel, the dog most favored by the royal family of Spain and immortalized in the court paintings of Goya. They were lapdogs, canine napkins for their owners to wipe their greasy hands on during banquets. I think this is why my mother bought him, even though he's not a show dog. She still has delusions of grandeur, of the old days when she had a buzzer under the dining room table that she'd push with her foot when she wanted the cook to serve the next course, the old days when my father would instruct the pilot to land the company plane so my mother could pee on terra firma. Now though, at forty-eight, my mother's a divorcee in a dim little two-bedroom apartment on Eighty-first and Park that the two of us have shared for the last four years.

My mother is one of those blazered geeks you see trotting poodles in formation, bribing them with liver snaps to stand still on a table while some stranger gropes their withers. She would never have done this if my father hadn't left her for a twenty-five-year-old, forcing her to find something to do in order to make a living. She should thank him; after all, she's always saying, "Dog training is the first thing I've ever done for myself. It's the first thing I've ever been really really good at it." I'm supposed to disagree with her, say she's a great mother. Ha.

Today Mom's showing Mr. Jeffrey, one of her prize dogs. This pug could make her.

"Puppy class, novice bitch, best of breed . . ." my mother mutters to herself as she takes down her favorite cereal bowl. I like to say novice bitch. It's like a bitch in training.

On this big day Mom's preparing her breakfast of champions—she weighs what looks like a cup of gravel on her trusty diet scale, pours some blue milk over it, then digs in, her chewing sounding like a wood chipper.

When she finishes, she puts her bowl on the floor where Waffles hoovers up the last bit of beige milk.

"Did you eat anything, Mary Beth?" she asks, peering over her reading glasses so she can actually see me. "Breakfast is the most important meal of the day. Are you getting taller, or is that hemline inching up?" She frowns, two wrinkles in her forehead cross like swords on a family crest. "I'd like to hear what the sisters have to say about that." Sacred Virgin Academy is supposed to be the strictest of the socially elite Catholic girls' schools in the city, a place where girls from good families can go and have the inner wayward slut disciplined out. I've been going there since I was three. My parents weren't taking any chances. A block outside of school we roll up the waists of our skirts to make them minis, stuff our ties in our bags, ditch the ugly blue blazers, push down our socks, undo an extra button on our white blouses to show off cleavage, and in my case, a little gold crucifix with a ruby in the center, caught between my tits. Could you die?

"I ate already."

"What did you eat?" she asks suspiciously.

"I had a doughnut and milk." I love to watch my mother's face scrunch up in disgust.

As usual I couldn't sleep. I lay in bed fiddling with the crucifix my father gave me for my confirmation, but I just couldn't lie still so I got up. Anyway it was already six, a slit of yellow light catching fire at the bottom of my shade. Sometimes I like to get up really early and just throw a coat over my pajamas, then walk up Lexington Avenue. It's completely deserted and eerie like a movie set, not a soul around except for recovering alcoholics riding their bikes to AA meetings, and doormen hosing off the sidewalks. It's like I own the world. At the Korean market I bought a chocolate doughnut, a carton of Quik, and a pack of Marlboro lights. I really wasn't hungry, the cigarette was okay, but that's about all. And of course, about twenty minutes later when I was in the shower, I threw it all up. As I was kneeling there trying to push my vomit down the drain, I almost started to cry, which I never do. I can go months and months without crying. But getting sick like that, it bugged me for some reason. It never had before.

When I was fourteen, my mother taught me how to throw up. She'd come home from a New York Kennel Club meeting and found me sprawled and groaning on the family room floor, skirt unbuttoned, legs akimbo, wallowing in a sea of shiny cellophane Little Debbie Snack Cake wrappers. The way she reacted you'd have thought she'd found me doped up and naked with a Puerto Rican boy.

After nearly making me beg her to make it better, she dragged me to my feet and pushed me into the bathroom. I felt full as the ticks I used to pull off of Waffles in the country, ticks plump as grapes that I'd explode with matches like little blood bombs. I had this vision of my mother holding my chin as she fed me spoonfuls of sweet pink Pepto-Bismol, then tucking me into her big bed with a glass of ginger ale.

In the bathroom she cranked the taps on full blast, little droplets of water spraying out of the bowl, hanging in the air like a fine misting rain.

"Here," she said, kneeling in front of the toilet the way we knelt together at mass.

"Come on," she said gently, and pulled me down beside her. "There's nothing to be afraid of."

I nodded. This was too weird. I stared at my mother's hand grasping the toilet seat; I couldn't imagine her touching a toilet. I could see the tiniest little nicks on her knuckles.

"Now, you want that garbage gone, don't you? Because that's what it is right now, just garbage," she said, her voice suddenly hard and purposeful.

I nodded again.

"Gone forever from your body. You want to feel light and clean, don't you?" she said as though she weren't just teaching me to puke but also offering to wash away my sins.

"Of course you do." She pushed my hair back behind my ears, and into the back of my blouse, split ends tickling my spine. "For safety's sake," she said.

"Just these two fingers," she directed, holding up her first and middle fingers pressed together. "That's good."

So I opened my mouth, leaned over the toilet, and stuck my fingers in my mouth. I felt that little pendulum of pink flesh in the back of my throat brush the back of my hand. I gagged, but nothing happened. I was failing her. Hail Mary, I prayed.

"Here, let me help you," she said, taking my hand and guiding it into my mouth, my teeth scraping the top of my hand. She was biting her lip, deep in concentration as she pushed my hand further and further until both of my fingers were well down my throat, the tips of my fingers touching my windpipe. She held my hand there, even as I started to gag, my stomach leaping like a trampoline, tears bouncing into my eyes. She let go just in time and everything came up—bright yellow fritos, my garish hot lunch of sloppy joes and fries, chocolate milk, and the barely digested Little Debbies, the cream still visible. My back arched like a cat as I heaved again, this time just at the smell of it.

"Don't worry; it get's easier," my mother said, then stood up and straightened her skirt. "You did very well. I'm proud of you." She bent down and patted my head, then turned the tap down to a trickle. I laid my head on the toilet seat and listened to the water run. I watched my mother walk away, her greyhound legs moving with purpose, high heels clicking on the tile floor. I studied her tight calves, the muscles massed in a ball, permanently shortened by a life in high heels, so that now it hurt her to walk in flats.

That was the closest we've ever been. That day I felt she saw me. She knew me. She wanted to help me, and I think I loved her then. I can't remember anything else she's taught me other than how to respond to a formal party invitation and when and where you can wear white shoes. Anytime I make myself throw up, I think of her. Sometimes I think, *See, take that. I am not fat, and I am not a child. I can take care of myself.* Sometimes I think, *I don't want to be you. I want to be just the opposite of you.*

This morning when I threw up in the shower I didn't think of her; I thought of Dr. Andrews. I had a three o'clock appointment. What was I going to wear?

"You're in bed," my mother says, stating the obvious.

"I'm sick," I say and curl up like a shrimp.

"It's that doughnut," she says. "Good Lord, Mary Beth, do you have any idea how many calories are in a chocolate doughnut? Do you? They are the atom bomb of the food world," she says, her eyes flitting around the room like a weapons inspector searching for warheads: an arsenal of candy corn, an underwear drawer stocked with Tasty-Kakes.

"I don't know about that," I say, rolling onto my back so I can see her upside down, "but a recent study found that the aroma of doughnuts is the single most arousing scent to men."

"Oh that's nice, Mary Beth; that's a very nice way to talk to your mother. Fine," she says. "But, I don't want to hear you complain about not having a boyfriend," she says. If only she knew. I would bet money that I've slept with more guys than my mother ever did.

"I'm sick and you're on me about my weight," I say. "I've been vomiting for days. Days."

"I'm just trying to help you," she replies, then pulls out her compact and vigorously powders her nose. "Beauty is power, dear. You better learn it now," she says as she crayons on a bit of shell-pink lipstick. A shade she's been wearing since she was a virgin.

"I know," I say, trying to sound forlorn, like she's always right and

I'm always wrong. I don't want to fight anymore today. I just want her to leave. I struggle to sit up and hunch my shoulders so I look pathetic.

"Do you need me to write you a note?" she asks.

I nod.

"Fine," she says as she puts on her blazer and straightens her lapels. She runs her hands quickly up the length of each leg checking her stockings for ladders.

"If you need me, you know where I'll be," she says and gives me a little half-hug. Mother-daughter photo op.

"Oh, I love love you, Waffles," she coos, ambushing the little bastard as he licks his groin in my bedroom doorway. She cradles him in her arms and kisses him on the belly. She shuts my door, and then a second later opens it. "Dear, do you think you will be able to use those tickets for the dog show?"

"I don't know," I say, annoyed. I'm sick after all.

"You know it would be nice if you took the smallest interest in what I do," she says.

I say nothing. What can I say.

"Well," she sighs. "That's the best ticket in town today, and believe me some people would give their eyeteeth to be there. It's a big day, Mr. Jeffrey, best of breed," she says as though this will entice me.

I shrug.

"If his owner calls, could you please tell her I'm already at the Garden, and tell her to keep the dirty laundry off the floor. I tell you if that dog eats another sock, saints protect us," she says, crossing herself and closing the door behind her with a ladylike slam.

I flip on the TV and have a smoke. Then I go into the kitchen and open the fridge. There's a wallet-sized studio portrait of Mr. Jeffrey on the door. A pug in profile in front of a blue satin curtain. It looks like a school photo. All he needs is a bow tie. What a runt. I think about taking a little nip of my mother's frozen Stoli, but I don't. My stomach hurts, but it's a good hurt; the insistent hunger pangs remind me that I have control. In one way, I am pure. Still, my heart is pounding like a ball-peen hammer on steel. I steal a Xanax from my mother's medicine cabinet and think about calling Phillip, but he's at work. Yesterday morning I'd stopped by his apartment at seven. As I was tiptoeing out of the apartment, my mother called sleepily from her bedroom, "Grab a banana."

I had to crack up.

At first he was mad that I'd just stopped by, as he always was, but once he had me tied up to his futon, in my school uniform, white cotton panties at my ankles, he was happy. Afterward, after he'd modestly stepped back into the boxers he'd left like a pair of fireman's boots by the bed, after he'd showered, and I'd wiped myself with his lame bondage gear—four Brooks Brothers silk neckties—after that, when I sat him down, and told him I was pregnant, he was mad again. Then he started to freak out, "You're seventeen—for Christ's sake!" he said, like I had to be reminded. Tears came into his eyes. He said, "I hate this. I really really hate this."

"Me too. I've never been in this situation before; I'm lost. I don't know what to do!" I wonder, if like my father, the tips of my ears turn red while I lie.

Phillip did know what to do. He figured it all out like the businessman he was—he was so good at figuring out profits and risks—I would get an abortion. There was no other choice.

Of course, just being a kid I don't have that kind of cash, even if my dad is rich. Phillip was good about that; there'd be no going Dutch, no way. We walked together to the cash machine, but not holding hands. It was so odd to be on the street with him in the daylight, him all grown up in his Wall Street costume—a dark gray Paul Stuart suit and Gucci oxfords—and me in my Sacred Virgin prison gear. As we walked, I started lagging behind him. I wanted him to slow down and walk with me, talk to me, but he was cruising. At one point, I let him cross the street without me, the traffic rushing through the space between us. I stood there with a girl in a uniform similar to mine, but she was maybe eleven. She had chubby thighs and her hair was brushed back into a low sophisticated ponytail and fastened with a tortoiseshell clip, which was the way I bet her mom wore her own hair. She was holding hands with her father and he was tugging on her ponytail and she was laughing like it was the funniest damn thing in the world. I don't remember if my father ever walked me to school. I just don't remember. When the light changed, the two of them literally hopped off the curb, and arm in arm, crossed the street. I thought, That girl has never even given a guy a blow job. She's never had a guy feel her up and tell her, You are so beautiful.

Across the street, Phillip was glaring at me. Hands on his hips he barked, "Come on, step it up," just like my father.

At the ATM he inserted his card then paused for a moment, turning his shoulder to shield the screen like some kid who thinks you want to cheat off them. He had some nerve.

"I've got to make sure I've got enough," he said in a low voice. "Shit," he said. "It's got to be money market."

He sighed, dug into his briefcase, and pulled out a slim black checkbook. Then, right there in the street, he wrote me a check. I held out my Algebra II book and he used it for a desk. His handwriting was shakier than a boy's; if he was a kid, I'd have said he needed Ritalin.

"Get a good doctor, a reputable man. Do you know what I mean, Mary Beth?"

I nodded. I knew what he meant—someone discreet. I didn't tell him I'd already made an appointment last week.

"This should cover it, don't you think?" he asked me, and I saw there a glimmer of who we used to be. Me sitting in his lap at Dorian's Red Hand, the bar where we went. The romantic dinners in expensive restaurants smaller than my living room, the clubbing and staying up until morning doing coke and smoking pot and talking about his dull Ohio childhood, the pressure of his body on top of mine, the time a homeless guy selling roses and giant stuffed chickens out of a shopping cart told him, "That's one beautiful girl, you best hold on to her," and he'd laughed and said, "Don't I know it, brother."

It was understood that the money was to cover "the procedure," a cab, some flowers for myself maybe, a box of chocolates, some bubble bath. He kissed me quickly on the lips, then pulled me to his chest.

"I'm so sorry," he said into my hair, holding me tight against his body, like he wanted to hide me inside of him. It felt good to be touched, to be held in place so tightly. Here I was. Then he pulled away, and took my chin in one hand. "Take care of yourself," he said, starting to cry again, and that was that.

Well, I was taking care of myself. I was a girl with a check for $2,000. As I caught the bus to school, I wondered how much money a thirty-three-year-old stock broker made. What would he have had to shell out if he'd wanted to make me an honest woman? Wasn't one month's salary the rule of thumb for what a man was supposed to blow on a girl's engagement ring?

I'd gotten gypped.

The doorbell rings. I peek through the fish eye and see Marco, our doorman, standing in the hall, grinning at me. "Your mother tells me you're sick," he says when I open the door. Marco is nicer to me than any other adult. I think it's because he and his wife can't have kids.

"Here, I thought this might make you feel better. You got a postcard from your father," he says, holding it up between his fingers like a magician pulling the lucky card you picked out of the pack.

"Oh really," I say, trying to sound bored; then I snap the card out of his fingers and close the door fast.

Marco reads all our mail, and I don't want Marco to tell me what my father's written.

I take it into the bathroom. These days I have to pee constantly. I turn on the tap, even though nobody's home, and go. In Japan they have toilets that when you sit down make the sound of water running so no one can hear you pee. Amazing.

Dad's card is basically a weather report. In Cancún it's sunny and warm. No surprise. I take it into the kitchen and read it again, between the lines, searching for subtext the way the sisters teach us in English class.

> Dear Mary Beth,
>   Hi kiddo! Isn't this sunset amazing? It's really beautiful here. The weather has been great, really cooperating. I've been on the golf course every day. It's heaven. Had a super lobster the other night at a restaurant on the beach. You'd love it. How's school? Be good.
>
> >   Love,
> >   Dad

Blah blah blah. Like he can't call me up? Like he can't pick up the phone and ask me how I am? I haven't heard his voice in weeks and weeks. I run my finger over his big, loopy script, watching my hand move. Is that how his hand moves?

"Be good," he writes.

"Love, Dad," he writes.

I throw the card in the trash, then pick it out. I am so weak.

I think about buying myself a beautiful pair of Italian leather boots with his credit card. He gave me my own charge because he knows how tightfisted my mother can be.

"I don't want you to do without," he'd said, pressing the card into my hand, like the key to some imaginary city, "but don't abuse it."

Abuse it? That card wanted it.

I like using his card; it's like he's buying me things. Sometimes when I'm feeling blue, I'll go shopping. I'll hold up dresses and ask, Would he like this? Would he think this looked pretty on me? Mostly though, I use his card because it's my right as his daughter; he owed me that leather coat, he owed me that handbag. Anytime I'm short on a tab, good old Dad steps out of the shadows to help me out. *Here, my dear, let me get that for you. No, no, I insist. My treat.* One day after field hockey practice I took the whole team out for sundaes on Dad's card. Did he ever get mad? Not really. He'd just say, "Be careful with that card, honey." Or when we got together for one of our quarterly dinners in the city, he'd say, "That's a pretty skirt. Did I buy that?" and for some reason I always lie and say no, even though I always make a point of wearing clothes he's paid for when I see him.

In my room I changed out of my uniform and into a pale blue cashmere sweater my grandmother gave me for Christmas last year, a knee-length blue flowered skirt, and a pair of black ballet flats, both from Mom. It's important, my mother says, to look nice when you go to the doctor. In case, I suppose, you die there.

The clinic's waiting room is full of slick, uncomfortable orange and yellow plastic chairs, bus station furniture designed to cause discomfort, to make loitering impossible, as if anybody would want to hang out here. The ceiling is low. Overhead one of the fluorescent lights has a bad tube. It keeps flickering, providing a kind of a disco effect. Inside the light are dead flies, all on their backs, legs up and crossed like reluctant virgins. How did they get in there in the first place?

In one corner, sort of hiding behind an electric-blue and lavender silk flower arrangement, sits a lifeguard type: blond, slightly wavy long hair; tan; good teeth. He's holding a Coach "Grace Kelly-style" purse on his knee, bouncing it the way you do a baby. His eyes are bloodshot, probably not from crying, but from pot. Stoned courage. A tall, dark-haired guy in khakis and a dark blue blazer stands looking at the selection of pamphlets—"So You've got Genital Herpes," "Infants 101," and "The Truth About Gonorrhea," which I once thought sounded like a travel brochure for some mysterious and secluded island that didn't welcome tourists. He's cute. When he sits down across from me, and accidentally drops the lavender cardigan he's been clutching, I smile at him and he looks confused. Thank heavens I didn't bring a purse— who would be its guardian? Certainly not the fat man in the shiny green suit dozing beside me, the day's racing form balanced on his knee. I say a Hail Mary out of nervousness. I haven't told a soul; not even my girlfriends know where I am, or what has happened. They wouldn't understand; they are still caught up in making out, and dry humping, playing the power game of stopping guys before things go too far. Well, too far is where I live. I think of my mother. What would she say? What would she do if she knew I was pregnant? I imagined the lightning crack of ice cubes being hurled into a glass. *Slut!* The slosh of vodka, as my mother, Zeus of the cocktails, prepared to annihilate me. *You are no child of mine!*

A rotund nurse with a mad scramble of red hair and the tiniest mouth I have ever seen shows me into a tiny, cool pink room. It's like being inside a cone of cotton candy. I hang up my jeans jacket and get undressed. I drop my Sweet Sixteen pearl necklace into the toe of my shoe and put on the blue robe, ties in the front. My hands are shaking so badly I can barely make a knot. The nurse takes my blood pressure. Her hands are cold and soft. She's humming. She makes no small talk. She just smiles at me and hums some tune like a polka. I can't tell what she's thinking. She scribbles down some numbers. I wonder if she's ever had an abortion, if she hates me for doing this.

"Everything normal?" I ask, wanting conversation.

She hums and nods, then vanishes.

It's freezing in here. I stand on tiptoe. I pinch my gut; I'm getting fat. I tell myself, no solid food for two days. The Muzak station is playing the hundred strings version of "Stairway to Heaven." That was my old boyfriend Michael's and my song. Now Michael, Michael would have come with me.

I pace for a while. My feet are freezing from the tile floor, so I finally climb up on the table. It's a huge stainless steel table, covered with white paper that comes off a giant roll, the kind you used in art class as a kid. On the ceiling someone, perhaps the red-haired munchkin nurse, has taped a *National Geographic* photo of a cool green waterfall buried in the jungle. It looks like a place you'd really have to hike to, a place that is special because so few people have seen it. It's a lovely distraction. That's what it is; and I laugh out loud—that's what Phillip called me once, a lovely distraction.

Where is Dr. Andrews? Usually he makes an appearance before the nurses take my blood pressure and temperature. It's like he's so happy to see me that he can't wait until they are done with me, but today, so far, he's a no-show. It's prom season, I guess. He must be backed up. Out in the gray-and-green-tiled hall, gleaming silver gurneys are lined up against the wall, like limousines waiting to spirit girls into recovery. Recovery is nice. It's quiet; it's like a war hospital in the movies, rows of white beds, girls lying there, some weeping, some sleeping. Some with IVs. Some girls are chatting with their neighbors. I wouldn't be surprised to see somebody, one day, break out a pack of cards. Anything for a distraction. Then the nurse comes by with a tray of cookies and juice. Everybody who can sit up does and takes one. Last time they were butter cookies with the imprint of a little schoolboy on them. I nibbled off his feet, then his stomach, and finally I ate his face. By the time you leave, you've had a nap, and your snack, and a nurse has given you a thick sanitary pad, dense and white as a snowbank. Leaving the hospital with this huge pad in your pants it feels like you're a girl again, like it's your first period and your mom won't let you use tampons because they might break your hymen. It's like your virginity has been restored, and you're a good girl all over again.

I wait. I wonder if Dr. Andrews is married. Does he have kids?

I close my eyes and think of Dr. Andrews. He's at least six feet six inches tall and thin as a weather vane, his graying hair is brushed straight back from his high forehead, and because he uses some kind of pomade, you can always see the furrows from his comb in his hair. He likes to wear those old-fashioned suits with high-waisted gabardine pants, and on the street he wears a felt fedora, which makes him look like an old movie star. He's from the Midwest; he told me that, and that as a kid he was clumsy and lousy at sports. He gew ten inches his freshman year of college. Sometimes he sounds a little like Jimmy Stewart. I love to hear him say my name.

The first time he asked me if I wanted a nurse to hold my hand during the procedure. He asked me if there was anyone waiting for me, or should someone call me a cab. I said yes someone was waiting for me, but I didn't tell him that Michael was loitering outside smoking like a fiend. Neither Michael nor I wanted him to come in. It felt too personal. Still, I didn't want the doctor to think I was a slut, or somebody who nobody cared about.

The second time he didn't ask me if I wanted a hand-holder; instead he told me jokes. *What did the little pig say when he fell down the steps? Oh, my aching bacon. What did the grape say when it got stepped on? Nothing; it just let out a little wine.*

Jokes, I now realize, that were all about pain. Maybe he was afraid that despite the anesthesia, I'd be in pain. He didn't want me to be in pain.

The second time he told me, "Mary Beth, you are a good girl with very bad luck."

I'd lied and written on my form that I was using a condom and a sponge, when in truth I was unprepared. It was my first and only date with Rocco, a gorgeous curly-haired Italian waiter from Mezzaluna. We ended up at the Plaza, at Trader Vic's. I took him up to the second floor to show him the ballroom where I'd gone to my very first cotillion. I thought about staying, Stop it, but it was over so fast; it was like an accident. It didn't seem so bad until he didn't call me, until I saw how he'd torn the hook and eyes out of my bra when he couldn't get it undone, until every time I went into the restaurant he had somebody else wait on me.

That time when Dr. Andrews asked, I told him that I was alone. I didn't tell him what happened, although I wanted to tell him, but I'd rather he think me mysterious.

Today, who knows, maybe Dr. Andrews will sing "Old Man River" to me and accompany himself on harmonica—that would be a nice counterbalance to the drone of machines, the awful sucking sounds. Today when Dr. Andrews asks me about the cab, I'll say, Can't you take me with you? Or, maybe you could just drop me on your way home?

Then we'll ride together in his car. He'll have lemon drops in his glove compartment, plus maps of all the prime foliage states. He'll buy me a tuna melt at the coffee shop. We'll talk. He'll like me. I'll tell him my really dumb knock-knock jokes, and he'll ask me if I want to go to the aquarium this weekend to see the seals, and I'll say yes, yes please.

There's a soft quick rap on the door. I sit up. Dr. Andrews has got my file pressed to his chest. He's wearing a dark blue suit today, with a very worn alligator belt. He pinches the bridge of his long nose and rubs his eyes for a moment.

"So, here we are," he says, closing the door behind him. He's been working too hard. "How are we feeling today?" he asks, sitting down hard on the metal stool, his knees sticking out like a praying mantis, and I believe he cares, but for some reason he's not looking in my eyes, but at my neck, or into my chest.

"Not so hot." I lean over and grab my stomach. Now I don't want to look in his eyes. Something feels wrong.

"Well, I can't say I'm surprised," he says, shaking his head a little. He seems angry. He attempts to rig up a smile, but he can't sustain it. It gets lost in a grimace.

"I'm sorry," he says. He shakes his head, and rubs his eyes again. I suddenly feel sick. I want to say, It's not my fault that this happened. Instead I just sit there and feel myself shrinking, getting colder and colder, and smaller and smaller.

He picks up a tongue depressor and starts turning it over in his hand like it's some kind of artifact he's never seen before. He's stalling.

"What is it?" I ask, nervous. My God, maybe I've got cancer, toxic shock or something.

"Mary Beth," he starts slowly. "As your doctor I have to advise you, that despite your age and good health, what you're doing here just isn't advisable for you. You know that, don't you? Do I need to give you the whole your-body-is-a-temple, sanctity-of-life spiel again?" He pauses; he's actually angry at me.

"Well, I wouldn't say my body is exactly a temple; it's more like a roadside shrine," I start to say, but he interrupts me.

"Now come on. This is what, the third time you've been here in two years, Mary Beth." He stops. I'm rolling my eyes, but I don't mean to. I want to hear the spiel again.

"Darn it all, forget medically—emotionally, psychologically, I'm concerned. You're a smart girl. I . . ." He looks flummoxed. He pops open the file, and extracts a pair of tortoiseshell half glasses from his coat pocket.

"You're what, a senior?" he says. "Where are you going to college?" he asks, squinting over the tops of his glasses.

"Princeton."

"That's a very fine school. Go, Tigers!" he says, some color finally coming into his cheeks.

"Go, team!" I say, making a triumphant fist. We both laugh, but it's a small, uncomfortable laugh. I hate the way he's looking at me, so disappointed.

"This is the last time, Mary Beth." He settles down at the end of the table. "I'm sorry," he says, and I think he almost means it.

"What do you mean?"

"Mary Beth, I like you. If you were my own daughter, this could not sadden me more. Do you understand? I'm going to write you a prescription for the pill, all right?"

"I don't need the pill. I don't want it," I say. "It's not like I'm really, you know, sexually active or anything," I say.

"This is it," he says, handing me the prescription. "I'm really very sorry."

I dig my fingernails into the palm of my hand. *But I have to see you again*, I think, *You can't leave me*. But I don't say it. I can't believe I'm losing him.

I lay down, scoot my butt down the table and stick my feet into the icy stirrups. The red-haired nurse comes in and lifts my feet out for a moment, then slides two folded-up paper towels into the stirrups, so they aren't so cold and hard. I don't know what to do with this kindness. I cross my arms behind my head like I'm laying out on a tropical beach. I'm casual and cool. Get it out of me, just get it out of me. But when he inserts the speculum and winches me open, when he goes inside me with the tube, my whole body cringes. Before I'd been so relieved, so ready, out out damn spot! Sayonara.

I try to see Dr. Andrews crouched down at the foot of the table, but he's tented by sterilized blue paper; a white mask covers his lips and nose, his head covered in a blue surgical cap, his eyes behind glasses that reflect the light. He's like a miner, bent over in concentration, prospecting inside me. This is the last time I will see him, and I cannot see him. My hands fly up to cover my face. He'd never asked me if anyone was coming to get me.

In the recovery room I lay still as a stick, feel the blood leaking out of me, soaking into the pad. I wish I could pray. I swear I feel as though something is wrong with me. Mary, give me a sign, I pray. I feel like a glass jar spidered with cracks, just waiting to shatter. Do I have to break for Mary's goodness to enter me? What has to happen to make me pure?

The room is quiet but for the hum of the fluorescent lights. Most of the others are sleeping, all except for a woman with gray streaks in her dark brown hair, who's wiping her eyes on the hem of the sheet, and the black girl beside me who has been staring at the ceiling ever since they wheeled her in. Forgive me, I pray. Forgive me.

"Is there someone waiting for you?" the nurse asks me when I refuse my cookies and juice, although I am ravenous. "Someone you can call?"

I think about my father standing in a pool of tree shade practicing his chip shot. His hand reaching out to stroke his chin, my chin. My mother at the Garden, surrounded by dogs. Her hands placed authoritatively on her hips, giving simple easy-to-understand dog orders: sit, roll over, beg.

I shake my head. "I've got cab fare," I say and turn on my side.

At the front desk I pay for the abortion on my father's credit card. I sign my name boldly, and I write on the bottom of the credit card slip, *Weather is here, wish you were beautiful.*

Halfway home I change my mind, and ask the cabdriver to take me to Madison Square Garden, though I don't know why exactly. Out the window I look at the girls on the street, girls my age smiling and laughing, talking on pay phones. I wonder who they are, if they are like me.

The last time I was at the Garden was for some ice show with my school. The nuns are crazy about ice shows. Today the ice is covered up, the hardwood floor is down, and they've laid down Astro-Turfy carpet, like half these dogs have even ever walked on grass. I can't see the show area but over the loudspeaker a voice is describing the dogs as they enter: "Belvedere, a plucky miniature schnauzer, is a stocky little playmate! This gay friendly little dog is Salome; she's a Lakeland terrier, we all know what feisty little showboats they are! She simply owns the ring!"

I walk slowly up the aisles half looking for my mother, half staring at the dogs. Some are locked in cages; others like a black-tongued chow are being fussed and picked at while they try to nap in their dog beds; then there are those ridiculous mutts who are unfortunate enough to be tricked out in gear only leather queens and Milquetoasts could appreciate, like the Yorkshire terrier in a studded leather harness and cap behind the wheel of a miniature red sports car, and the tea cup Chihuahua in an ascot and monocle curled up in a miniature armchair. They seem sad and bewildered, but maybe it's just me. I mean, maybe it's not such a bad life.

"Princess Cortina d'Empazzo is a saucy Italian greyhound bitch," the disembodied voice booms. "Dogs smile with their tails. Why, I think she's flirting with the judge! Naughty, naughty!"

I feel queasy. Where is my damn mother? Two aisles over, I spot what looks like the pug ghetto. A man with pencil-thin mustache presses a paisley handkerchief to a pug's snout like it's a child he is imploring to blow its nose. On the next table is another pug who could be Mr. Jeffrey, but to be honest, all those dogs look alike to me. It's like sometimes when I see a picture of my family, each of us looking like the other, blond, gray-eyed and square-jawed, I think that we look like a subspecies of man: Upper East Side *Preppus erectus*. Overbred, and inbred. Linked by our infirmities. One day we'll be just like the pugs whose noses and eyes constantly leak mucus because years of overbreeding have made their nasal cavities collapse.

"You should be home in bed," I say to myself, and I'm right. It's just too bad if my mother doesn't believe that I came, not to mention that I came sick! Maybe if Mr. Jeffrey wins, she'll forget she even asked me. She'd never miss me. There really is no point in staying.

I make my way toward the exit past the poodles, the Afghan hounds, the corgis, and the Pekingese. I wonder if I'm pale, if I'm walking funny, if anyone can tell what I've just done. Hail Mary, I pray.

I'm about to leave when I hear, "Mary Beth!" and for a moment I freeze; it's like the Virgin Mary heard my plea. I turn and see my mother running toward me. She's hunched over, taking mincing little steps, her pink lips pursed in anger. She's furious. She knows exactly where I have been, and what I have done. My God, did someone from the clinic call her? Or can she just tell by looking at me? Run, I think, run. But I don't move, I close my eyes, and a strange sense of relief wells up inside me. I never expected this connection from her, and I'm surprised that it pleases me. I wait for her to hit me, or start yelling, but when I open my eyes she is just standing in front of me glaring. There is a dog, a pug, Mr. Jeffrey, I presume, tucked inside her blue blazer and secured under her arm like a hairy football.

"Thank God you are here," she says, her whole body trembling, even her perfectly lacquered up-do is shaking a little, like a tiny yellow volcano. I half expect to see steam rise out of it. Throw a virgin into the volcano! Appease the gods; save yourself!

"What?" I ask, confused. Was she worried about me? I feel something in me give way, get soft.

"You won't believe this animal," my mother hisses and gives the pug a squeeze that makes his already bulbous eyes seem to bulge. I stare at my mother who is glowering at Mr. Jeffrey, oblivious to me. I don't know which one of them is uglier to me right now. My mother doesn't know what I've done. She doesn't know shit. How stupid can I be?

"Come with me," she says and grabs me by the wrist. Before I can protest or shake her off she drags me into the women's bathroom. I have no say. What can I say? I don't understand what's going on. What I do know is that taking a contestant off the floor and into a restricted area, like the women's bathroom, is strictly against the rules and could get my mother disqualified. The thought of my mother getting nailed makes me smile. I follow her into the wheelchair stall. She locks the door. She flips down the toilet lid and puts Mr. Jeffrey down. His glossy black marble eyes are bugging out of his head. He's snorting and sniffling like mad. Mr. Jeffrey knows something is up.

"Can you believe it?" my mother says, like I know what's going on. She puts her hands on her hips, and stares down at Mr. Jeffrey in her Alpha Male power pose. He starts to whine, stamps his little paws, and halfheartedly tries to leap off the toilet but my mother catches him mid-flight.

"No way, buster," she says. He squirms in her arms, and tries to bolt again, but my mother will not be deterred. I have never seen her like this, so take-charge. She presses her hand down on the back of his head. "I need your help, Mary Beth. Now. This is serious. I really need you to help me with this," she says, working her hand down his little barrel chest and back to his potbelly, then back to his thumb-sized penis where she begins to manipulate his groin, which just seems to increase Mr. Jeffrey's sniffling, his cold dog snot spraying my face.

"No way," I say, crossing my arms across my chest. My heart is slamming against my rib cage. "This is beyond revolting."

"We have to do this fast. Lord help us," my mother prays. "I know what you did, Mr. Jeffrey," she says in a kind of scary singsong. "I know what you did, you sick, weird little dirty underwear-loving dog, and I'm not going to have you ruin this day for me. No, I'm not. We have come so far, Mr. Jeffrey, so far."

"What did he do?" I ask. I'm feeling wobbly and light-headed. What I really want to do is go home and sleep for a week.

"I'll show you," she says and turns Mr. Jeffrey around so his butt is facing me. His tail is curled up in tight curlicue, his puckered and pink little anus quivering. She wedges his head between her legs, then closes her knees on his shoulders so he's held in a vise of her thighs. She starts massaging his belly again, pushing on his sides.

"Okay, do you see anything yet?"

"See what? What do you mean?" I ask. Mr. Jeffrey is whining and shaking as he lowers his rump down onto the toilet seat. She hoists his hips back up.

"Do you see the sock?" she says, her voice starting to break, her tortoiseshell half-glasses slipping down her nose.

"You're joking!"

"No, I am not joking. I most certainly am not joking."

She squeezes Mr. Jeffrey again, and he grunts and snuffles, like he's enjoying it. Then he emits a short gusty fart and I see a little something white poke out of his ass. At that moment the door to the womens' room opens and my mother shoots upright clamping her hand over my mouth. I want to scream, *Hey lady, we've got a pug in here!* but I don't. I am so weak. Once my mother is sure I've got the message, she takes her hand away and starts to pet Mr. Jeffrey, leaving her other hand firmly over his muzzle.

We hear the unbelting of pants, the unzipping, the press of flesh to toilet seat (no paper down, no crouch) which makes my mother wince. Finally there is the sigh, the stream, and the rezipping, the rebelting. Mr. Jeffrey starts to whine. It's time to change my pad; it feels heavy and cold. My mother looks at me; she looks like she could cry. I could too.

"Are you all right down there?" someone with a pleasantly clipped British accent inquires.

"Oh yes, I'm fine. Just a little, you know—female trouble," my mother says, smiling like the woman can see us. I smile too.

"Oh right," the woman replies with restrained empathy.

Thank God the woman doesn't check under the stall. She does, however, take a damnably long time washing her hands, but finally she leaves.

"All right, that's it," my mother says. "Let's do it."

She resecures Mr. Jeffrey between her knees, and there it is. I step back in horror and bang into the stainless steel sanitary napkin disposal. My mother raises her head, she actually looks concerned, and in that instant Mr. Jeffrey pulls his head out from between her legs and sinks his teeth into her on the forearm.

"Bad dog!" she shrieks and clamps her knees tight on his head. I can see the angry imprint in her skin. Mr. Jeffrey is subdued now, but I am furious. What the hell is wrong with him?

"Grab it, just grab it and pull," my mother hisses, but all I can do is watch tiny beads of blood welling up on my mother's arm. My stomach is singing with hunger pains. My head is in a fog. All I want to do is put my head down on the toilet seat and rest, but I don't. Instead I lean down and pinch the slick bit of cloth between my thumb and forefinger and I start to tug. It makes a disgusting sound, like a wet cork being pulled slowly out of a bottle.

"Careful, careful, for heaven's sake, you don't want to pull out his entire large intestine," my mother says, trying to peer around and monitor the state of Mr. Jeffrey's asshole. "Oh Lord, please don't let there be bleeding of any sort, none. That would be the end of me."

I pause. My mother's French twist has come undone; strands of hair stick to her pink lips. She needed me.

As I gently tug out the shit-stained fabric, I realize that what I am extracting from Mr. Jeffrey's ass is a pair of little boy's jockey shorts. First the crotch appears; then one stretched-out leg hole, and then the other, are extruded from the dog's butt. I pull and pull, until the waistband snaps out of his anus and victory is in hand. I stuff the soiled underpants into the sanitary napkin disposal. My mother slumps in relief against the wall.

"Thank God," she says and crosses herself.

Mr. Jeffrey nuzzles my mother's thigh, licks her arm where he nipped her. She rubs his ears. All is forgiven.

My mother pushes open the stall door. The light in the bathroom is bright. In the mirror, the two of us look roughed up, as though we've been in a rumble. We both start to laugh, I laugh until I can't breathe.

"Thank you," my mother says, touching my shoulder like I might think she was talking to somebody else. "Really. That wasn't any fun."

"It's okay," I mumble, embarrassed by her gratitude.

"Oh, look at the time," she says, wiping her eyes. She hoists Mr. Jeffrey up into her arms. He sits there very straight, looking stoic and human, like a hairy dwarf with dreadful allergies.

"You'll stay, won't you?" my mother asks. She turns on the water and runs her hands under the stream. She splashes a little water on her face, then heads back into the handicap stall to get a piece of toilet paper. "Please stay; we'll go for ice cream afterwards, my treat," she says like I'm a little kid who can be bribed. She puts Mr. Jeffrey down on the floor, and he immediately begins sniffing at my calves. I wonder if he can smell blood. Does Mr. Jeffrey know what my mother could only imagine in her very worst nightmare? I lean against the bathroom stall door and watch my mother blot her face with the tissue, then drop it into the toilet. The tissue floats in the bowl like a paper angel waiting for somebody to pee on it. "Oh come on, say you'll stay," my mother says. "You'll like it. I know it."

"You don't know what I like," I say in a voice that seems too loud. My head is full of static; my mother's lips are moving but I can't hear what she is saying. She reaches out and grabs my arm and it's funny the way she slides to the floor like a rag doll, like I'm pushing her down, but I'm not, I don't weigh anything. I'm just a kid. For a moment she looks afraid of me; then she pulls me slowly into her lap. We're wedged in tight between the toilet and the wall, my feet sticking out of the stall. My mother smooths my skirt down over my knees. I'm afraid that I'm dying right here on the floor by the toilet. I'm bleeding to death. I want to tell my mother something, but I'm not sure what. I listen to the water running in the toilet. It's so soothing. My mother's breath hums in my ear. I think I hear her say, "I'm here."

THE GOOD CHANCE
CHICKEN

Each day at dawn, the lumps of vertebrae at the top of my spine began to ache. My bones and muscles tried to help themselves, to fix the bent shape that furniture moving had made out of my body. When I woke up, when the pain pushed me out of bed, right then was when I tried to convince myself that I hadn't thought of Cass; she was not my first conscious image, even if I had, even if she was.

My building wasn't quiet in the morning. Everybody was up and busy, making breakfast, listening to weather reports, news, and soap operas in Spanish. Luz's family was as loud as anybody's. They had salsa music on and there was the sound of pots banging and water running; then they'd yell to be heard over all of that. I slowed on their landing. I stopped in front of their door and found myself sniffing air, trying to suck in Luz's scent. Their door opened. I didn't move. My heart sped a bit and my lungs crinkled up and I was sure I'd just made a noise like air getting sucked out of a paper bag. A man came out.

He was dark colored, with one of those funny haircuts that's just a little longer in the back. He had a gold necklace with OCIDES spelled out in shiny wide letters. The Tasmanian devil from cartoons? Built with strong little legs and a huge chest that supports a thick head? That was Ocides, except human, and big, bigger. I was sure he was Luz's father and I wanted to ask him about Luz—I'd given her little brother Alfredo a tiny gold statue of a man, to give to her.

Ocides nodded at me. For all he knew I was coming to check the gas, or the cable—I was nobody in particular to him.

"Hey," he said. Then I knew I'd heard his voice before. When I left for work in the early early morning, I could hear him singing in the shower, his deep voice coming through several walls.

"Eeuh ay," I said, which was all I could get out; then I followed him down. I thought about how it was nice of him to say hello to a stranger.

Outside I went over to White Castle and ate a quick breakfast in a bright orange booth. Seven of their little egg and cheese sandwiches, hash browns in the shape of a brick, coffee that burned even though it wasn't hot—and I was ready for my day. I thought, no doubt, that Ocides is an all-right guy.

We moved a sleepy couple from a loft down in Tribeca to a house in Riverdale. They didn't have much—and what they did have was light. Some people are like that—lightweights, with tons of furniture made of bent birch wood and spindly bits of steel, without books, with posters in thin frames that we have to hold close to our bodies, so that they won't blow away in the wind. They did have a whole bunch of change, and like all rich people, they made us pack it up. Rich people are funny that way—you'd think they'd give us their change or give it to beggars or donate it somewhere—but they move it out to the country.

We were all quiet during the move, because the lush grass of Riverdale was beautiful in early September, and I think we all knew enough not to mess it up by yapping. We came back into the city and I got Vince to drop me at a Hundred and Tenth and Broadway, where all the college kids are, and then I walked across, back home through the park. I had to walk slow—what with all the plastic bags of small change I had stuffed down into my socks and sneakers. When I got out of the park, I leaked change a bit, so there were little pools of it behind me. I looked back and the change glittered in the garbage-colored street.

I stepped into my local Chinese take-out, Hong Fat. Shiny photos of different dishes covered the walls. The place was half full and boiling hot, with everybody waiting for their order and only one couple eating at a table, both of them slurping up their lo mein and drinking Snapple iced tea through straws. I looked at the wonderful pictures, of briny fresh lobster and crab, of carefully arranged slices of duck and eggplant, and wondered why the hell they didn't bother to imitate them, why there was always so much green pepper and water chestnut and never enough chicken. But nobody complained and I didn't get that, how they could show you one thing and give you another and still, everybody would accept that fat gap as a given.

Then Luz walked in. A vein in my neck throbbed for a second and popped my head up an inch. I asked myself, Think about God much? The answer was no, and I thought, Well think about God now, 'cause it's time to give up some thanks.

She had on shiny black Adidas warm-up pants, a white short-sleeved T-shirt, and black mules. She looked like a young woman from the neighborhood, but also—she looked dressed up, like she was there to meet somebody. The place was loud with the sizzling noise of boiling oil tossed around in a battered aluminum wok.

Two cops walked in. They muttered something about an opportunity. A dish highlighted in gold was called Good Chance Chicken. A love song on the radio: If I could get just one chance with you. But I stank! I looked down at my sweatshirt, at my blue jeans stained with cooking grease that I'd wiped off a pan I'd packed that morning. A man in front of me ordered wontons and hot and sour soup, $3.95. I pulled my shirt away from my skin. It was my turn. I could feel my heart beat; the word "chance" chanted over and over till it felt like I was back in Peewee hockey and my brother and his friends were whispering "spaz" louder and louder until I dropped my stick. I shook it all off. She was right behind me.

The counter guy looked at me, silent, expectant.

I said, "Hey, good to see you. Make me what's good, chicken and vegetables the way the cook likes them, maybe the Good Chance Chicken, and give me seven egg rolls."

The guy gave me the half smile that I deserved since he'd probably seen me a hundred times. I stepped aside, so that I was next to her. But she didn't order. She turned to me. She said nothing.

I said, "I—we met the other day, with your brother, Alfredo . . ."

"Yes. Seven egg rolls? Why?"

"You say, why seven . . ."

I couldn't very well say the truth, that usually I gave them away on the walk home. I couldn't think straight. It was scary. I don't even like egg rolls.

"I save them?"

"Yeah," she said. "Maybe you'll have extra, you want to share them, I'll buy one from you, then I won't have to order." She gestured to the woman behind her, who went ahead.

"I'll give you them," I said.

We stood there, looking.

"I can't eat all seven," she said.

She turned and put her elbows behind her on the counter and faced the front of the store. I dared to take a split-second glance and I saw her breasts jut out, the slow rise and fall at the top of her chest as she breathed. She stared straight forward. She had her hair down and loose, and she took it and pushed it around so it came down over her right shoulder. Her hair was shiny, smooth.

I paid and we walked out, with her in front of me. Now that we were outside the restaurant, I had no idea where we would eat.

She said, "Tell me your name again."

"I'm Kelly, and you're Luz, right?"

We shook hands. It was cool outside after all that food heat and her hand was firm and I got in that extra second of touch. The physical feeling of her was astonishing—I had not touched a woman in months. The truth flashed at me. I had gone dateless for more than a year, sexless for sixteen months. The only woman I'd ever made love with was Cass. And we were long over and now all I had of her was what I woke up with, the stupid longing part. I wondered if Luz noticed, if this new prickled desire moved with me, if it was something she could smell.

"Alfredo says you're nice to him," she said, "and—thank you for the little golden man." She smiled. It took all I had to keep from saying that I stole it and I stole it for her.

"Good," I said.

A man interrupted. "You got egg rolls?"

He was on my right, a man in a dark coat, with an earless Mickey Mouse hat, and I knew him; I reached in and found an egg roll, hot in its little paper sheath. I handed it to him, and then he reached into the bag and grabbed a packet of duck sauce.

"Clarence," I said, "you making it okay?"

"Not bad, Kelly, thanks."

He held the food and smelled it. Then he put his hand on my shoulder, gave me his deep nod, and left us.

"Let's go back to your apartment, or you'll give it all away."

"Right, right. Yes," I said.

I gave egg rolls to a few more people, whose names I did not know. Luz walked along next to me and I turned to her and saw that I had not walked along the street with a woman in so long—the experience was almost new—but I did take care to walk on the curbside, and to make sure not to bump up to her too close—not to box her in.

Then someone yelled for me, "Hey hey! Kelly! Where you been?"

Jimmy Charney sat on a stoop a few houses before my building. He was smoking and his knee was going up and down, fast. He was so thin that you could see his bones jangling under his canvas jacket, his clavicle, the pointed ball of his elbow. Jimmy had been with Miracle Movers back when I'd just started. Now he lived with his mother in a building all too near mine.

"Hey, uh, Jimmy—"

"No, no! I see you're with a lady; don't let me bother you now— only, your bet came through the other night, at Hooligan's, and the bartender asked me to tell you if I saw you, that's all, you can collect on Tuesday—and listen, maybe I'll see you down there soon, right?"

"Uh—"

"Say no more; we need to meet soon is all."

He got off the stoop and waved. His body was amazing—all thick ribbons of muscle around bone—dope-addict thin, and you could see the tension in him—ripples of strength showed through just below his ears and along his jaw. He'd been fired for petty theft and people said he had to support his mother's methadone addiction. He bopped down the street, away from us. I hadn't made any bet at Hooligan's. I did not want him to be interested in meeting with me.

"That your friend?" Luz asked.

"No more than anybody else," I said.

We went upstairs slow and polite. I tried to let her go first.

"No, you go," she said.

I went up. I guess she didn't want me behind her, looking at her body.

"Stairs are good for you, huh?" I asked. She said nothing, only kept her breathing even and matched my steps. When we both passed her landing and she was still with me, that's when my heart began to really beat.

Inside, we didn't eat. We weren't hungry. I put the bag in the fridge.

We sat in my two chairs. She had one of those twenty-five-cent packs of Big Red, and she took out two sticks, rolled them, and gave me one. Big Red doesn't fix your breath, I don't know why, but it doesn't. I chewed madly in the hopes that it would help, but it was fruitless.

"I once had a friend like that guy we just saw on the street, you know, a girlfriend, who was always hanging around, always wanting something, and finally I told her, fuck off, you know? Don't come around me."

"Yeah?" I said.

She wove her accent in and out, so that she allowed her Spanish to crease her English. She caged out my space, paced it off, touched my few books while she spoke.

"So I'm in eighth grade and I'm coming home from school, two of her friends throw me up against a building, they've got me pinned and there she is, all huffed up and angry at me? Her friend gives her a scalpel, out of nowhere, a scalpel, little shining thing—she comes rushing up, bangs my head against the wall, cuts me here, see?"

She held up two fingers and showed me four cuts, on her jaw, the shadow of her neck, a nick on her collarbone. She had to push aside her shirt for me to see.

"They laughed at me. I went home and got my father's baseball bat and came back out; they were all on a stoop, and I came up and I hit her friends and they ran; then I hit her on her back and on her head and all these guys had to hold me back and I was hitting everybody in sight. That girl went into the hospital."

"Don't worry," I said, "I'm not going to try anything."

"I know. I'm just telling you a story." She smiled. "Sometimes you have to tell a story, just to keep things straight. 'Cause who knows who you are, and I'm in your apartment and all—"

"I just think you're so—" But she interrupted me. The energy in that room pulsed, wide waves of it coming off us. I believe in all that, pheromones, smell, stuff deep below talk. She kept walking, pushing, afraid, maybe, of our connection.

"You go to school?" she asked. She stretched and put her hands behind her head. But then she saw me watch her—catch the rise and fall in her chest—and she put her arms down, over her front.

"No, I quit a few years ago."

"So what do you do?"

"I move furniture. Do you—go to school?"

"Two classes a semester, at John Jay. I have to help my mom a lot, and I work, at Duane Reade, on Fifty-seven and Broadway."

I imagined her there, behind the counter, ringing up toothpaste and quart bottles of Coke. She'd be there, beautiful, and when the customers looked up, they would gasp. She would spend much of her time looking at the ceiling, thinking of other things. The managers probably gossiped about her. They probably spent a lot of time behind her, messing with her cashbox.

"What's your mother's real name?"

She giggled.

"Migdalia."

"How'd it turn to Queen?"

"It didn't. The first time you saw her, she said, 'Quién?' and then you thought she was saying her name, so you called her that."

"No."

"Oh yeah." She nodded.

We sat at the table and I heard my stomach make noise and so did she and then we just laughed together, with the radiator making its first bangs of fall, and the dirt on my clothes and her beauty and my stupidity.

"Now my father calls her Queen, my son does, Jahaira, we all do, now, 'cause of you."

"Your son?"

"You knew that, right? Alfredo is my boy."

"I didn't know that. That's good, he's a beautiful boy."

I thought, When we get married, he can be the ring-bearer. I didn't ask about a father. She must have been very young when she had Alfredo. Selfish, I hoped that the father was a stranger now.

"He is beautiful. And I love him, don't get me wrong about that. He's my responsibility and I bring him up right. I pay for his clothes; I do his schoolwork with him. He's going to be just fine—"

"I didn't say—"

"I just don't want you to go thinking I don't care about my boy. Not that I care what you think or anything . . ."

I saw that I needed to look at her, to speak slow.

"No. I know Alfredo. I like him. We have fun together sometimes; you know, we play ball in the hallway."

She kept looking at me, searching my eyes.

"Okay," she said.

She was suddenly leaned forward, angled and serious.

"Why'd you move up here?"

"It was kind of this fluke thing, not a particular choice; it was money mostly—"

"Everybody said because of drugs, but that was too stupid; who would move all the way to a place because of drugs?"

Then she looked pleased. I got up and went to the window and she did too, and the street below was not pleasant or beautiful, but our place there, above, was legitimate, our tenement castle, our spaceship, our first date. Down below people pissed in the street, were mugged, were suddenly a little bit cool on that September night. And we were near each other.

"Now, I have to go."

And I thought, This is the only thing that can make me happy, is me with her, is this.

"I hate it here," she said. She waved her hand out over the street. "I hate it here."

I could say nothing. They were much more her streets than mine.

"I'm going down now, I promised I'd help Alfredo with his math and it's almost time for his bed."

"You have to go?"

Between us a half doe-eyed look, like we were younger together. Her looking up, me looking down.

"Yes, I have to go."

"Luz, listen. Let me take you out on a date, soon."

"That would be nice." But she was already crossing the room.

"To Hanratty's. Friday night, maybe, at eight?"

"Yes, but we'll meet there, not here." She came back halfway and held out her hand and I was able to hold it again.

"The little golden man? I found him for you—I stole him for you."

"Yes. It's good. Thank you," she said.

Then she moved away, closed the door behind her.

I will learn to hate it here too, I thought. I will take her hate inside me and share that too. I stole for her. She'd smiled when I said it, and that felt good. I believed that before I had met her, I knew only discontent. My heart rushed up and pounded inside of me. I will steal it all for you.

Sheila Kohler

CRACKS

Fiamma fainted in chapel this morning. The teachers do not know we make ourselves do it, though they suspect we do. They even had a doctor brought in to examine us, but he said there was nothing wrong with us. He said he had never seen such a healthy group of growing girls. We do look healthy. Our skins are gold with all the sunshine, and our hair and teeth look very white in contrast. Weekdays we wear short-sleeved white blouses and green tunics with their big *R*s embroidered on our chests and our short green socks. Our tunics are worn four inches from the ground, measured kneeling, so you can see our knobby knees.

Perhaps Fiamma did not make herself faint. Perhaps she just fainted. The girls on the swimming team take turns fainting in chapel. We all know how to do it. Before Communion, while you are on your knees and have not had any breakfast, you breathe hard a few times, and then you hold your breath and close your eyes. You sweat and start to see diamonds in the dark. You feel yourself rush out of yourself, out and out. Then you come back to the squelch of Miss G's crepe shoes, as she strides along the blue-carpeted aisle to rescue you. She makes you put your head down between your knees, and then she lifts you up and squeezes your arm. Miss G is our swimming teacher, and she is super strong.

You lean against her as you go down the aisle and feel her breath on

100

your cheek, and the soft swell of her boosie. Your heart flutters, and you see the light streaming in aslant through the narrow, stained-glass windows: red and blue and yellow like a rainbow.

Miss G leads you out into the cool of the garden. You sit on the whitewashed wall under the loquat tree in your white Sunday dress and undo the mother-of-pearl button at your neck. Miss G sits on the wall beside you and smokes a cigarette, holding it under her hand, so Miss Nieven, our headmistress, who has an M.A. from Oxford, will not notice if she comes upon her suddenly. When Miss G tells you to, you take off your panama hat and set it down on the wall. Then you lean your head against her shoulder. You get to sit there under the cool dark leaves of the loquat tree and feel the breeze lift the hem of your tunic very gently and watch Miss G blow smoke rings until she asks if you feel all right now. Her voice is deep and a little hoarse, like a man's.

Meg Donovan, who is a beauty and comes from Barbeton, says she thinks Fiamma might be preggie. Meg's mother often fainted when she was preggie. One time Meg saw her mother fall down from the table where she was turning around, having a hem pinned up. Meg has five sisters, and they are all at our school. She says her father says they should name a wing of our school after him because of all the tuition he has had to pay.

Di Radfield, whose thin lips dip at the corner ever since her father committed suicide in the bath, says Meg must be mad. Fiamma has not even got the curse, so how could she be preggie? Ann Lindt wonders who the father could be. There are no men around here except for the night watchman, John Mazaboko, and the servants, and Sir George's bones and those of his dog, Jock. Fuzzie, who wants to be an opera singer like Mimi Coetzee, says, "Maybe you can do it to yourself in the dark if you cross your legs and rock the bed."

In our school the only snow we have at Christmas time is made from cotton wool, and the holly is made of plastic. It is so hot we sweat when we eat the roast turkey and the roast potatoes and the gem squash, and when they flame the Christmas pudding, the light outside is so bright you can hardly see the flame. The poem we read does not make much sense to us, as April is not the cruelest month and it breeds nothing out of the dead.

Our school is surrounded by farmland. No one is here except the teachers, who are mostly spinsters from England, and the girls. The teachers clasp their hands to their hearts and look across the dun veld to the distant horizon and talk about the lilac in May. The girls loll in the leather chairs in the common room and talk about boys. They lie out on the lawn and listen to Elvis Presley singing "Nothin' but a houn' dog" on the gramophone. They sleep over sums in the classrooms or whisper in the library, as they pretend to look up Latin words. They move their mouths in silent prayer in the chapel and ask God, please, please, let Miss G choose me for the swimming team.

Near the school a few mangy cows graze, and mud huts stand, and wattle trees line the riverbanks, casting their thin shade. The river is hardly a river, just a few pools of dark, trapped water where the mozzies breed. Sometimes it does not rain for months. The earth cracks, and the soil strangles the roots of the flowers. The dust roads lie dry and white as shells, and in the afternoons when we walk, there is dust on our lace-up shoes. No fan-shaped sprinklers wave back and forth in the evenings to cool the air, and we are not allowed to take baths. The smell of sweat mingles with that of sweet dusting powder and Mum's deodorant and the 4711 that we splash behind our ears and pour down our fronts. Once the thatched roofs of the rondavels caught fire and the night watchman, John Mazaboko, had to come running with his hose.

The graves of Sir George Harrow and his faithful bullterrier, Jock, rest in the shade of a frangipani tree. The school once belonged to Sir George. There is a portrait of him in the library, wearing a monocle and looking old and dried out. Under his portrait it says he was a High Commissioner. The graves are out of bounds, but we sometimes run there to lie down on the cool marble slab and fold our hands on our chests and play dead.

Fuzzie was playing "All things bright and beautiful" loudly on the upright piano when Fiamma fainted. Fuzzie thumps when she plays the piano, and we make the gesture for an organ grinder behind her back. Even so, you could hear the dull thud when Fiamma's head hit the back of the pew. Then you could hear Miss G advancing down the aisle, her starched khaki jumpsuit rustling and her crepe-soled boots squelching, coming on valiantly, head held high, like a knight in armor. Miss G looked beautiful and brave, and the chapel looked like a castle.

Fuzzie says Miss G has an *aquiline* nose, which means she looks like an eagle.

Miss G is lots of girls' crack. When you have a crack you see things more clearly: the thick dark of the shadows and the transparence of the leaves in the light and the soft glow of the pink magnolia petals against the waxy leaves. You want to lie down alone in the dark in the music room and listen to Rachmaninoff and the summer rains rushing hard down the gutters. You leave notes for your crack in her mug next to her toothbrush on the shelf in the bathroom. If you accidentally brush up against your crack, and feel her boosie, you come close to fainting.

Sometimes Miss G calls the twelve of us on the swimming team into her room and tells us to shut the windows and shutters. We sit in the half-light and listen to her talk. She tells us to watch men in their bathing costumes, how they swell when they come near a girl. She makes us feel we are the snake charmers. She says Miss Nieven is a lezzie with Miss Lacey, the English teacher, whom Yeats once loved. Miss G has seen them in the moonlight in Miss Lacey's square green Chevrolet.

Fiamma has misty gray eyes and pale freckles and thick dark hair. She walks very straight, as if her head were a crystal vase she was balancing on her shoulders. Fiamma comes from the lake district in Italy, and she is the only girl in the school who is an R.C. They let her into our school, but she has to come to chapel with us.

She lives in a big villa with many servants. She is supposed to be a princess or something like that, and before she arrived, Miss Nieven told us to be polite and treat her kindly.

We learned about Bloody Mary in history and how she killed lots of people. She was an R.C. We read a poem by the greatest poet in the English language, according to Miss Lacey, and he asks God to avenge the saints slaughtered by the R.C.s. Perhaps Fiamma saw someone slaughtered, and she was thinking about it when she fainted in chapel. Perhaps that is why they have sent her away from her lovely villa, which is near a blue lake and mountains.

Fiamma has very white skin and suffers terribly from the mozzies. Fuzzie says Fiamma bathes in champagne to keep her skin so white.

Di Radfield says it is milk. Maybe that is why it attracts the mozzies. Fiamma has big red welts on her calves and her arms. She spits on her mozzie bites and says the mozzies are eating her alive. Ann Lindt told her to use repellent, but Fiamma says it stings too much.

Fuzzie says Fiamma fainted because someone gave her the Black Spot. The Black Spot frightened Fiamma because she believes in vendettas like all Italians. Fuzzie can sing "La donna é mobile" from *Rigoletto*.

We torture all new girls. We make them eat bitter aloe or swallow cod-liver oil. Sheila Kohler tried to make a new girl put her head down the toilet, but the girl refused. Sheila Kohler said, "But you have to," but the girl just walked away.

Ann Lindt says she does not think Fiamma would have fainted because of the Black Spot. Ann Lindt knows everything. She reads *The Manchester Guardian,* which is sent to us from England on special thin airmail paper and pinned to the bulletin board, where it flaps about in the breeze that comes in through the open windows. Ann Lindt told us we were in danger of war over a crisis in the Suez Canal. She asked Miss Nieven why the natives do not have the vote. Miss Nieven said democracy takes a long time to develop.

Ann Lindt has to wear thick glasses because she is always reading. She reads books by Winston Churchill, who was attacked in an armored train in the Boer War. She sits in the windowsill in the early morning before we get up and reads Winston Churchill's *Great Contemporaries* and looks up the words she does not know, words like *internecine* and *belligerent.* She says they do not read *Treasure Island* in Italy and so Fiamma would not even know that if someone gives you a piece of paper with a round blackened circle on it, it means they are going to kill you.

Most of us came here as boarders at five or six because there were no proper schools where we lived. We left our parents on distant farms or small towns. We traveled alone or in little groups for days on dusty trains through the dry veld. We arrived exhausted and confused, stumbling through the long, narrow dormitories, lit only by Matron's torch, and finding our beds among strange sleeping girls. The sheets smelled damp and funny. We lay awake listening to the dry wind clashing in the palm trees and tried to count the stars.

We cried for our mothers until Matron came and told us to be quiet, we would wake the other girls. When we got to the hiccupy stage she took our temperature with a thermometer that she keeps in a small glass of Dettol. Her name is Mrs. Looney, and we think she is, too.

Even now sometimes, we lie awake sniffing and hiccuping and imagining our mothers: they come to us in the half-dark, their soft breaths on our cheeks as they sing us familiar songs or recite rhymes we know: *She shall have music wherever she goes.*

At first we saw our mothers' faces as we tried to untangle the knots in our hair, or when we left our soap in the big bath with the feet in the bathroom under the stairs. We thought we heard our mothers calling our names, and we ran down into the bamboo at the end of the garden, catching glimpses of them parting the bamboo and stepping toward us in green silk dresses, but it was the cry of a sparrow hawk or the wind in the leaves.

We made up imaginary friends. Fuzzie's is called Margaret, which is her real name. We call her Fuzzie because of her curly hair. She runs around the hockey field until the breath rasps in her chest, talking to Margaret. At night in the dormitory Fuzzie tells us stories of Chinese girls who have blue eyes and blond hair, and Zulu maidens as pale as lilies. Ann Lindt interrupts and says such things are not possible. But we like to fall asleep to the sound of Fuzzie's voice. We feel ourselves spin out into the darkness, round and round, like a leaf on a lake.

Before she fainted in chapel this morning, Fiamma rose at dawn and went to swimming practice. Fiamma may be an R.C., but she is an excellent swimmer. Miss G says she can teach anyone to swim fast. All you have to do is to desire it. Miss G says desire is everything. We all like the way she says *desire.*

Miss G made us all race this year, now that we are in the senior school. She said we could choose any stroke we liked. She made us wait forever on the grass in our thin black costumes, while she strode up and down the edge of the pool with the yellow whistle in her mouth. Miss G's hair is glossy as a blackbird's and cropped so short you can see the bristles at the back. When she strides up and down you can see the shimmer of sweat on her strong arms and the dark shadow of the shaved hair between her strong, brown legs.

We felt the sun burning the skin on our shoulders puce. We licked

powdered sugar from the flat of our palms for energy. Then Miss G
called out our names and had us line up. Our legs felt watery, like the
reflections of legs in water. We giggled and squirmed and pulled the
straps of our green plastic caps away from our chins.

She lifted her black gun in the white air and fired. We heard the
crack of the gun. Birds shot up in the air. We flung ourselves across
the water for the two lengths. We splashed and kicked into one another. Fiamma left the rest of us behind after a few strokes. When
Sheila Kohler saw she was not winning she threw her hands up in the
air and sank down into the water.

Fiamma says her house is surrounded by regular gardens with gravel
paths and ancient trees and a stone wall by the lake. She says the house
is old and large and filled with flowers, and the cannas flame red and
orange at the edge of the lawns. There are flowers in every room—
roses and sweet peas and strelitzias. There are lilies and peonies and
baby's breath. There are flowers everywhere, she says—on every table
and cabinet and inlaid chest, on every marble mantle piece and even
on the tops of bookcases. In the entrance hall there is a forest of flowers. Fiamma maintains the whole house looks like a hothouse.

She says there are many old paintings lit up with little lamps over
the gold frames. Mostly, they are so dark you can hardly see the half-
peeled fruit or bleeding hares. In one of the paintings she says there
are two women staring at you, face-on, with a sort of dead expression.
Their hair is done up high on their heads and their stiff boosies are
bare. One of the women holds a nipple of the other gently between her
long white finger and thumb.

Di Radfield says she woke up early, too, before chapel this morning
and saw Fiamma hunting for her swimming costume. Fiamma is always losing things. She is used to having servants pick up her clothes
from the marble floors of her big villa. Fiamma brushes her cheeks
with a toothbrush every night before she goes to bed to make them
glow. She adds an Alka-Seltzer to the flat water to make it fizz. She
curtsies when she shakes hands with a grown-up.

Miss G says that no one will tell us the truth about life, certainly not
that bunch of spinsters who know nothing about it. She says, "Think
of the water as your home. Learn to do without breath. Stay light."

She tells us not to roll about or twist our shoulders or lift our heads too high in the water, but to suck a little air from the side of our mouths. She tells us not to make any splash, to slice silently through the water.

We all wore our panama hats and our white Sunday dresses with the mother-of-pearl buttons down the front for confirmation, because Miss Nieven said this was not a fashion show. When we were confirmed, we had to go to confession for the first and the last time in our lives. Sheila Kohler cried afterwards. She said she had told the minister she had read banned books, but she was not sorry, because they told the truth. Ann Lindt said Sheila Kohler was just trying to get Miss G's attention.

We know who has the curse and who does not because we play Truth in the dormitory at night. We put our hands into a pile and then pull them out. Someone sits on the sidelines and calls out Stop, and whoever has her hand at the bottom of the pile has to tell the truth. That's how we learned that Meg Donovan let a boy put his finger up her winkie. Di said she was jealous of Meg and followed her around for days like a dog. Di says we get the curse early because we live in such a hot country, but Fiamma is an aristocrat and they do not get the curse as early as commoners, because they have blue blood.

Di Radfield says she had finished swimming practice this morning before anyone else arrived. She says she saw the whole thing. Miss G was at the swimming pool early, striding up and down the edge of the pool. Then Fiamma got out of the pool and did a perfect swallow dive from the high board, opening her arms on the rising sun and orange sky for Miss G.

Di Radfield says she remained silently in the shadows in the changing room, waiting to see what would happen. She watched Miss G follow Fiamma into the changing room, going toward Fiamma with the light behind her. Di could not see Fiamma's face, because her back was turned toward Di. Slowly Fiamma slipped her arms out of her swimming suit straps and folded down the top of her bathing costume. She spread her arms out on either side and shook her shoulders in a sort of dance. Little drops of water fell onto the concrete floor from the tips of her fluttering fingers. She stepped out of her swimming costume. Di saw her naked back, the bare white shoulders, the damp skin, only the cool morning air clothing her. All the while Miss G was watching Fiamma, and her face looked red and wet, her mouth slightly open. Then Miss G moved toward Fiamma slowly, put her arms gently around her. Miss G lowered her dark head to Fiamma's boosie and sucked. Di could hear her sucking like a baby.

When they had finished, Fiamma floated out of the changing room, leaving the door open. Through the open door Di saw the grass shining white in the early morning light and the soft yellow flowers on the mimosa trees like snow on the thin branches. Di Radfield put on her tunic quickly and picked up her panama hat and ran down the bank toward the school.

Di Radfield says she wanted to cry, because Miss G has never even grabbed her boosie, but instead she decided to tell Miss Nieven what had happened.

At evensong in chapel Fuzzie plays "Now the day has ended / Night is drawing near" on the upright piano, but she gets stuck on the first two lines and plays them over and over. The odor of incense is in our nostrils. Our sunburned faces float like pink petals in the dim light. We are worn out with the sun and talking about Fiamma. It is the sad time on Sunday night, and we cannot recall our homes.

Miss Nieven rises for the sermon. Her shadow looms long and thin on the wall. She tells us Fiamma will have to stay in the san for a while, that the doctor has to check her out. She has sent Fiamma our good wishes, as she knows we would have wanted her to. She says that this is the sort of thing that happens when you behave in a foolish way. She read "When I was a child I spake as a child . . ."

On our knees we watch Di Radfield flip her hair back from her face and breathe out hard. She holds her breath and closes her eyes. We look for Miss G but we already know she is not there. We know what has happened to her and that she will not be back. Miss Nieven is coming to the end of the prayers, and Di's time is running out. She is beginning to sweat, and she turns pale, but we know she will not be able to slump sideways into the aisle. She will not see diamonds in the dark.

DANCING A SAD THOUGHT

For only ten dollars, you can get an hour introductory class *and* a half-hour private lesson at most of New York's dancing "academies." When I finally decided, at the age of thirty-two, to learn the tango proper, I was surprised and a little pleased by the pages and pages of dance schools listed in the yellow pages. Just by their ads I could tell these businesses were fiercely competitive. I knew the ten dollars was only the wiggling worm, the first free fix, yet I anticipated with a very basic pleasure being fawned over, sold something. In the end, however, all the schools seemed the same, and I chose the school that claimed to have taught a famous actor to dance; it seemed an appropriately random enough reason on which to base a decision.

It was summer, and all of us in the first introductory class were embarrassingly freshly showered and sweaty and smelling of toothpaste. If the rest were anything like me, then each of us had anticipated that fateful encounter with our one true love, whom we'd recognize at a glance across the floor, while simultaneously anticipating a room full of desperate clods, and obviously each of us had figured, in the face of either event, that we should at least be clean. The class ran this way: Anthony, the group instructor, would show us a basic step, then have the men and women form different lines. The lines would collide to form separate couples, then each couple would try out the step as Anthony counted out the timing for us. Next came the order "Switch!"

and each woman would rotate clockwise to the next man. There were fifteen women and eleven men, which meant that there were always four women during each rotation who had a choice: stand still and watch the couples on either side work out their figures, or hold out your arms and practice your steps with a ghost. Early on, I figured this was some sort of character test, and I watched to see who would stand, how awkwardly they would stand, who would dance, and how unself-consciously they would dance.

When I finally got around to taking tango lessons, which is to say when I finally got over my humiliation of wanting to take tango les-sons, it was the small gestures that surprised me; the slight push of my partner's hand, the brush of his knee on my inner thigh, his persis-tent fingers on my back. It was so intimate, and this intimacy was so public, and ran so parallel to the impersonal, it was pornographic. And every time I thought this, felt the slight stir of sex, and the faint shame of sex, I felt even more ashamed, and even more sexed by the indiffer-ent, formal framework of our meeting.

My private instructor's name is Ivan and he possesses a strong Slavic accent and even stronger Slavic face. Our first few lessons together I want to ask him if tango is popular among Eastern European immi-grants, or if he's an exception. I want to ask him all about his life because I love anyone different, but I don't because not only might it be rude, but I also actively remind myself that I'm only one of many students. He's got a strong, well-proportioned face and blue eyes, thick black hair and skin so white you can see the beard beneath its just-shaven smoothness. I'm sure that with the close physical contact many students develop a crush, and I decide almost immediately that I will absolutely not fall into such a rut. Instead, I decide, he should develop a crush on me. It's an almost arbitrary decision. After all, the school has at least half a dozen male dance instructors, and I could have been paired with any of them. Ivan has come into my life like the majority of my friends and most of my lovers; with an erratic luck.

In truth, I've wanted to tango ever since I first saw Gomez grab Mor-ticia in a TV sitcom from my childhood, *The Addams Family*. The show was based on a series of *New Yorker* cartoons by Charles Addams, which focused on the lifestyle of a particularly macabre family. The cartoon characters were ghoulish and droll, and the producers of the TV show spent the first season trying to duplicate this. But it wasn't their oddness that attracted me, for I was odd myself, something I alternately courted and despised. The Addamses, for all their quirkiness, were still a very tight-knit family; the producers quickly picked up on this and later season episodes underscored the Addamses' "functional" attributes. Essentially, *The Addams Family* went from being about outsiders to *Father Knows Best* in drag. And while the Addamses retained their genuine eccentricities even with the tinkering of their family dynamics, this was still an era in which the shape of television sitcoms distinctly American was being defined. Unlike earlier comedies, which traced their roots to rowdy and uncensored vaudeville, most sitcoms in this country after World War II consisted of episodes built around recurring, easily digested morals. Typically, these morals underscored honesty and hard work. Oddly, these morals were usually "learned" by eventually becoming discovered as the actions that would have prevented the preceding half hour of comedic antics in the first place. Whatever immoral fun took place could be presented by producers "safe" in the knowledge that ultimately it was all for the "good."

Still, when I was watching the Addamses, and without knowing how little I knew, I had only an exaggerated, silhouetted impression of what made a tango a tango. Along with my friends, tango, to our adolescent minds, was like sex or our crippled math teacher, or what we thought sounded very much like Chinese; all things easily made fun of. On a regular basis throughout elementary and junior high school, usually accompanied by fits of insidious laughter, I would find myself grabbing someone's arm in mine, dramatically pointing it straight out toward one end of the room and then following it with a stealthy, sidling gait, all to be followed some ten steps later by the abrupt maneuver and thrill of dramatically changing arms and direction so as to glide awkwardly, no matter how slick I believed we looked, back to our original starting point.

But unlike mimicking the math teacher and chortling in pseudo-Chinese, tango continued to stake its claim on my desires even in private. And because I didn't know what real tango was, the tango I actually desired was the laden moment itself, when the mood would overcome Gomez—it seemed a mood that easily overtook him, and I wanted that impetuousness as well—and Gomez would yell, "Tanggo!" abruptly turning his torso and full attention—and oh, how I wanted attention turned on me with such focus—toward Morticia, tossing whatever he was holding behind him, it did not matter if it was a priceless vase or ticking bomb (yes, I wanted that too, that knowledge of how worth was fluid, that money and danger were valueless when up against passion) simply so that he, Gomez, could better stretch out his open hand toward his beloved wife. Whatever else was going on, when Gomez and Morticia had to tango, they tangoed.

As I was performing my own pseudotango in those childhood basements, I had no idea just how complicated the tango was. And complicated not just in its actual maneuvers, but that its very history was tangled and shadowy.

My first surprise was to learn just how sad tango is. That very first group lesson, Anthony, the head instructor, emphasized the importance of "tango face." "You have to look like you just came from a funeral," he told us. You rarely, if ever, look your partner in the eyes, something that distinguishes tango from most other dances. This sadness is embedded in the physical gestures of tango, but is easiest to see the lyrics of tango songs. Love in tango is not the simple boy-meets-girl-and-they-live-happily-ever-after type of love. Most tangos are about suffering from love. And if they aren't about suffering from love, then they are about suffering from poverty, or social oppression. Their lyrics outline lives filled with bad luck, hunger, isolation, and God's indifference. One of the best-known definitions of tango comes from Carlos Gardel, one of the great tango singers of all time. "It's like dancing a sad thought," he said.

As soon as this unexpected underside of tango showed itself to me, I became even more curious. I set out to learn as much as I could. The basic, physical facts were easy: a basic defining feature that separates tango from ballroom dances (even though tango is often defined as a ballroom dance, to the horror of its purists) is timing. Except on the contest floor, it's not a neatly laid out dance. It's a lot like jazz, with the lead dancer improvising, slowing down and speeding up as he feels the need, doing whatever figure he fancies at that precise moment. It's tango's lack of choreography, its reliance on inventiveness, that makes a lot of traditional ballroom dancers avoid it; most people tend to favor the more structured, "safer" dances, such as the waltz and foxtrot.

But it was the history of tango—it took a while for me to get familiar enough with it to drop the article "the"—that surprised me most of all. The origins of tango are still under debate. In Argentina, tango is widely danced by all levels of society, and is endless fodder for Argentinean intellectuals and a source of cultural identity for nonintellectuals. There, the debate over tango's history gets vicious, with ruined marriages, lost tenure, and even, in at least one case, a duel. There are thirty-three official histories of the tango, but most people agree that ur-tango first appeared in the mid-nineteenth century in the Río de La Plata region in South America, the region that has a foot in both Brazil and Uruguay, and then culminated into recognizable tango form in Argentina. It was a "low" dance, danced in brothels and in the street and commonly by "Negroes." What's distinctive about tango is that it actually crossed economic and racial lines on a regular basis: black men, visiting the brothels, were actually allowed to dance, in public for the first recorded time, with white women. Upwardly mobile landowners would dance on the same floor as ex-slaves, and often men would dance with other men. It was a deeply scandalous dance, something most upper-class Argentineans, along with lesbianism and infanticide, wouldn't even admit existed. Most important, and perhaps most dangerous from the upper-class perspective, tango obliterated social lines. What scandalized the upper classes was not the sexual metaphor of tango, but the identity of those partaking in the metaphor. Sex in many forms is an effective way of reiterating clearly marked structures of power, but somehow tango, uniquely, avoided this. Even if it was only for those brief moments on the dance floor, tango actually equalized partners, no matter what their sex, race, or class.

I didn't know this at first. Before I ever started the tango, I had decided it was a sexist dance. But in truth, in my lessons with Ivan especially, it hardly seemed to do with him being a man. Acting out the Hegelian theory of the enslaved master, Ivan depended upon my following even more than I did his leading, and my most persistent mistake was in anticipating his next move. The first lesson more than a dozen times he stopped, put my arms down for me, stepped back, and looked straight at me with those beguiling eyes: "No, no. You're not listening to me. You don't know how to just wait and listen."

He got that much right. I thought of all the men in my life who at one point or another—standing in their doorway in jeans, naked in my living room, in their silk ties on their way to work—telling me the same thing. It surprised me, you know: I always thought I'd *like* being led, like taking no responsibility for the course of things. I like taking control when I'm adept, there being few pleasures quite so exquisite as being elegant at something, but I'm always just a little bit more happy to be passive. Still, there are a lot of rules, a lot of boundaries. And yet, somehow, I'd never anticiated *this:* the slight sweat I could feel through his shirt, and, as silly as it sounds, just how close he'd stand next to me.

I remember when I was finally relieved of my burdensome virginity. I'd pictured the event a million times in my head, had read a score of writings about it, looked at a hundred photos, yet somehow the actual, tactile fact of having to part my legs so wide surprised me. It was morning and the light was coming in and his cats were sitting on the floor idly watching us. Their hair floated in a thin line of early sun. Unaccustomed to such a position, my left hip suddenly cracked loudly into the silence. Embarrassed by the volume, I looked up at him, my first lover; a new, small island of doubt forming in an already large sea of doubt.

At each of my private weekly lessons, I try to drop little asides to Ivan about my exciting, fascinating life.

"I can deduct all this, you know, because I'm a writer. I'm going to write about the tango."

"You must your feet more quickly in the turn move," he replies.

"Of course, I might have to miss my lesson next week because I'm waiting to hear from my agent if I have to fly to Burma."

"Perhaps it is time for shoes with proper leather soles for you to buy. These boots you always wear; they are for a boy on a farm, not for tango!"

In the group lessons my fellow fledgling men practically demand that I lead, for they have no idea how to maintain a proper frame. Here, quite unlike the ideal Ivan, I am thoroughly disgusted by the general and everyday reality of most men's ineptitude. It is no wonder, I think, that I don't know how to listen. Ivan *knows* how to hold me. Here, in group class, I find myself forcing the correct space between myself and my random partners, pressing them too hard simply so that they will resist and thus create at least a portion of the correct tension required to hold me. This inexperience, combined with the predictable routine of steps required for such clumsy practice, not only accentuates but fosters my desire to be in control. This only ruins me worse for the private lesson. Initially, Ivan simply tells me when I'm not listening to his signals, but as the weeks wear on he takes a more definitive form of action: When I don't listen, he physically pushes me away. We stand there for a moment, squared off, the other couples in the large space spiraling past us.

While I was watching the Addams family tango, I had no idea that I was also watching a cultural fallout of the tango in the worst, bourgeois capitalist terms. To understand this, you have to look at another popular TV family closely related to the Addamses: the Munsters. The Munsters, you see, unlike the Addamses, were working-class: Herman Munster worked as a manual laborer in a cemetery, while his wife Lily was the quintessential housewife, commonly seen preforming domestic chores, though usually with a twist, as when she dusted by actually spraying dust on the furniture. In contrast, the Addamses were infinitely wealthy. Gomez was always spending millions at the drop of a hat, and there were continual references to gold mines and trunks filled with jewels. Often, Gomez, who had a number of university degrees, could be seen reading a stock market ticker-tape: When he lost one fortune it was greeted with a casual shrug, suggesting there was plenty more where that came from.

Unlike Lily, Morticia was never seen preforming menial tasks: she wore a binding black dress that would have prevented any such effort anyway, a dress that also happened to be based on a style made popular in the early twentieth century by tango dancers. The Munsters, who never once tangoed, were lower-middle-class and bore a physical freakishness they could not escape, nor could ever wish to escape, since it was always crucial to the plot that they consider themselves as adhering to the norm. The Addamses, on the other hand, were decidedly upper-class. Though the immediate family, the two parents and the two children, chose to be surrounded by freaks, they themselves were physically normal: Their freakishness was based instead on eccentricities carried to the extreme, eccentricities supported by Gomez's boundless wealth and ego.

The point of all this is that the tango itself was just another dance in the global scheme of things until it got taken up by the French in the early twentieth century. To the cultural imperialists of that era all exotics served the same function: to amuse a class of people at the same time it helped solidify their economic and social position. Traveling shows of "exotics" showed men dressed as gauchos performing the salacious tango. In reality, gauchos had little do with tango, and to have them equated with it was not only historically incorrect, but as absurd as something else often featured in these shows of foreign exotics—African Americans dressed up as American Indians. It didn't actually matter to the Europeans that someone had gotten it wrong, because any gradation of social or cultural importance that didn't directly relate to their class was highly inconsequential. And so it was with tango. It was a "low" dance that offered the thrill of slumming, and if its intricate social importance was obliterated by the good times, no one particularly noticed, or cared.

Tango became all the rage, sweeping its way across Europe during the 1910s and 1920s. And then, with the brand of bourgeois respectability placed upon it by Europe, tango was redefined for Argentina, and somehow became the dance of choice. Tango's golden age in Argentina, which lasted from about 1930 to 1955, was fueled by the dubious nationalism of Juan Perón, who wanted to regain Argentina's national pride, yet wanted to regain that pride by making Argentina appear as European as possible. For Perón, who pushed the tango as a dance of cultural identity, tango represented the perfect tool of propaganda. It has a history far too complicated to contain and thus easy to forget, and an allure far too seductive to dismiss.

After my first six-week lesson cycle was over, I talked the man I was seeing into taking classes with me. I was sure it would save our relationship. Because he'd never danced, he had to take the first-level classes, and I opted to take that first level over again with him, something the instructors generally encouraged. That was a mistake. Stephen had what my writing students call a "white boy" way of dancing, which, in his defense, I like to think is the result of listening to a lot of acid rock during the seventies. What really shocked me, though, wasn't Stephen's lack of rhythm, but my impatience with him. Me? I'd always thought I was the perfect lover, the perfect partner. All those years of loneliness it never occurred to me that I'd have trouble loving someone, only that I'd have trouble finding someone to love me. Yet, here on the dance floor with someone who loved me, I found myself turning into what I'd always referred to as a bitch.

"No, no, no," I'd tell him, trying to shove his hand onto the right place on my back. When he wouldn't hold me with enough tension, I'd let my body collapse against his, causing him to trip. Often, I considered slapping him. Sometimes, as the music played and we practiced our steps, I'd catch a glimpse of us in the huge wall mirror: with Stephen's tall good looks and my tiny figure we made a pretty good-looking couple, but I couldn't let it rest; immediately I'd start picking apart what was wrong with his head position, whinily insist he hold my hand up higher. In retrospect, I'm amazed he never slapped me.

For all its emphasis on machismo, tango is one of the unsung heroes of the modern feminist movement. Both upper-class and bourgeois European women now not only left the house unaccompanied, something unheard of only a few years before, they actually allowed complete strangers to hold them so immodestly at the *thés dansants* that were becoming all the rage across Europe. Women also used these tea dances as arenas for experiments in smoking in public, as well as to show off shocking fashions that revealed thir natural shapes. Well-bred matrons were known to swoon at the very sight of a sex-laden tango. *Except . . .* the original scandal of tango, back in the slums of Argentina, had to do with its class and race relations; once Europe co-opted it, the scandal was transferred to its erotic content, and once that happened, it was ready to become a product. Tango started appearing in films and in plays and by virtue of this alone converted into something viewed openly wicked yet privately desired. In other words, a highly salable product. The loud moanings of sex not only drowned out the more complicated cries of racial economics, it also shifted the scruples of tango into a new, and far less threatening, form. The historical result of prohibiting sex has been to make it seem even more desirable. The beauty of that, from the imperialist's point of view, is that the sin of sex overshadows the taboo of blurring the barriers of class and skin color.

Once, I got stuck in the airport for a few hours with a man I was interested in. We looked through magazines to pass the time and inevitably found ourselves taking the "How much do you know about sex?" quiz in *Cosmopolitan*. When he answered the question, "How many orgasms can a woman have in one session of lovemaking?" with C, four or less, I looked at him in shock. Didn't he know? Men own 99 percent of the world's real estate and rake in 78 percent of its earnings, despite the fact they only account for 44 percent of its workforce. Didn't he know the one sure thing women have to lord over men? When I answered, E, unlimited, my friend wouldn't believe me and we almost fought about it, until I forced him to look up the answers in the back of the magazine. We sat there quiet for a few moments, a silence filled with his embarrassment, and then a whole group of stewardesses passed by us, pulling their compact luggage on squeaking wheels past a giant rubber tree, their tight, luridly colored pants matching the carpet they walked on, decorated with the airline's infantile logo. My friend's eyes watched their back ends as they walked away from us. I watched him watch them, and then he looked back at me and somehow now, inexplicably and perhaps unjustly, the embarrassment was mine.

Months later, after too many drinks, we ended up in bed, and we both remembered. He dared me. I lay back while he watched and I set to work, just to prove something. After more than he was untroubled by, he started accusing me of faking it, so we quit. Something uncomfortable had happened between us, but why didn't we know how to say it, how to stop it, or, for that matter, how to keep it going? It had stopped being pleasurable early on, but I kept thinking I had to prove it, prove it, prove it. Prove what?

At the end of what was to be our final lesson together, Ivan broke all my illusions. He took me into his office and sat me down.

"Do you want some coffee, some tea?" he asked.

It was the first time he'd ever not rushed off to his next student at the end of a lesson, leaving me feeling slightly awkward and abandoned there in the school's hallway. A wind of hope breezed through me as he leaned intimately forward to tell me something.

"This, as you may remember, is the end of your first six-week lesson cycle." His accent tangled the consonants. "You would like to buy the next cycle, yes?"

I looked at him, half amused, half tired of the whole thing. I felt vaguely guilty, vaguely ashamed. Around us poorly framed posters hung askew on the walls: exotic, passionate poses of men bending dramatically and sexually over limber, provocative women, the costumes all seventies-style sequins and the makeup and hair pushed to a Long Island mall extreme. I knew now that these poster poses came from competition tango, which is different from actual tango in that it is all choreographed; the dramatic poses all set up beforehand, all premeditated in their effect: They have little to do with the raw, unpredictable drama that surfaces unexpectedly when you dance tango freestyle, with sincerity.

"I'll take a check, if you want?" he asked, hopefully.

The truth is that I never did get Ivan to give me a glance even remotely colored by desire. The truth is that I never did become a particularly good tango dancer: I wanted the emotion, the passion, but I balked at the work.

P . S .

It had been a long time between drinks of water for Louise Brown. It was an early spring outside her office window, and if she craned her neck between the stacks of applications and the stacks of folders that hemmed her windowsill, she could see that beyond her little cubicle the world was full of boys.

Shaggy boys with bandannas leapt through the air like eager golden retrievers to catch a Frisbee with an open jaw of a palm. There were boys without their shirts on. Boys smoking pot and boys flirting and hundreds of boys, it seemed, leaning into hundreds of lank, skinny girls, with lank, skinny hair, in lank, skinny skirts; all these couples hanging out on the great, grand limestone steps of the central library of the university. They were half Louise's age, the boys were, and they all looked like they were getting plenty. What had happened to her life?

She turned to the application in her lap. This particular young man wanted to be a sculptor, he wanted to be a Master of Fine Arts, and he wanted this divine transformation to occur at the very fine institution where she was now acting admissions coordinator. Louise sighed heavily and reached for a cigarette, knocking over another pile of folders with a roughened elbow, an elbow that years ago her ex-husband, Alan, used to massage after her bath with cream. The folders slid to the floor, spilling all those forms covered with sloppy pen and ink that had explicitly stated in bold print: TO BE TYPED ONLY. The floor was a mess. Fighting back the urge to weep, she leaned over, started straightening up. Warshofsky, Evans, Aguado—she'd re-alphabetize all of them in record time. Louise picked up another folder. Turetsky, Scott.

Scott fucking Turetsky.

And for a moment, her heart stopped. It did that now and again, a little mitral-valve-prolapse action, a familiar suspension of her most vital organ, like a dancer's leap, she and her life supports hanging in the air, bridging two moments in time. Then came the crash in her chest, the heavy beating of a desperate bird's wings, the poor thing (her heart) banging up against the sliding glass doors of a patio.

Louise caught her breath. Scott Turetsky. She petted the outside of his folder.

There had been a Scott Turetsky when she was a girl growing up in Larchmont. Her Scott Turetsky had been a painter and a printmaker (a printmaker!), and she'd loved him from afar from the moment she first saw him, which was registration day freshman year of high school. He had a girlfriend then—Scott Turetsky always had a girlfriend—a beautiful hippie chick, Roberta Goldman, with long, flowing red gold hair and long, flowing Indian skirts and toe rings and earrings and bracelets around her upper arms, one bejeweled job gracing her left ankle. When the two of them, Scott and Berta, as he called her, walked into the school gym arm in arm that morning, the seas parted, and they skipped to the head of the line, directly in front of Louise. Scott's hair was long then, too. It was thick and black with silver gray streaks, like a smattering of frost had wafted down and graced it; and it was unbrushed and matted in a long, loose ponytail that was tied with a rubber band.

Three years later, after Berta had been replaced by Trisha the dancer, and Trisha had been replaced by Theresea Longo, the dark-eyed daughter of the proprietor of the lone Italian restaurant in Larchmont, and after Theresea had been dallied with and sent back to the kitchen, he was hers. Scott Turetsky was hers. They dated hot and heavy the summer before her senior year. Scott had just returned home from several months in Italy; his parents and his grandmother had refused to continue wiring him advances on his inheritance, so he had come back from Europe to work off his coming art-school expenses in a local food emporium called Cheeze Bazaar. Louise would wait for him to sweep and close up shop, and then they'd ride around for hours in his beat-up old red truck. He was full of Italian phrases and romantc stories, and she spent hours listening to him while brushing out his long salt-and-pepper locks. They broke up just weeks before he was to drive up to Rhode Island to go to art school. "It's only fair to you," Scott said, one afternoon in the truck, *after* she had given him a blow job. "I don't want to hold you back; I want you to have a wild and adventurous life." Louise. Wild and adventurous.

It was the drive to Rhode Island that killed him.

He'd never even gotten to school, never got to test his mettle as an artist, never had time to regret his decision, to come to his senses, go crawling back to Louise, to grovel in the dirt. He'd never even had a chance to miss her.

Nor was she granted the booby prize, the status of being his girl-friend at the time of his death. In fact, Scott Turetsky had just started up a little end-of-summer thing with her best friend, Missy, so Louise had none of the dignity of widowhood, which Missy dined out on for years.

Now she looked down at the folder. Dare she peek inside?

Turetsky, F. Scott.

F. Scott? The name was written in at the top of the application in a tight and even hand. Not typed, of course, but in a rich black ink, perhaps a fountain pen—which her Scott Turetsky had favored, the wealth and elegance, the gravitas of oily ink. The letters had nice full curves to them before they feathered away into nothing. She glanced further down the paragraph. His address was left blank. A post-office box. A post-office box in Mamaroneck. Mamaroneck, the sister city to her native Larchmont.

She read on. Date of birth: August 28, 1973.

Her Scott Turetsky (not an F. Scott Turetsky) had been born August 28, 1961. She knew this because he also had died on August 28— August 28, 1981—a fact that a lot of people in her town had valued as having some mystical if useless significance but that she had only found creepy and fitting and somehow round: a kid dying the moment he turned twenty, just as he became a man.

More, there was more. This Scott Turetsky, F. Scott Turetsky,was about to graduate from the Rhode Island School of Design. He was a painter and a printmaker. He favored large, oblong canvases, like her Scott Turetsky had, and he painted only in oils, too, although unlike her guy, he liked to layer the paint with linseed oil until the colors melted slightly under its weight, "like brown sugar burning," said his essay. He liked to "caramelize" the "hues." F. Scott Turetsky had also spent a year in Italy, where he spent most of his time "eating gelati, drinking wine and looking at art, sitting in churches, spending my Bar Mitzvah money." There was an ironic edge to his essay; it was gently self-mocking but full of self-love as well. "I believe in myself. I guess you could say I believe in myself totally. I want to live wildly and adventurously, which might be interpreted as hubris but is honestly the way I feel about myself."

F. Scott Turetsky had three recommendation letters, two from the high priest and priestess of RISD and one from Louise's very own high school art teacher, Ms. Cipriani. "While I don't normally approve of high school students painting nudes from living models, Scott's portrait of his girlfriend is reminiscent of one of Matisse's cruder odalisques."

Louise was reeling. Berta, Trisha, Theresea Longo, all of his exes, captured in full flower, their finest hour, at the art show of the senior class. It was a town scandal, Rabbi and Mrs. Turetsky loyally at their son's side, holding their heads high; the girls aflutter, instant celebrities. Her Scott Turetsky had never immortalized her own naked, nubile image—he'd promised but had never gotten around to it. He'd rather (his words) make love to her than reduce her to a work of art.

She looked down at F. Scott Turetsky's application. A phone number: (401). Without hesitating, she picked up the phone and dialed. The phone rang one time, two times, three; exhausted, she almost rested the receiver in its cradle. But she hung in there. Four rings, five rings, six rings. On the seventh, someone picked up.

"Hey," said a mysterious young man.

"Hey yourself," said Louise.

Why on earth did she say that?

"Baby," he said.

"This is Louise Brown," Louise said. "From Columbia, School of the Arts, admissions."

"So you're not my baby," the young man laughed.

No. Apparently not.

"Is this F. Scott Turetsky?" she asked, all business.

"Yeah," he said. "Sure." And then, "Louise Brown from the Admissions Department, you're not going to believe me, but I was just about to pick up the phone. I forgot to send in my slides. This must be some weird psychic phenomenon, you know?"

"You're telling me," Louise said.

It was a Wednesday, the day of F. Scott Turetsky's trumped-up interview. Louise had scheduled him at the end of the day. This way she could spend the better part of the morning in Emporio Armani trying to find a skirt that looked like one she had bought in the House of Shalimar in 1979. Nineteen seventy-nine. Six years after F. Scott Turetsky was born. She finally settled on a gauzy eight-tiered swirl that flirted about her ankles. After she paid up—a small down payment on an apartment—Louise slipped into a local coffee shop, made her way into the bathroom and changed, shoving her jeans into the wastebasket in the corner. She looked at herself hard in the mirror—how rough her skin seemed, how large her pores were—and then took her long brown hair (hair she had blown dry straight for the first time in seventeen years that morning) out of its clip and fastened it in a silky loose braid. Another look he'd liked.

Back at the office, F. Scott Turetsky was late by three-quarters of an hour. Louise was prepared for this. He'd always been late before. She'd taken to telling him that the movies started half an hour earlier than they actually began. *Midnight Express.* How hard she'd grabbed his right hand when the hero bit out his fellow prisoner's tongue. So hard, Scott Turetsky's left hand fell from its working position on her breast.

It was 5:48 exactly. Louise, practcally apoplectic, knew this, for she was staring at the clock when F. Scott Turetsky knocked on her office door, which she'd left an inviting halfway open.

"Hey," he said.

"Hey yourself," said Louise, a little too jovially, before turning around. "Come on in."

She sounded like an admissions officer.

F. Scott Turetsky came in. Louise swiveled in her chair and sized him up. He was the right height (five feet ten inches), the right weight (155). Actually, he looked a little thicker, but he was four years older, four years older than when she'd last laid eyes upon him. His eyes were the same flawed cobalt blue (brown specks). F. Scott Turetsky wore baggy jeans and a big, striped baggy polo shirt; his dark hair was shaved close to his pretty head. It was shaved in patterns in the back, the New York skyline, but among the darker patches of his stubble, Louise thought she could see a smattering of silver frost.

So it was him. A little older, perhaps, a little more handily equipped with a set of laugh lines. But it was him. Or some facsimile—a clone perhaps, a ghost. It was him.

That or his identical nephew.

It was him, now with a tattoo braceleting his wrist, crawling up his arm. When he turned to close the door, she could see a blue-and-green serpent inked across his neck.

It was him, but a variation.

F. Scott Turetsky was sitting in her office.

God.

Louise began to talk. She appeared to herself to be reciting the entire course catalog in a bureaucratic drone. But inside, inside! "Hey," she wanted to call out, "it's me, it's me—it's me inside this grown-up body. Under the aerobicized muscles, the thickening skin, under the permanent tan line on my left ring finger, under the scars—inflicted by life, by disappointment, by my weaknesses and jealousies and flaws, inflicted by you!—it's me, it's me, your Sugar Magnolia, your Cinnamon Girl!"

She wanted to crawl across the floor, unzip his pants and suck on his cock.

Instead she went on and on about School of the Arts course offerings while she drank him in.

He was slow, flirty, a little shy, asking questions and then answering them himself, as had always been his way.

"I mean, hey, you know, I'm like a rube, raised in the burbs. Providence ain't much of a city. . . . Will I get eaten alive here? I mean, hey, Ms. Louise Brown, is there any hope in the Big Apple for a small-town loser like me?" He flashed her a killer smile.

"Sure, there's hope," he said, answering himself. He was really smiling now. "There's always hope—right, Louise, you're thinking that there's hope for me. I can tell. I can tell what you're thinking, and it's hopeful. I can read your mind."

At an outdoor café on Upper Broadway, they ate burritos and drank margaritas, letting the sheer force and volume of the begging, amputated homeless drive them inside. And so it was a piece of cake getting him back up to her apartment, with both of them already three sheets to the wind.

Ha. She'd wrangled a beautiful young boy into her home, one she prayed was still in possession of a pair of muscular ridges that rode the knobby track of his spine, of a hairless back, of an abdomen that she remembered came in sections. How long had it been since she'd slept with a body that didn't slide?

How long had it been, honestly, since she'd slept with anyone?

Louise needed this night! So she finagled F. Scott Turetsky upstairs, pushing away the fear that her own age might prove a deterrent. Somewhere deep in his abnormally young psyche, F. Scott Turetsky might also remember their other life and miss her nubile image, but then again the Scott Turetsky that she knew had been less than appreciative of her corporeal gifts. She had been so waiflike and slight back then. It had been hard, when she was dressed, to distinguish her breasts from her ribs. Once, after sex, Scott Turetsky had insisted on lying on his side on his bed—his penis now a little kickstand—and examining her naked. He had Louise parade back and forth like a model—an embarrassed, awkward and shy model, with hunched-over shoulders and hands that fluttered about in a weak little fan dance to hide herself. After ten agonizing minutes, Scott declared her pretty OK—which made Louise's head feel light and her cheeks flush hot—if only her butt were a little higher. Then he jumped up from the bed, cupped it in his hands and lifted to prove his point.

Too bad Scott Turetsky didn't live long enough to fall victim to a slow metabolism, a balding head and a thickening gut like the rest of the male members of their high school class. Too bad some heartless woman somewhere didn't get to pinch his love handles and giggle when he was striking out as an artist in New York and most needed her support. Too bad someone in as good shape as Louise was right then didn't suggest he take up jogging while, dressed only in socks and a blue striped buttondown and totally vulnerable, he was getting ready to go to work at his uncle's car dealership in New Jersey.

Too bad that, unlike the rest of them, Scott Turetsky got to die when he was perfect.

But with F. Scott Turetsky, Louise had the hometown advantage. She knew F. Scott Turetsky would have a penchant for older women.

She remembered Scott Turetsky telling her this himself when they were lying naked in Manor Park one night seventeen years before on a blanket made up of their cutoff shorts and black concert T-shirts, her lacy white bra curled like a kitten at his ankles.

It was ex post facto, and over before she knew it, and she was antsy and he was spent, and they were lying a foot apart and not touching on the hot, moist lawn that led up to the little local beach, a tiny pathetic spit of sand—his words punctuated by the obscene wet slap of the sound.

In order to get a conversation going—it was embarrassing, lying apart and naked like that, her thighs squid white in the moonlight; it was embarrassing, to have been as dry as a desert and not to have come and not to have had the time to properly fake it—Louise was bemoaning the fact that she was getting older. A senior. Used goods. When so many pretty skinny little freshman girls were dying to take her place.

She reached out her hand to his.

She didn't want to lose him. No matter how self-centered he was, no matter that he was a lousy lover. She was seventeen. What did she know but lousy lovers? None of that mattered, not the strange pungent mix of his "natural" deodorant and his body odor, his silly affectations, his incredible self-love.

"Not to worry," said Scott Turetsky. "I really dig older women. I mean really old, like thirty-four or thirty-five. As long as they're still in shape. Strong girls. That's when they're at their sexual height. For a guy, it's nineteen. So you're lucky. You're catching me at my peak."

Then he rolled over and mounted her again.

But in her apartment, as an adult, making out on her couch with an older but still young F. Scott Turetsky, Louise changed her tune. I'm lucky, she thought, I'm so very lucky to be here now with him. And it seemed like in the four intervening years—four years F. Scott Turetsky time—he had picked up some pointers. He was passionate, kissing up and down her neck. He was passionate, worrying at her earlobe. His body was familiar. So boyish and so beautiful. When he pulled his shirt off over the back of his head, his once hairless chest now sported curly black spirals around the nipples, and farther down, in the bottom quadrants of his stomach, it got curlier and thicker still, leading a woolly path to his groin.

Louise thought, I can't believe how lucky I am. To have a second chance.

"Wait a minute," said F. Scott Turetsky. "Don't you want to talk?"

Talk?

"You know, get to know each other a little, before, before you and I make love." Here he reached out his hand, took hers in his dry palm.

Make love?

When was the last time anyone had seduced her just by putting her off?

Scott Turetsky. He'd done the same thing their first time in the back of his truck. He'd gotten her going until she was crazy, and then he'd stopped short, so that Louise was so loose and trembly she felt that if someone were to pull a secret thread she would unravel and fall apart. He'd stopped her, because he was the sensitive one and she the over-eager, anxious slut. He'd stopped her, even though he'd done it with Berta and Trisha and Theresea Longo and probably half of Rome, while this was Louise's first anything. The experienced Scott Turetsky had Louise Brown the virgin begging for it.

Now she was older, wiser.

"OK, F. Scott," she said. "Let's talk."

F. Scott combed his fingers through her fingers. "You're hands are so beautiful—they look like Georgia O'Keeffe's. Are you an artist?"

"No," said Louise. "I'm the School of the Arts acting admissions coordinator."

"I know that, Louise Brown." He smiled at her shyly. "But what are you in your heart?"

In her heart, that wobbly, faltering muscle, that generator of panic and fear? What was she in her heart but lonely?

"I don't know," said Louise softly. She hated him.

F. Scott Turetsky's right index finger grazed her collarbone.

"Everyone's an artist in their heart."

She didn't have time for this. But F. Scott Turetsky was going on. See, his parents were willing to spring for his tuition. He knew he should probably just move out to Williamsburg, get a day job and paint his ass off, but he'd never really been out of school before, and he guessed—his finger exploring the hollows above her breasts—he was a little scared. Of the real world.

Oh God, thought Louise. I'm not seventeen anymore—I don't have to listen to this.

She decided to take matters into her own hands. Literally.

"Hey, this is all right," F. Scott Turetsky said.

In a minute, they were both naked and on the floor, existential crises now mercifully forgotten.

He stopped for just a moment to pull his wallet out of his jeans. He plucked out a condom, a fluorescent yellow lubricated Sheik, and said, "Is this all right? I mean, I wouldn't want you to do anything you didn't want to."

That same old Scott Turetsky line.

"It's fine," said Louise, "it's good." And when he fumbled a little with the rubber, she said under her breath, "Come on."

Once cloaked, F. Scott Turetsky stuck out in front of himself like a luminous yellow wand.

He rolled on top of her, so Louise turned the tables this time, and she rolled on top of him. "Mmmm," said F. Scott Turetsky, "whatever the hell you want."

Who was this guy, this cute young guy, this M.F.A. applicant that Louise was now fucking? Was he really her beloved Scott Turetsky, her old lost love reincarnate? Or was he just some kid whom she'd practically picked up from the street?

What did it matter, now that she was finally getting a piece of what she wanted? Weren't there always going to be Scott Turetskys and F. Scott Turetskys, a new crop every generation, coming off the sexy-bad-boyfriend assembly line?

She'd met more than a few of them since her divorce. Producers, war correspondents, videographers. After thirty they grew their hair long again; they wore it in ponytails. And these guys were always off somewhere, Bali or Morocco or Bhutan, and they were always hopelessly in love with some Peace Corps gal or an Iranian photographer or a gorgeous mixed-race actress who just got cast in an upscale miniseries; some woman who jerked and jerked and jerked them around, who jerked them around so much they couldn't help jerking you around, too, these Scott and F. Scott Turetskys. It was the trickle-down theory of romance.

But now Louise was on top. She was on top and liking it. This F.

Scott Turetsky had melted into a blissful and helpless puddle between her hips. Every few seconds, he would arch up or thrust or twitch or something, a little weak smile teasing at his lips, but at best his rhythm was syncopated and close to annoying; so, soon, through caresses and a careful squeezing of her inner organs, Louise seized control of the situation, F. Scott Turetsky giving up.

When they were young, Louise and Scott Turetsky, the summer nights in Larchmont were thick with the scent of pollen and perfume, the smell of gasoline, of pot, of cigarettes, of bug spray and his deodorant. Their young naked bodies were softened by the filmy haze of suburban starlight; they were as blurry and unreal as if a cinematographer were viewing them through a layer of shimmery gauze. When they were young, Louise would spread her legs and let Scott Turetsky enter her, whether she was ready or not, whether it hurt her or not, and she'd say, "I love you, Scott; I love you, honey," in intervals of about seventy-five seconds. She counted. She counted the intervals between her words of encouragement and the moments until it was over. Sometimes, sometimes it felt like his fucking her went on forever; then other times it was over before she knew it.

But when it was over, when he had come, when he had finished, he would completely collapse, sinking down on Louise, his hipbone grinding into her pelvis; the weight of his body flattening out her lungs, making it hard to breathe; the soft, tender tissue of her vagina aflame and burning—so much so that after a couple of rounds of this, when she peed later, even in the shower, it would sting. And she'd think, Someday I will find someone who loves me; someday I'll get married and have a husband; someday sex will be something I like, I love—it will be something good.

Now, in her apartment with F. Scott Turetsky, it was Louise who was keeping it going, getting him to the brink, then pulling back, then getting him to the brink again. The poor kid was all shiver and moan.

"Oh God," he said, "thank you. Thank you, God, a lot."

With a slow in and out she pleased him.

Only when he gave up the ghost did she finally allow herself to come. And then they slid away from each other in a loose knot, on her living-room floor, F. Scott Turetsky's right arm slung haphazardly across her waist as he lightly, lightly began to snore, while Louise tried to even out her own breathing, to calm her racing heart.

Now she was lying half-clothed—for she still had her T-shirt on—on her floor with a boy half her age, dead asleep, in her arms, with a boy she didn't know. His mouth was open, and a little spit bubble breathed in and out of the corner. She smelled his buzzed head; it was as sweaty and sweet as a baby's. What had she done? She could lose her job for this. Now that he'd slept with her, maybe this strange kid thought he could gain admission to the graduate program of his choice. Or worse yet, he just might fall in love.

She wriggled out from under his arm. She covered him with one of her sofa throws. Then she got up and went into the kitchen, looking for a cigarette. In the cookie jar was her emergency pack. She tapped one out and lit up. Smoking, she went back into the living room. A beautiful naked boy was sleeping on her rug.

She'd fucked him.

When they were young, when they were done, Louise would trace the words "I love you" across Scott Turetsky's still-panting moist back with the tip of her right forefinger—employing the same hope and delicacy with which she might have traced those heartfelt words on a steamed-up backseat window. And she'd say, "That was great, Scott—I really love you," which was true. The second part was true: She really did; she really did love him. She loved him and she loved him and she loved him, and she was never going to get over him, no matter what anybody had to say about puppy love and life experience. No, Louise never was going to get over the stupid dead boy she loved with all her heart when she was so ridiculously, improbably young that it should have been against the law.

It should have been against the law back then to have been as young as Louise Brown once was.

And now, at last, she's old.

INDELIBLE

The only other person in the Laundromat, a blond woman in her twenties, stood at the folding table across from John. He tried not to notice her. He sat resting his right foot on his left knee, his chin propped up by both hands. The buckles of his black leather jacket dangled over the edge of the bench, the lace of one Doc Marten untied. He was clearly succeeding in his attempt to look forlorn, but the woman didn't seem to care.

John noticed that the woman's underwear alternated in colors as she folded it and popped it into her black gym bag. Pink, light blue, yellow, light green. Easter colors, he thought. He considered telling her, but lately, whenever he met a woman he wanted to talk to, his mind flashed forward to the inevitable moment when they would no longer be speaking to each other. So instead of speaking to her, he stared into the washing machine in front of him and watched as the suds turned from white to gray to charcoal black. He thought he might begin to cry.

He'd been testing the colorfastness of a new design he'd silk-screened onto a T-shirt. The ink he'd used had been labeled indelible on the front of the tube, but—he discovered later—water soluble in smaller letters on the back. He wondered how anything could be both simultaneously. But first he wanted to perfect his original, most personal design: a simple doodle of a locomotive with cockroach legs. He had been leaving it as a tag since college. He tagged everything with it: buildings, street signs, bathroom walls, cocktail napkins, the ankles of women while they slept.

John thought maybe he could make some money with it because people were always asking him what it meant. On good days it was a cockroach turning into a locomotive, on bad days it was a locomotive turning into a cockroach, but most days it was just a locomotive with cockroach legs and when people asked what it meant John just rolled his eyes in a way that made them feel stupid for asking.

As he watched his latest failure pass into the final wash and rinse, he considered his options. It was nearly summer and outside the open door of the Laundromat people were walking by in shorts and T-shirts and less. It seemed the entire neighborhood was becoming a clothing-optional society. The Laundromat was set down from the sidewalk by a short flight of stairs and lit by only a few bare bulbs, so the outside world seemed unnaturally bright. He watched the disembodied legs as they marched by the window—women in shorts, miniskirts, some in thigh-high boots. Perhaps it was time for a change. Perhaps he should retire the black leather jacket or at least stop wearing it to the beach. Maybe it was time to stop dying his hair. It was possible he'd feel better if he went home and shaved his head. But what he really wanted to do was talk to Mary.

John glanced back at the woman with the Easter-colored underwear.

Mary had left behind a small drawer full of black underwear when she packed up her car, and took off across the country promising to send postcards from the road. She and John had been friends for a long time, meaning that they hung out in the same crowd, but rarely spoke to one another. They ended up getting together unexpectedly at a New Year's party a year and half ago. It was a small party and at one point everyone was gathered around exchanging stories about the fucked-up couples they knew. Mary said, "What I don't understand is why any of you are surprised. I mean, how many couples do you know who aren't fucked up in some way?" John turned to her and said, "We're not fucked up." He meant it as a joke, but when he said it he saw something soften behind her eyes and he thought it was possible he really did like her.

After the party, he walked her back to her apartment, and she invited him in to hear stories about the strange people she met while temping. He ended up staying the night.

Later, when Mary packed her car and left town, John realized that he was the kind of man who could sit up all night if there wasn't someone there to turn out the light and tell him it was time to sleep.

Now, when he sees people that they both knew—people who were probably there at that New Year's party—he tells them, "Mary's doing really well," even though he hasn't heard a word from her since she left. He imagines her living in New Mexico, in a little mud house she'd built with her own hands. He sees her melting snow for water, living off sprouts and doing laundry by hand. Never mind the fact that when she lived in the city she filtered the water twice, sent out for pizza, and sent everything to the cleaner's, including her underwear. He always thought Mary had the capacity for unrecognizable change, and he was sure she was happy now. If she ever decided it was time to move on, she could just hose down her little mud house till there was nothing left and no one would ever know she had been there.

He remembered sitting in a café with Mary and speculating on the status of the other couples sitting in the room. At the next table, a boy and girl held hands across the table and exchanged information on their ethnicities. "Does your mother speak *any* English?" the boy asked. Across the room, a woman in an Anne Klein suit approached an apparently estranged friend who had been trying to ignore her. John and Mary watched as the women squealed and embraced. A few tables away, another couple sat in silence, the woman staring away from the man's gaze; he reached across the table and grabbed her jaw to pull her attention to him.

"I'm a cynic," Mary said. "Lately I look back on all my relationships and it seems that they were all either extremely temporary or inextricably permanent."

John asked, "Which one am I?"

Mary thought for just a moment. "You," she said, "seem to fall somewhere in between."

It was on this very same date—an early one—that John told Mary the story of "Monkeys! Clowns! Circus!" He'd been trying to impress her by saying something clever and ironic, but nothing he came up with seemed to do the trick.

"You're not the first man to tell me that," Mary said to his final attempt.

"No," John said. "But I am the first man to ever say, 'Monkeys!

Clowns! Circus!' " His eyes widened with each word, as if he was casting a maniacal spell.

"What?!"

"Monkeys! Clowns! Circus!"

Mary shook her head. "I don't understand."

"Only my sister and I know what it really means," he said.

Mary looked down at her menu. "So what does it mean?"

John told her the story of how—maybe twenty years earlier—he and his older sister, Ginger, were playing one afternoon at the foot of her closet. While John pulled toys arbitrarily from the shelves, Ginger grabbed his hand and said, "Listen to me. I'm about to tell you something very important . . . because what I'm about to say is something we will remember for the rest of our lives."

John dropped Barbie and G.I. Joe to the floor, he was so struck by Ginger's serious tone. It seemed she was about to say something she'd been thinking over for a very long time.

"Monkeys! Clowns! Circus!" she said. "Only you and I will know what it means."

John nodded, pretending, as usual, that he understood.

They kept the words to themselves, using them only on special occasions when nothing else would make sense. They would whisper it in each other's ears during their parents' arguments or, when they were older, write the words on the bottom of a particularly melancholy letter. "It's over between me and Lynn," his sister once wrote. "Maybe I'm not a lesbian after all. Love, Ginger. Monkeys. Clowns. Circus."

John told Mary, "We should have something like that. Our own special code."

"Well," Mary said. "Okay . . ." She looked over the menu for inspiration. "How about . . . White Cheddar Cheese Burger Pizza."

"Great," John said, but he was disappointed. He'd been hoping for something a little more personal.

A few nights later, after dinner and a movie and some drinks downtown, John said to her, "You know what I'm in the mood for?"

"What?" Mary said, keeping her eyes on the "Don't Walk" light blinking across the street. She was holding her latex jacket with one hand and smoking with the other. John loved watching her.

"I'm in the mood for some White Cheddar Cheese Burger Pizza," he said.

"Really?" Mary said. "This late? Aren't you still full from dinner?" She hadn't even remembered.

John watched the girl in the Laundromat fold her shirts and place them carefully in the black bag. She ran her hands over her jeans and tossed them back in the dryer for another quarter's worth of heat. He turned back to his washer and his newest mistake entering the spin. He remembered the first time he introduced Mary to his sister Ginger. They met for drinks, and after two rounds Mary decided to go home early. "You guys can stay and do your brother-sister thing," she said. He worried that he hadn't paid enough attention to her.

Ginger said, "I just don't think she's a very nice person."

There was a small black bag left beneath Mary's chair—one of those nylon, all-terrain, floppy briefcases. "Are you sure it's hers?" Ginger asked when John grabbed it. "I mean it looks like something a businessman would take with him into the jungle."

"No," John said. "It's hers. I'll give it to her when I meet her for breakfast in the morning."

As he carried the bag home, he grew curious about what might be inside. It seemed both heavy and empty, like there was a small weight hidden somewhere inside. When he got back to his studio apartment, he carried the bag straight to the bathroom. He closed the bathroom door as if for privacy, sat on the toilet and carefully undid the zipper to the bag. He looked inside. There was a gun resting in its holster. A .357 Magnum. He lifted the gun to see if it was loaded, but got nervous and put it back in the bag, left the bathroom, and shut the door. He called Ginger to ask what he should do.

Ginger said, "I don't like that woman."

"But what if she was planning to kill herself? What if I give it back to her and she shoots herself? But if I tell her I'm not giving it back, she'll know I looked inside."

"Maybe she's shooting heroin," Ginger said cheerfully. "Maybe she just carries it for protection when she goes to score her supply."

"No," John said. "If she was carrying it for protection, she'd keep it more available. She was planning on doing something with it. She had some kind of plan." He was always certain that Mary, unlike him, had some kind of plan.

When he met Mary in the morning, he held the bag up cheerfully and oversmiled. "I have your bag," he said.

"What are you talking about?" Mary said. "That's not my bag."

Sitting in the Laundromat, watching the washing machine go into its final spin, John wondered if maybe that had been the attraction to Mary. That he thought she could carry a gun. That with her anything seemed possible, even if it wasn't.

The woman in the Laundromat was folding the last of her laundry and putting it away. John was sure he had never seen her before, and wondered if their meeting might, therefore, be fate. Then he thought perhaps he *had* seen her before, in some type of commercial, but he couldn't remember which one. She looked up and caught John looking at her. He allowed himself the fantasy of her spread out across the folding table, modeling underwear for him. But in his fantasy, he imagined the underwear was black, and the bra, like Mary's, unsnapped in the front. He looked back at his reflection in the glass window of the washing machine.

He thought back on his and Mary's decision to move in together, and how they had probably arrived at it more out of boredom than out of any sincere desire. In fact, he was certain now that it was out of desperation that Mary had moved in. She had been arguing with her roommates, he remembered, and had been spending more and more time at his place until finally it seemed to make more sense for her to bring all of her things over. Mary moved in on a Saturday in October, the first cold snap of the season. She emerged from a taxi wearing a strange oversized pea coat, and carrying a suitcase in each hand. John grabbed the few boxes out of the trunk and Mary pulled out three odd black tubes and carried them under her arms. He felt let down; he'd been expecting a truckload of curious objects, each with a mysterious history she might share. Instead, all she seemed to have were a few boxes of used books.

Later, she showed him how the black tubes, when placed properly together, formed the frame for a small dining room table.

"It's held together by tension," she said. "Like everything else."

John was alarmed by how much time Mary spent at home. She stopped taking temp assignments, saying she was looking for something more permanent, but the Sunday *Times* was stacked unopened in the recyclables each week. Meanwhile, John found himself getting less of his own work done. Every time he started drawing anything—a doodle of the locomotive with cockroach legs, a preliminary sketch for a mural with a circus theme—he found Mary looking over his shoulder asking, "But what does it mean?"

Meanwhile, his sister Ginger seemed to be enjoying her single life, telling him at every opportunity, "I don't know why that woman is still in your apartment." To which John replied with a shrug, "Monkeys. Clowns. Circus."

In the end, they were staying together because they thought briefly that she might be pregnant, and neither of them wanted to suggest what the other was already thinking. When she told him it wasn't true—that it had been a mistake, everything was fine—the first thing he said, without thinking, was "I guess we don't have to stay together anymore." He thought it was probably what she was thinking too.

For several days they didn't speak to each other at all. He sat alone wondering how anything so permanent could have been so temporary, but still he felt it was something they would work out together. When he came home and found Mary packing, he almost said, "I'll go with you," before he realized that she was leaving to get away from him.

If he knew where she was now, he might call information to get her number. He wouldn't talk to her, though. He just wanted to see if she would pick up, to know that she was there.

John opened the washing machine and pulled out the wrinkled shirt. He stretched it in his lap. The locomotive with cockroach legs had turned into a gray cloud in the middle of the shirt. A man with homemade tattoos on his arms mopped up and down the aisles, pausing to remove sheets of lint from the dryers. John remembered someone—was it Mary or Ginger?—telling him that dust and lint are made mostly of human skin. He watched the man's tattooed arms—the ink blurred into his flesh—as he gathered the sheets of lint into a large ball and tossed it away.

The woman brushed by John with her small black laundry bag. She paused for a moment and looked down at his lap.

She said, "You need to let it set first, before you can wash it."

John watched as she walked out into the street. His eyes followed her legs as they passed the window and disappeared. He looked back at the gray cloud resting in his lap and thought of a new design: a shirt that read WATER SOLUBLE in large letters on the front and INDELIBLE in smaller letters from behind.

X O

It started like this: I was sitting on a bench in Tompkins Square Park reading a copy of *Spin* I'd swiped from Hudson News, observing East Village females crossing the park on their way home from work and wondering (as I often did) how my ex-wife had managed to populate New York with thousands of women who looked nothing like her but still brought her to mind, when I made this discovery: My old friend Jonah Kaplan was a record producer! It was right in *Spin* magazine, a whole article about Jonah and how he'd first made his name on a group called the Tiny Ants that went platinum six or seven years ago. There was a picture of Jonah receiving some kind of prize, looking out of breath and a little cross-eyed—one of those frozen, hectic instants you just know has a whole happy life attached to it. I looked at the picture for less than a second; then I closed the magazine. I decided not to think about Jonah. There's a fine line between thinking about someone and thinking about not thinking about someone, but I have the practice and the self-control to walk that line for hours—days, if I have to.

After one week of not thinking about Jonah—thinking so much about not thinking of Jonah that there was barely room in my head for thoughts of any other kind—I decided to write him a letter. I addressed it to the company he worked for, which turned out to be inside a green glass building on Park Avenue and 52nd Street. I took the subway up there and stood outside the building with my head back, looking up, up, wondering how high Jonah's office was. I kept my eyes on the building as I dropped the letter into the mailbox directly in front of it. "Hey, Finko," I'd written (that was Jonah's nickname). "Long time no see. I hear you're the man, now. Congrats. Couldn't have happened to a luckier guy. Best wishes, Scotty 'Darts' Haussmann."

He wrote back! His letter arrived in my dented East Village mailbox about five days later, typed, which I guess meant a secretary had done it, but it was Jonah all right.

"Scotty, baby—Hey, thanks for the note. Where have you been hiding yourself? I still think of the Dildo days sometimes. Hope you're playing that slide guitar. Yours, Jonah," with his little wiggly signature above the typed name.

Jonah's letter had quite an effect on me. Things had gotten—what's the word? Dry. Things had gotten sort of dry for me. I was working for the city as a janitor in a neighborhood elementary school and, in summers, collecting litter in the park alongside the East River near the Williamsburg Bridge. I felt no shame whatsoever in either of these activities, because I understood what almost no one else seemed to grasp: that there was only an infinitesimal difference, a difference so small that it barely existed except as a figment of the human imagination, between working in a tall, green glass building on Park Avenue and collecting litter in a park. In fact, there may have been no difference at all.

I happened to have the next day off—the day after Jonah's letter came—so I went to the East River early that morning and fished. I did this all the time, and I ate the fish, too. There was pollution, yes, but the beauty of it was that you knew about this pollution, unlike the many poisons you consumed each day in ignorance. I fished, and God must've been on my side, or maybe it was Jonah's good luck rubbing off on me, because I pulled from the river my best catch of all time: an enormous striped bass! My fishing pals, Sammy and Rob, were shocked to see me catch this superb fish. I stunned it, wrapped it in newspaper, bagged it and carried it home under my arm. I put on the closest thing I had to a suit: khaki pants and a jacket that I dry-cleaned *a lot*. The week before, I'd taken it to the cleaners still in its dry-cleaning bag, which caused a breakdown of some kind in the gal behind the counter—"Why you clean? You already clean; bag not open; you waste your money." I know I'm getting off the subject here, but let me just say that I whipped my jacket out of its plastic bag with such force that she went instantly quiet and laid it carefully on the dry-cleaning counter. *"Merci pour votre considération, madame,"* I said, and she accepted the garment without another word. Suffice it to say that the jacket I put on that morning to visit Jonah Kaplan was one clean jacket.

Jonah's building looked like one where they could implement tough security checks if they needed to, but that day I guess they didn't need to. More of Jonah's good luck flowing down on me like honey. Not that my luck was generally so bad—I'd call it neutral, occasionally edging toward bad. For example, I caught fewer fish than Sammy, though I fished more often and had the better rod. But if this was Jonah's good luck I was getting today, did that mean that my good luck was also his good luck? That my visiting him unexpectedly was good luck for him? Or had I somehow managed to divert his luck and siphon it away for a time, leaving him without any luck today? And, if I *had* managed to do the latter, how had I done it, and (most important) how could I do it forever?

I checked the directory, saw he was on forty-five, took the elevator up there and breezed through a pair of beige glass doors into his office waiting room, which was very swank. The decor reminded me of a '70s bachelor pad: black leather couches, thick shag rug, heavy glass-and-chrome tables covered with *Vibe* and *Rolling Stone*. Carefully dim lighting. This last was a must, I knew, so musicians would wait there without putting their track marks and bloodshot eyes on display.

I slapped my fish on the black marble reception desk. It made a good hard wet *thwack*—I swear to God, it sounded like nothing so much as a fish. *She* (blonde highlighted hair, polar blue eyes, pink mouth, the sort of chick who makes you want to lean over and say to her, oh so sweetly, "You must be *really* intelligent; how else would have you have gotten this job?") looked up and said, "May I help you?"

"I'm here to see Jonah," I said. "Jonah Kaplan."

Her eyes on me felt like tweezers. "Is he expecting you?"

"Not at this moment."

"Your name?"

"Scotty."

She wore a headset that I realized, when she spoke into a tiny extension over her mouth, was actually a telephone. She said my name and waited with the tiniest curl to her lips, like she was hiding a smile. "He's in a meeting," she told me. "If you'd like to leave a message . . ."

"I'll wait."

I deposited my fish on the glass coffee table next to the magazines and settled into a black leather couch. Its cushions made little animal sounds, squeaks and murmurs and sighs, and filled the air with the most delicious smell of leather. A deep comfort seeped through me. I began to feel sleepy. I wanted to stay there forever, to leave my apartment on East 6th Street and live out the remainder of my life in Jonah's waiting room.

True, it had been a while since I'd spent much time in public. But was such a fact even relevant in our present "information age," when you could scour planet earth and the universe without ever leaving the green velvet couch you pulled from a garbage dump and had made the focal point of your East 6th Street apartment? I began each night by ordering Hunan string beans and washing them down with Jaegermeister. It was amazing how many string beans I could eat: four orders, five orders—more sometimes. I could tell by the number of plastic packets of soy sauce and chopsticks included with my delivery that Fong Yu believed I was serving string beans to a party of eight or nine vegetarians. Does the chemical composition of Jaegermeister cause a craving for string beans? Is there some property of string beans that becomes addictive on those rare occasions when they are consumed with Jaegermeister? I would ask myself these questions as I shoveled string beans into my mouth, huge, crunchy forkfuls, and watched TV—weird cable shows, most of which I couldn't identify and didn't watch much of. You might say I created my own show out of all those other shows. I did it with a certain artistry, I think, which is why it was a pity I didn't know how to record on my VCR, which I'd bought on the street and therefore lacked instructions for, because I think what I made of those shows—the combination—was better than the shows themselves. In fact, I'm sure of it.

Here was the bottom line: If we human beings are information-processing machines, reading X's and O's and translating that information into what people oh so breathlessly call "experience," and if I had access to all that same information via cable TV and any number of magazines that I browsed through at Hudson News for four- or five-hour stretches on my free days (my record was eight hours, including the half hour I spent manning the register during the lunch break of one of the younger employees, who thought I worked there), if I had access to all that same information (and if I won my prolonged dispute with the owners of 1001 East 6th Street, my present information-gathering techniques would be gloriously enhanced by a small rooftop satellite dish encased in an electrified cage—the source of our dispute—that would semipermanently disable anyone who touched it), then technically speaking, was I not having all the same experiences those other people were having?

I tested my theory by standing outside the public library during a gala benefit for heart disease. I made this choice randomly: I was reading magazines in the periodicals room, having been banned from Hudson News by the owner, a mentally unbalanced individual who refused to believe it would be in his best interest to allow me to spend long stretches of time reading in his store rather than stealing hundreds and hundreds of magazines from him, which I would otherwise be forced to do, or firebombing Hudson News, as I would most certainly do if he dared to call the police or throw me out (which he subsequently did, and I use the word "throw" in the quasiliteral sense).

At closing time, as I was leaving the periodicals room, I noticed well-dressed individuals tossing white cloths over tables and carrying large orchid bouquets into the library's grand entrance hall, and when I asked a blonde gal with a notepad what was going on, she told me about the benefit party for heart disease. I went home and ate my string beans, but instead of turning on the TV, I took the subway back to the library, where the gala was in full swing. I heard "Satin Doll" playing inside, I heard giggles and yelps and big swoops of laughter, I saw approximately one hundred long black limousines and shorter black town cars idling alongside the curb, and I considered the fact that nothing more than a series of atoms and molecules combined in a particular way to form something known as a "stone wall" stood between me and those people inside dancing to a horn section that was awfully weak in the tenor-sax department. But a strange thing happened as I listened: I felt pain. Not in my head, not in my arm, not in my leg; everywhere at once. I told myself that there was no difference between being "inside" and being "outside," that it all came down to X's and O's that could be acquired in any number of different ways, but the pain increased to the point where I thought I might collapse, and finally I limped away.

Like all failed experiments, that one taught me something I didn't expect. One key ingredient of so-called experience was the delusional faith that it was unique and special, that those included in it were privileged and those excluded from it were missing something. And I, like a bystander unwittingly inhaling toxic fumes from a hidden vent, had, through sheer physical proximity, been infected by that same delusion, and in my drugged state had become incapable of implementing my airtight logic. I was planning to repeat the experiment—to visit the site of a gala benefit shortly after its conclusion, when the toxic fumes had dispersed—I just hadn't done it yet.

I went to the blonde receptionist's desk, balancing my fish on two hands. Juice was starting to leak through the paper. "This is a fish," I told her.

"Oh, God," she said.

"Tell Jonah that pretty soon it's gonna stink."

I sat back down. I heard the receptionist whispering into her telephone headset. My "neighbors" in the waiting room were a male and a female, both of the corporate persuasion. I sensed them edging away from me. "I'm a musician," I said by way of introduction. "Slide guitar."

They did not reply.

Finally, Jonah came out. He looked trim. He looked fit. He wore black trousers and a white shirt buttoned at the neck but no tie. I understood something for the very first time when I looked at that shirt: I understood that expensive shirts look better than cheap shirts. The fabric wasn't shiny—no, shiny would be cheap. But it glowed like there was light coming through from the inside. It was a fucking beautiful shirt is what I'm saying.

"Scotty man, how you doing?" Jonah said, patting me warmly on the back as we shook hands. "Sorry to keep you waiting, buddy. Here, c'mon back to my office." He had his arm around my shoulders and was steering me toward a hallway.

"Hey wait—I forgot something!" I said and ran back to get the fish.

As I slung the bag from the coffee table into my hands, a little fish juice dripped from one corner, and the corporate types both jumped to their feet as if it were nuclear runoff. Jonah waited for me at the entrance to the hallway. I noticed, to my infinite joy, that he'd had a hair transplant. The track lighting illuminated his skull, which gleamed a little with sweat, and I recognized those plugs, which looked like grass when we first put it into the park, before it takes and evens out.

"Shopping?" Jonah asked, eyeing my bag.

"Fishing," I told him.

Jonah's office was awesome, and I don't mean that in the male teenage skateboarding sense—I mean it in the old-fashioned literal sense. The desk was a giant jet black oval with a wet-looking surface, like the most expensive pianos have. It reminded me of a black ice-skating rink. Behind the desk was nothing but view—the whole city flung out in front of us the way those street vendors fling out their towels packed with cheap glittery watches and belts. That's how New York looked: like a gorgeous, easy thing to have, even for me. I stood just inside the door, holding my fish. Jonah went around to the other side of the wet black oval of his desk. It looked frictionless, like you could slide a coin over the surface and it would float to the edge and drop to the floor. "Have a seat, buddy," he said.

"Wait," I said. "This is for you." I came forward and gently set the fish on his desk. I felt like I was leaving an offering at a Shinto shrine on top of the tallest mountain in Japan. The view was tripping me out.

"You're giving me a fish?" Jonah said. "That's a fish?"

"Striped bass. I caught it in the East River this morning."

Jonah looked at me like he was waiting for the punch line.

"It's not as polluted as people think," I said, sitting down in a small black chair, one of two facing Jonah's desk.

Jonah stood, picked up the fish, came around his desk and handed it back to me. "Thanks, Scotty," he said. "I appreciate the thought; I really do. But a fish will surely go to waste here at my office."

"Take it home and eat it!" I said.

Jonah nodded and smiled, but he made no move to retrieve the fish. Fine, I thought, I'll eat it myself.

My black chair had looked uncomfortable. I'd thought, lowering myself into it, This is going to be a hellish chair that makes your ass ache and then go numb. But it was without question the most comfortable chair I had ever sat in, even more comfortable than the leather couch in the waiting room. The couch had put me half to sleep—this chair was making me levitate.

"What can I do for you, Scotty?" Jonah said. "You have a demo tape you want me to listen to? You got an album, a band? Songs you're looking to have produced? Tell me what's on your mind."

He was leaning against the front of the black lozenge, ankles crossed—one of those poses that appear to be very relaxed but are actually very tense. As I looked up at him, I experienced several realizations, all in a sort of cascade: (1) Jonah and I weren't friends anymore and never would be. (2) He was looking to get rid of me as quickly as possible with the least amount of hassle. (3) I already knew that would happen. I'd known it before I arrived. (4) It was the reason I had come to see him.

"Scotty? You still there?"

"So that's what happens when you get to be a big shot," I said. "Everyone wants something from you."

Jonah went behind his desk, sat down and folded his hands in a pose that looked less relaxed than the first one, but was actually more so. "Not necessarily," he said. "But I haven't seen you in years, Scotty. You write me a letter out of nowhere; now you show up at my office—I've gotta assume you didn't come here just to bring me a fish."

"No, that was extra," I said. "I came for this reason: I want to know what happened between A and B."

Jonah seemed to be waiting for more.

"A is when we were both in the band, chasing the same girl," I explained. "B is now."

I knew instantly that it had been the right move to bring up Alice. I'd said something literally, yes, but underneath that I'd said somehing else—we were both a couple of ass wipes, and now only I'm an ass wipe; why? And underneath that, something else: once an ass wipe, always an ass wipe. And deepest of all: You didn't get her. I did.

"I don't know about you," Jonah said, "but I've busted my balls."

"Ditto."

We looked at each other across the black desk, the seat of Jonah's power. There was a long, strange pause, and in that pause I felt myself pulling Jonah back—or maybe it was him pulling me—to Chicago, our hometown, when we were two of four Flaming Dildos; back to when Jonah was one of the lousier tenor-sax players you're ever likely to hear, an odd-looking kid with prematurely thinning hair and my best friend. I felt a kick of anger so strong it filled me with nausea, the kind that makes you black out before you can puke. I closed my eyes and imagined coming at Jonah across that desk and ripping off his head, yanking it from the neck of that beautiful white shirt like a knobby weed with long, tangled roots. I pictured carrying it into his swank lobby by those plugs of hair and dropping it on his blonde receptionist's desk.

I rose from my chair, but at that same moment Jonah got up, too—jumped up, I should say, because when I looked at him, he was already standing. He didn't look afraid, but I smelled that he was. Vinegar—that's what fear smells like.

"Do you mind if I look out your window?" I asked.

"Not at all," Jonah said and stepped quickly aside.

I went to the window. I pretended to look at the view, but my eyes were closed.

After a while, I sensed that Jonah had moved nearer to me. "You still doing any music, Scotty?" he asked in a friendly way.

"I try," I said. "Mostly by myself, just to keep loose." I was able to open my eyes, but not to look at him.

"You were something on that guitar," he said. Then he asked, "You married?"

"Divorced. From Alice."

"Oh yeah," he said slowly, pretending this was something he'd known once but not cared enough about to remember. "I heard you two had gotten married."

"Four years," I said.

"I'm sorry, buddy."

"All for the best," I said, and then I turned to him. He was standing with his back to the window. I wondered if Joah ever bothered to look out when he was alone, if having so much beauty at close range meant anything at all to him. "What about you?" I asked.

"Married. Three kids." He grinned, and then the grin failed, and I smelled vinegar again. Suddenly, I knew what Jonah was thinking—that I'd come up here to take away these gifts life had shoveled upon him, to wipe them out in a few emphatic seconds. This made me want to yell with laughter. Hey, "buddy," I felt like saying. Don't you get it? There's nothing you have that I don't have! It's all just X's and O's, and you can come by those in a million different ways. But two thoughts distracted me as I stood there, breathing Jonah's fear: *(1)* I didn't have what Jonah had. *(2)* He was right.

Instead, I thought of Alice. This was something I almost never allowed myself to do—just think of her, as opposed to thinking about not thinking about her, which I did almost constantly. The thought of Alice broke open in my mind, and I let it fan out until I saw her hair in the sun—red, her hair was red—and I smelled those oils she used to dab on her wrists with a dropper. Patchouli? Musk? I couldn't remember the names. I saw her face with so much love still in it, no anger, no fear, none of the sorry things I learned to enjoy making her feel. Come inside, her face said, and I did. For a minute, I came inside.

I looked down at the city. It's extravagance felt wasteful, like gushing oil or some other precious thing Jonah was hoarding for himself, using it up so no one else could get it. If I had a view like this to look down on every day, I thought, I would have the energy and inspiration to conquer the world. The trouble is, when you most need such a view, no one gives it to you.

I inhaled a long breath and turned to Jonah. "Health and happiness to you, brother," I said, and I smiled at him for the first and only time: I let my lips open and stretch back, something I very rarely do because I'm missing most of my teeth on both sides. The teeth I have are big and white, so those black gaps come as a real surprise. I saw the shock in Jonah's face when I grinned. And suddenly I felt strong, as if some balance had shifted in the room and all of Jonah's power—the desk, the view, the levitating chair—suddenly belonged to me. Jonah felt it, too. Power is like that; everyone feels it at once.

I turned and walked toward the door, still grinning. I felt light, as if I were wearing Jonah's white shirt and light were pouring out from inside it.

"Hey, Scotty, hold on," Jonah said, sounding a little shaken. He veered back to his desk, but I kept walking, my grin leading the way into the hall and back toward the reception area, my shoes whispering on the carpet with each dignified step. Jonah caught up with me and handed me a business card: thick, sumptuous paper with embossed print. It felt precious. I held it very carefully.

"President," I read aloud.

"Don't be a stranger," Jonah said. He sounded bewildered, as if he'd forgotten how I had come to be there; as if he'd invited me himself and now I were leaving prematurely.

Outside the building, I walked directly to the box where I had mailed the letter to Jonah. I bent my neck and squinted up at the tower of green glass, trying to count the floors to forty-five. And only then did I notice that my hands were empty—I'd left my fish in Jonah's office! This struck me as hilarious, and I laughed out loud, imaging the corporate types seating themselves in the levitating chairs, one of them lifting the wet, heavy bag and then recognizing it—"Oh, God, it's that guy's fish. . . ."—dropping it, revolted. And what would Jonah do? I wondered as I walked to the subway. Would he dispose of the fish forever then and there, or would he put it in the office refrigerator and take it home that night to his wife and three children and tell them about my visit? And if he got that far, was it possible that he might open up the bag and take a look, just for the hell of it? I hoped so—I knew he'd be surprised. It was a shiny, beautiful fih.

I wasn't good for much the rest of that day. I get a lot of headaches—tension headaches, I guess they are, but the pain is so intense that it throws off bright, excruciating pictures. That afternoon I closed my eyes and saw a burning heart suspended in darkness, shooting off light in every direction. It wasn't a dream, because nothing happened. The heart just hung there.

Having gone to bed in the late afternoon, I was up and out of my apartment and under the Williamsburg Bridge with my line in the river well before sunrise. Sammy and Rob showed up soon after. Rob didn't actually care about fish—he was there to watch the East Village females on their early-morning jogs, before they went to school at NYU or to work at a boutique or whatever it was East Village girls did with their days. Rob complained about their jog bras, which didn't allow enough bounce for his satisfaction. Sammy and I barely listened.

That morning when Rob started up, I felt an inclination to speak. "You know, Rob," I said, "I think that's the point."

"What's the point?"

"That their breasts don't bounce," I said. "It hurts them. That's why they wear jog bras in the first place."

He gave me a wary look. "How do you know that?"

"My wife used to jog," I said. "She told me."

"Used to? You mean she quit?"

"She isn't my wife anymore. I don't know if she still jogs. She probably does."

It was a quiet morning. I heard the slow *thop, thop* of tennis balls on the courts behind the Williamsburg Bridge. How can they stand playing tennis this early? I wondered. But they were probably looking over at me and thinking, How can he stand fishing this early, or at any time? I'd had joggers stop to warn me, "You shouldn't eat the fish from this river, you know. It's very polluted." Girls, mostly. "Thanks," I'd say. "I wasn't planning to eat it." They'd jog away, satisfied, Rob's head bobbing as he watched them. Aside from the joggers and tennis players, there were usually a few junkies out by the river in the early mornings. I always looked for one particular couple, a male and female in thigh-length leather jackets, with skinny legs and ruined faces. They had to be musicians. I'd been out of the game for a while, but I could spot a musician anywhere.

The sun rose big and round and shiny, like an angel lifting her head. I'd never seen it so beautiful out there. Silver poured over the water. I wanted to swim in it. Pollution? I thought. Give me some more. And then I noticed the girl, one of the joggers. I spotted her peripherally because she was small and freckled and ran with a high, leaping gait that was different from the others'. She had light brown hair, and when the sunlight touched it, something happened that you couldn't miss. Rumpelstiltskin, I thought, straw to gold. Rob was gaping at her, and even Sammy turned to look, but I kept my eyes on the river, watching my line for a tug. I saw the girl without having to look.

"Hey, Scotty," Rob said, "I think your wife just ran by."

"I'm divorced," I said.

"Well, that was her."

"No," I said. "She lives in Chicago."

"Maybe she's your next wife," Sammy suggested.

"She's *my* next wife," Rob said. "And you know the first thing I'm gonna teach her? Don't clamp them down. Let them *bounce*."

He and Sammy broke up over that one.

I looked at my line, flicking quietly in the sun. My luck was gone; I knew I wouldn't catch anything. Soon I had to be at work. I reeled in my line and began walking north along the river. The girl was already a long way ahead, her hair shaking with every step. I followed her, but at such a distance that I wasn't following her, really. I was just walking in the same direction. My eyes held her so tightly that I didn't even notice the junkie couple heading my way. They were almost past me by the time I recognized them, huddled up against each other, shivering. They looked haggard and sexy the way young people can for a little while, before they just look haggard. "Hey," I said, stepping in their way.

We must've seen one another twenty times on that river, but the guy looked at me through his sunglasses as if he'd never seen me before, and the girl didn't look at me at all. "Are you musicians?" I asked.

The guy turned away, shaking me off. But the girl looked up. Her eyes seemed damaged, and I wondered if the sun hurt them and why her boyfriend or husband or whatever he was didn't give her his glasses. "He's awesome," she said, using the word in the male teenage skateboarding sense. Or maybe not, I thought. Maybe she meant it in the literal sense.

"I believe you," I said. "I believe he's an awesome musician."

I reached into my shirt pocket and took out Jonah's card. I'd used a piece of Kleenex to remove it from yesterday's jacket and place it in today's shirt, making sure not to bend or fold or smudge it. Its embossed letters reminded me of a Roman coin. "Call this man," I said. "He's a record producer. Tell him Scotty sent you."

They both looked at the card, squinting in the harsh, angled sunlight.

"Call him," I said. "He's my buddy."

"Sure," the guy said without conviction.

He won't call, I thought. "I really hope you will," I said, but I felt helpless. I could do this only once; I would never have that card again.

While the guy studied the card, the girl looked at me. "He'll call," she said, and then she smiled. "I'll make him."

I nodded and turned, leaving the junkies behind. I walked north, forcing my eyes to see as far as they could see. But the freckled jogger was gone; she'd vanished while I looked away.

"Hey," I heard behind me, two ragged voices. When I turned, they called out, "Thanks"—both at the same time.

It had been so long since anyone had thanked me for anything. "Thanks," I said to myself. I said it again and again, wanting to hold in my mind the exact sound of their voices, to feel again the kick of surprise in my chest.

Is there some quality of warm spring air that causes birds to sing more loudly? I asked myself that question as I took the overpass across the FDR onto 6th Street. Flowers were just coming open on the trees. I trotted underneath them, smelling their powdery smell as I hurried toward my apartment. I wanted to drop off my jacket at the dry cleaners on my way to work. In fact, I was looking forward to it. I'd left the jacket rumpled on the floor beside my bed the afternoon before, and I would bring it in like that—all used up. I'd toss it on the counter very casually, daring the gal to challenge me. But how could she?

"I've been somewhere, and I need my jacket cleaned," I'd say, like anyone else. And she would make it new again.

A GOOD GERMAN

"I was born into the Battalion," he told people, the way someone else might say "I went to Harvard" or "I fucked Madonna," and then he could take center stage and talk about it for a while or, depending on his mood, he could act annoyed when someone asked, "What was it like?" Sometimes his saying it was wasted: none of their victims had been famous and so a lot of people didn't recall hearing about Ned's Battalion at all. Sometimes Ben said he'd been born into the Manson family. Unlike most of the lies he told, that one was intended not to deceive but to assist, to make what he was saying easier to comprehend.

Lora, the woman he lived with, thought she understood. "You weren't really part of it." "Yes I was," he said. "Could you kill a black man? A Jew?" "Same as killing white." She asked, "Could you kill a white Christian?" He didn't think so. He didn't know. "I don't want to hurt anyone," he said, and meant it, but even the word *hurt*—whether thought or spoken—made everything that wasn't right well up inside him.

"It's never been like this with other men," Lora said. "It's not just your dick inside me, it's all of you. I can feel all of you moving inside me, Ben," and when she said that, he came, not with hard thrusts, he just melted, and felt an emptiness as great as any he'd ever known because if he could fool her without even meaning to, then even deception was out of his control.

Ben always felt good while he was talking. He liked an audience, enjoyed telling true stories as much as lies. When the State sent him to therapy, it was too easy: He chatted about his memories and the pain remained unreachable, without catharsis. The only words he ever stumbled over: "I should have been able to do something." Like everyone else, the therapist reassured him: "You were just a child. What could you have done?" "I don't know." After all these years, he still didn't know, as inadequate now as ever.

He didn't mind talking to reporters on the twentieth anniversary of the shootout and Ned's death. On-camera he came across both candid and ironic, a graduate student (though he'd just dropped out again, which he didn't mention), he was employed (yeah, right, minimum wage and no benefits at the video store). He had a roof over his head and a girlfriend. How terribly normal (though at age twenty-eight he should have had much more, though the first woman he'd ever lived with still referred to him as "that little sociopath"—and back then he'd been relatively tame). The reporter asked, Are you Ned's son? He'd once believed a cowboy named Beauregard Lake was his father. "Once the authorities came in, I was attributed to Ned, like a painting."

Strange his wounded little face had found no takers. Ben was not adopted. After attribution, he went to group homes and foster care.

Ben says what he thinks they want to hear. A rifle completed Ned, gave him something to do with his hands. Usually he strutted around, shoulders back, his hands flapping like idiot-mittens loosely attached to his wrists. In the classroom Ned hunched toward them over the lectern, bearded and simian with his fingers curled, his elbows bent and flexing. Ned needed a shoulder-strap to complete him, if not the rifle, then his guitar. He'd sing in his funny high voice and the guitar bounced with the rhythm or (though Ben doesn't say this on-camera) just bounced as though he were prodding it with an angry erection. He started the boys on muzzle-loading rifles, to learn what he called "scrupulous care." Ben liked it well enough, keeping his firearm clean, keeping it free of dirt and oil when loading, keeping his hand steady, pouring black powder into the pan, as Bobby or was it Buster smeared powder on his face. It looked to Ben like warpaint but Bobby said

"Look, I'm growing a beard, I'm a man." And Ned hit the boy across the face with the rifle stock and there was blood mixing with the powder and Ned held his handgun to Bobby or Buster's head: "Is it a toy?" he asked. "Do you think this is a game?"

What he sees in his head, and doesn't say, is Ned's penis, which he only remembers seeing once, though his therapist, suddenly hopeful, had made him talk about it again and again. The boys were all circumcised. God's covenant they were told. Ned had done it to them himself, but Ned's was purple red and wrinkled. It looked uncomfortable, angry, as though it caused his rage because it hurt him. It looked somehow oily and wrong-sized, not fitting right. To amuse the therapist Ben had said "like a novelty condom, from some factory behind the Iron Curtain." Ben imagines the loose skin, bagged and swollen like a blister and remembers that as a child he'd thought, Let me cut it off. He left it to the therapist to guess whether this was classically Oedipal or, because you must hurt to heal, well-intentioned.

He watched himself on the evening news, pleased that from his face, you could never have guessed what he was thinking. You would not guess how different he is from other people.

He's always been different, funny.

"Why do you want me?" he asked Lora. "I'm such a mess." "Your life is a skittish horse," she answered. "You're doing a pretty good job riding it." A Lora metaphor. She had recently become Native American; she had the skin and hair and cheekbones, the almond eyes to prove it, born to a Danish mother who met her Tibetan father in a refugee camp in India. "That makes me Indian," she said smugly, "don't you think?"

Lora can talk about Ben for hours, for days, on the phone long-distance with her best friend. Her fascination with him, the elusive source of his appeal. You couldn't look at him without thinking of sex, not that he usually looked aroused, but rather stunned and arrogant and a little sad, like a teenage boy who's just come. He always looked like he'd just had some; it was all aftermath or afterglow. Until you actually became his lover, you never saw who or what had aroused him, so you could imagine anyone or anything which soon became everyone and everything. He was so passivey voracious. His life seemed to leave him both enervated and energized—eyes dreamy, body loose and toned. He wore baggy pants and a gangbanger's bandanna; then shaved his scalp like a skinhead to go with his black pants and Doc Marten boots. He got dressed each day to invite reprisal but looked too baffled to provoke it. (Lora on the phone to a friend: "I want you to care about him because I do.") His somnambulist sweetness—eerie, comic and endangered as a naked sleepwalking child. The surprise of that sharp intelligence, the sudden flashes from behind those always-a-little-stunned eyes. He looked his wiliest when fast asleep, eyes squinted shut, sharp chin tucked into his own chest, or hers, or anyone's.

Now he lies awake beside her, because the torrential rain against the roof and windows could be aspen leaves shivering; the whistling in his ears could be the wind or a rocket or a belt; a car backfires unless it's a driveby shooting. Ben is sleepless and wracked, waiting. He's like a man with a head wound: the hyperawareness he needs to compensate for what is shattered makes him feel slow and dulled and yet exquisitely responsive to any stimulus, at the mercy of being more alive.

On the TV news, he looked untouched, saved. He was just a child, or as he prefers to say, a good German. Claire looked just as he remembered her. "I come up for parole again six months from now," she said. "In May. And this time I'm really hoping." After the shootout, she'd fled with the girl Susannah. She hadn't chosen Ben. She left him behind, which probably meant she hadn't been his mother. He'd called her his mother, her and so many others, all the grown-up women in the Battalion were called The Mothers. "Life is for the living," Claire told the reporter. "I don't think about Ned. I don't think about the people we killed. It's over for them," she said. "The only part I think about—I think about the children."

And that must be why he's hypervigilant and sleepless, in this state of urgent rather than passive receptivity: he knows Claire thinks about him. He's waiting for Claire to be released, waiting for her to come for him.

He started to remember things, like the anthro seminar he'd been closed out of, the T.A. breezily explaining, "*Sacrifice* is overenrolled; all the self-mutilators signed up." He noticed things that had been there all along: personal ads (the many people who were willing to do things to him); carpentry ads ("Need a Dungeon? Customwork—Discreet"); the sign for the shop on the second floor—*Body Piercing—Your Choice—With or Without Pain*. ("You pay more for pain," said his friend Terence, "but it's worth it." His thumbs moved along Terence's ears, he held his friend's head, he might pull it off and keep it, the soft warm mouth, the trumpet-player's callus just a hint of roughness at the margin. Terence milked him, sucked him dry, a clean and blessed relief like a bullet in the brain.)

At work, he stood behind the curve of his raised counter like a pharmacist or priest, checking out videos, taking the money or punching the membership card, handing out receipts and complimentary paper sacks of stale popcorn. One night with business slow he got a little crazy, pulling open drawers and slamming them. If he found glue he knew he'd sniff it, and when he took out the stapler he regarded it and handled it and turned it over and considered it, its hinge like a door, and he put it down and then suddenly slipped his index finger onto the bed and slammed the top down, shocking himself less with the pain than with his own indignant *ouch*.

Hurt me, he asked Lora.

"How can I hurt you?" she asked, meaning not "in what manner would you like?" but rather expressing the impossibility of compliance. Finally she screwed up her face and pinched him—doubtless the most evil thing she'd ever done to her little brother as a child.

When Lora first knew him, both his ears were pierced. He wore a ring in one nipple. Why? Because it looked hot—a simple ordinary cosmetic procedure. Now he's ringed in both, as though waiting to be hitched into harness. When he'd had his ears pierced, if he remembered right, it hadn't hurt. Even the nipples, which are obviously sensitive, hadn't been very bad. There was nothing to it. Otherwise, how could ordinary people riding BART or in the video store, at parties, in classrooms, on the ferry, on the street all display everything he had and often more?

Each time he had something done, he was surprised by the pain and then forgot it. The pain of piercing and of tattooing were incidental. Pain had not occurred to him then as something to enter into; he had concentrated on not feeling when surely what he'd needed was to feel. He wanted the unbearable, to know what happened once you got there.

Maybe Lora was right, once you opened the door, there was nothing to stop you; there was no telling what you might do.

In bed, he clung to her. (He, of course, could not hurt Lora; the very idea of bad things happening to her filled him with dread.) They held each other and he was safe for the moment and grateful, the softness of her skin, the strength of her dancer's legs. Then he shut down, a quick flick of the switch before he could whimper, please help me. As though she knew, she stroked his back, so lightly, lightly.

"When we still had the draft," he told Lora, "it was almost impossible to get classified a conscientious objector. The presumption is—unless you're a very rare exception—the government knows we're all ready and able to kill."

The abyss had always been there, but he had explored it the way a geologist might. He had studied the natural history of torture and murder. He could be irreverent. He could be dispassionate. He'd once counted on his intellect to save him.

He had been to so many schools and knew all sorts of things; his mind buzzed if he didn't keep it occupied. Now he was auditing Turkish at Berkeley; he'd already tried Russian and Gaelic and Greek. He moved from one study to another. As soon as the words and sounds became at all familiar, the buzzing in his mind started up again and drove him crazy—a miniaturized winged demon, like a mosquito or a fly. Sometimes the humming sound seemed so clearly separate from him, he moved his hands to brush it away or slapped his temple hard and fast to kill it.

The whole point of extreme pain, he thinks, must be to stop the mind. When you're feeling, for once you can't be thinking.

Ben thinks. He has studied and read. He knows all kinds of things. For example: The Maya kings and shamans perforated their penises with awls, they inserted cactus spines, turning the most sensitive flesh into spiked clubs in acts of self-torture. They pierced their tongues and ran cords through the holes. (He wants to run and hide as he describes it; he is sick with a sickening vertigo.) They bled all over sacred objects. They reached ecstasy that way; entranced, they opened the portals to the other world.

As a boy he had once met an Indian man from the northern plains.

Ned invited him to speak in the Bible class room. The man, who wore his hair in two black braids, said, "The Creator gives us everything. What can we offer the Creator? There's nothing we can give him in return except ourselves." He had just come from the Sun Dance. He rolled up his sleeve and Ned had the children go up to see the small pinpoint scars, seven in a vertical line. The man unbuttoned his ribboned shirt, took it off, then turned and showed them his back, where he'd been cut with razors, opening flaps to hold the pegs of chokecherry wood and the thongs. He said it so casually, as if this were entirely normal but electric shocks ran through Ben's marrow, nerve lightning and zipzag nausea. The Indian man said, "We were fastened to a tree. You pull forward four times. On the fourth time you must pull off. You pull off from the tree, that's how you leave a flesh offering, so it's not just your blood, it's your flesh." Ben looked at the scarred, lacerated back, afraid of the man, and of Ned, and of his own need to vomit. (After the talk, did the Indian man go home? What had become of him? According to Ned, Jews had left behind their Scriptures, the only thing of value, and so the world could now be rid of them. The redman had to be preserved only long enough to know his secrets.) The Indian man had turned to face them, tears glistening in his eyes, and Ben's mouth opened, receptive to fascination. He understood these weren't tears of pain or terrible memory. There was no pain in the man's face, his eyes dreamy, focused far away, his heart moved by some very strong and beautiful emotion.

"They did it for God, for the gods," Lora said, the expert on things spiritual, or so she claimed to be.

She said, "You don't even believe."

But he had believed, at least in something, intermittently: He was Catholic for a while—for the cannibalism, he told her. And then Sufi. He had whirled dervish-style. He went to Sufi gatherings where most people didn't speak English, where he could be greeted, given a glass of tea and a sheepskin to kneel on, be accepted yet never incorporated, he could find the reassurance he craved without the surrender.

"What makes you think God came first?" he said. "They invited the gods as an excuse. The drive was there first, the sexual drive towards bloody sacrifice and pain and mutilation. They had to justify it. That's the reason people invented God."

* * *

"Do you have an awl?" Lora asked. She sat on the rag rug, crosslegged, her skin all honeycolored with the sun coming through the window, making the room flow beyond its walls, ripe and bursting.

"In the tool box." He hadn't done anything with it. Awls and cactus spines are, perhaps, consecrated, but really, there are so many things at hand you can hurt yourself with. A clothespin. A can opener. Until Lora spoke, using the awl on himself had not very seriously occurred to him.

She asked, "Can I have it?"

She took off her sandal—"It's loose"—and screwed out a new hole in the leather strap.

She was practical to the point of obtuseness at times.When he described her to people he said things like "decent" and "sweet." He was on-and-off sure he didn't love her. He thought he was only with her because he was so scared; he had begun to scare himself. She held the awl and knew what he was thinking. She wasn't so oblivious after all: "I know guys who do stuff like that," she said. "Gay Mormons. They do it because they feel so guilty."

"I don't feel guilty," he lied. "None of it was my choice. I was born to it."

"So were they."

What does she want from him? He can never tell these days if she is trying to discourage him from his path or if it intrigues her. She brings it up herself now. Is she concerned, or curious and avid? Maybe she knows his weakness, the words as substitute for the act. Maybe she knows what she is doing.

Lora came home, "Hello, sweet," and cried out to find him lying on the couch, bristling with silver whiskers, his face full of needles and pins. "Ben! Ben! What are you doing?"

He said, "Somewhere there's a voodoo doll with a helluva headache." He hadn't pushed the needles in very deep, this was just a tryout. (He is being clawed, ripped open, torn apart. He longs for a wash of endorphins—the word is benign and makes him think of euphoria and of dolphins. Or, failing that, pain distracting him from inner pain.) But he had not been able to force himself to penetrate tissue. He'd pushed the points in obliquely, let them enter slantwise just under the skin. Now just moving his lips made most of them fall out. He and Lora knelt, running their hands over the cushions and floorboards and rag rug to retrieve them.

"Jeepers Creepers!" Lora expressed aggravation with false childishness, "Holy Guacamole!" and then got bitchy, like a woman: "Now I can't even walk barefoot in my own home. If you need to hurt yourself—go ahead. Do it! Do it! But for real. I don't know how you can stand it. It's your problem, but now it's driving me crazy. Get it over with already." Did she mean it? Or was she the reverse psychologist on the pavement calling up to the window, Go ahead! Jump!

He has the hollow needles now. Brand new. He often forgets about safe sex, but he won't risk AIDS with dirty needles. The reason these fresh needles are hollow is so that when you push them through your body they gouge out tunnels of flesh. This was not self-hatred, he thought. It was a quest for self, a road he wished he didn't have to walk alone. He imagines a brotherhood, of people cutting one another with razors, anointing each other's wounds, sharing unacceptable secrets and then accepting them. (Maybe Ned didn't really hate the Jews he killed; he made the women kill them with him so that they could never leave him.)

He tries not to wonder about the woman called Madame Maritza who did his nipples, what would make someone do this for a living. Anyway, he can't afford to pay someone to do it to him now. And though it seems a person cannot possibly do this to himself, he wants to. How about one in his nose, one beneath his lower lip, one in the dimple over his mouth, one in each cheek and even, yes, the eyebrows—more holes than he can possibly afford to fill with studs and rings. Of course, he's not doing it for the ornaments.

"Hey, it's OK," he remembers Lora saying, "your wiring just wasn't done by the union." He imagines the zigzag network, the circuitry of nerves—tearing it all out and starting over. Extinguishing the sizzle in the marrow, but first putting his finger right there, on the burning spark.

He would like to amputate that finger. He thinks of cutting something off—the finger or maybe just a joint of one, maybe a toe. He doesn't like the word amputate. He much prefers dismember. Could you do it with a knife? Will he need an axe? A kitchen cleaver? Even severing a little toe would be a marvelously complex matter, not just flesh and bone, but a microcosm of the body: muscle and tissue, arteries, veins and blood and what little he has of fat. Can you do it to yourself? Who can he get to help him? There are Mayan carvings showing self-decapitation. If he killed himself, that's the way he would most like it to be: pull his own head right off.

Will there be a lot of blood? There's something so horrible and somehow better about not just gouging flesh, but breaking, splintering, hearing the crack and break of bone.

He thinks about it till the sight of his fingers and toes sickens him. He hasn't acted. They accuse him by their very presence, stuck to his body like stolen things.

This is just another trial run, but he has to start somewhere. He's getting closer. When he shaved this morning, he thought of cutting his throat. Now he has the hollow needles. Now he has the bowl of ice cubes. (It's a good thing he has no mother. What mother could bear to be his mother, to know such things about her son?) He's got Thelonious Monk on the tape-player. Lora at rehearsal. He's got his flesh—the medium for him to work with—sitting with him on Lora's couch.

He picks up an ice cube and it sticks to his skin, then shoots out from his fingers, slippery as it starts to melt. He has better luck with the next and brings it toward his cheek but then refuses this most simple anesthetic, closing his hand around it, unwilling to thwart the pain. He unbuckles his belt, though he hasn't planned this; pulls it loose with an unpremeditated jerk. He drops his pants. The ice cube moves to the crack of his ass and something feels so right, some knowledge of instantaneous contradiction, in this case the not-feeling numbness and then the intensity of opposite sensations: burning cold; icy water melted by body heat.

He holds the piece of ice beneath him and presses so that it begins to enter, then sits with a jabbing violence upon Lora's couch. He stabs a needle into his nose. The pain is blinding. It tears through his eyes and right into the brain which approaches but does not reach blackout and in wavering tells him this is nothing, this is minor. The hurt he feels just proves the pain isn't big enough to grant an adrenaline rush or the mercy of shock. He needs more. He tears into the flesh below his lower lip and cries out confused with how terrible it is and how amazing and with the ice cube melting as it moves up inside him. If he withdraws the needles now, he'll leave puncture wounds, incompletely ravaged flesh, but he can't bear at first to push them through, and anyway, he has more needles. He goes about it methodically, opening one wound and then another, bit by bit till each needle is filled with its share of him. Into his nose, though the needle jams halfway through. Then there's a brief gush of blood. Into his cheek, his eyebrows, though a person cannot do this to himself, not just because of pain which he doesn't feel now, but the blood spilling into his eyes to blind him, and now he has no grasp, his fingers slick with it, not spurting but pouring, and seeping into his mouth and throat and leaking a little around the needles which for the moment still plug the new holes. From his lower lip, where he's gouged sloppily, it's dribbling and burbling till he sucks it in and swallows and he wants more as though he's forced open some rusty tap and gotten for his efforts only the few gurgles waiting in the line. He bleeds on Lora's couch. He should have thought of that. He stumbles entangled in his fallen pants and through the apartment spotting the rag rug and the linoleum. He should have done this in the tub so that's where he lies down. The sounds coming out of him seem to come from somewhere else and they distract him till pain overwhelms all distraction. Pain shoots his eyes out and shoots to his groin and all the way to his toes. The pain goes so deep, not at all like the razor slash, the cross he draws now across his chest, it's so amazing, so sharp, you don't even feel it. The sting comes later; the blood first makes an outline, a sign, and then a thin red sheet. He tries to force the needles through with both hands. A sharp point emerges inside his mouth, the spike passing through soft tissue and mucous membrane till he can touch it with his tongue. He could jab his tongue, prick it, open it, pull cords through it. Anything is possible. Everything tempts him—his navel, for example, his penis, or the webbing between thumb and forefinger, that convenient intimate place from which he has from time to time sniffed cocaine. He pinches the flesh, tests it. It's asking for a needle.

It is remarkable to him the way a body in shock does not shut down but simply goes about its business. Presumably this design feature was built-in in the interest of survival. That's its ordinary use, that he's adapted for his own extraordinary purpose. (His mind is detached and still working, he can think this. He's a smug automaton, a self-congratulatory machine that bleeds.)

Then suddenly he's suffering again and there's a time-lag till he understands why the trance is broken:

"Oh my god, what have you done, what are you doing?" Lora is screaming. "That's enough. Ben! Enough!"

But it isn't.

A. M. Homes

HIS CONFESSION

The summer I was nine my mother died. But before that happened something else happened, many things happened, and though I bore witness—and more—it was never clear to me what or why. I have forever played upon the sequence of that strange summer when time did literally change hands and the clock took to wildly spinning around. It would have been like a strange sweaty dream, a nightmare, except that when I woke, when the leaves turned and fall finally came around, I was alone. My life had been cleaved, irrevocably divided into a before and after.

That my family, my mother's family, never again mentioned her by name, never offered any explanation, was a detail I took as proof of my guilt, my own sick sense that I played a part in things. That nothing was offered kept me from asking, kept me convinced that they knew, they all knew—it was my fault. At nine, it did not occur to me that it might have been their guilt, the undeniable idea that something in their own actions had caused this horrible end. At nine, I was not so smart; I was only crazy with sorrow, furious that I'd been put up to such a thing.

Without even trying, without even knowing what was happening, without so much as an effort, in fact with only a plea, "No!"—a kind of pathetic begging, "No"—asking not to be brought into this, with nothing but my presence, my person, my love for my mother, I was drawn in, implicated. And despite my will—the will to remain who I was, as I was—there was confusion, uncertainty, the weakness of my person and then an unknowing of my will. And it did happen, it all happened. My desire confused itself and while I had once been sure that I had not acted, I became equally sure that I had—one often gets what one wants. Three weeks later, I became her murderer, or so I have always secretly said to myself.

If you want to know what led to what, how it came to be, I can only tell you my part. My story is mine only at times such as these when one must first take responsibility and then one's punishment.

So as not to go entirely around about it, backwards and forwards, confusing you as I so often confused myself, I will tell you what I remember. I will tell you what I've told no one else.

Wonder: Why do I draw you so close and pretend to trust? And it is pretend, a game, my game, played because I am so bored and desperate and beyond myself, because I have little to lose, because I have no one and nothing, because I am in this alone. Perhaps I am deluded, crazy to think that if I can make you understand, can re-create the events of a certain June and July, have you feel them as I felt them, then you will turn sorry for me, will do something for me, help me, relieve me. Perhaps you will then be willing to do what no one has ever done: exonerate and excuse me from this debacle that has become my life.

It begins with breakfast. Morning in June. I wake up, dress and go down to find my grandmother in my mother's kitchen, my grandmother hovering over my mother's stove.

"Over easy or sunny side up?"

"Up," I say, forever an optimist.

My mother's absence is not mentioned, is simply skipped over as though I might not notice. Through the day, silence builds. Unacknowledged, it multiplies. By dinner I feel I might explode. Within the rage is the frantic rumination that this day is a repeat of the morning two years before when I woke to find that while I'd slept my father had died. My father had died, seven men had been called, and while I dreamed they lowered him like a piano, eased him down the stairwell with a rope tied round his chest, his body too long and slowly going stiff to carry around the corners. And when I was told, I went to his room, thinking it wouldn't be true, thinking it a cruel tease, around the corner and through the door I found the bed stripped, the mattress bare and everything else in its place, as it was, as it should be.

That day and this day and over and over again, I curse God for my sleep, for so much lost at night, for the necessary slumber that deprives me of the events in my own life.

"Where's Ma?" I finally spit at supper.

"Charlottesville," my grandmother says. "Charlottesville," as if the name of a small southern town will tell me what I need to know. "It's a good facility," she adds. "They had my sister there once."

Facility for what?

Dishes done, she climbs onto a dining room chair, takes a suitcase from high in the closet, goes to my room and makes a swift transference of the contents of my drawers.

The bag is carried downstairs and set by the door, where it waits until morning when a horn blows outside and my grandmother picks herself up, pins on her hat and instructs me to collect myself, and pulls the door closed tight behind me.

In the middle of June I disappear. I am taken from my own life and set down in the home of the near stranger, who by some bit of poor fortune birthed the babe that is my mother. And there in my grandmother's house, I am given the same treatment of disdain and distrust that she'd previously reserved for her only child.

"There would have been others but the doctors advised against it," I heard her say. "Runs in families. Why make trouble when you've already got trouble?"

"How long will she be in Charlottesville?" I ask one morning.

"Well, that depends now, doesn't it?"

She squeezes the blood of an orange into a glass and sets it before me, thick with the meat of the fruit, with seeds I am afraid to swallow for fear a citrus grove will grow inside of me, its branches reaching up through my stomach into the back of my throat, tickling me.

"No seeds," my mother always said. "Spit the seeds."

In anticipation of the orchard within, I drink hesitantly. I cough and try to discreetly spit the seeds into my hand.

"Swallow it," my grandmother says. "No one wants to see you regurgitating at the table."

I swallow and cough again. Frightened, I cough harder.

"And don't choke yourself."

"My sister Sue was that way too," she says to her friends, like-minded women who spend afternoons in her living room, taking teas, rare-rooted brews they make themselves. There is a chorus to their discussion, an oft-repeated chant among the witches, "Crying shame. It's a crying shame."

"Sister Sue was that way too," my grandmother repeats.

"Crying shame. It's a crying shame."

Sister Sue, that way too. Round and round in my head, the echo, the incantation. What way? What way? Crazy like a loon. A loon?

I think of my mother, porcelain and milky glass, wandering, like walking and sleeping at the same time. Out the back door and into the woods behind the house, a white dress evaporating in the trees. She walks into the woods and returns hours later decorated with twigs, leaves, wild flowers, each hand carrying something she's found, oblivious to the cuts, scratches on her arms and legs. She comes out of it, rises to the surface and asks, "What happened today? I've already forgotten." I fill her in. I tell her what happened—but only to me; it seems pointless to tell the rest, pointless and unnecessary.

"Too much electricity in my head," she says rubbing her temples, "Too much."

My mother is the former Tomato Queen. Queen for a day in Morgan County, in the tiny town of Bath of Berkeley Springs, buried in the Mountain State, West Virginia.

"You and I," she says, a few days after she's back—we're still staying at my grandmother's house. "We'll take a little trip. We'll go back, to where I was raised, the old home."

My grandmother, bent over the oranges, elbow bearing down, shakes her head.

"It's not up for discussion," my mother says. "I'll have my boy with me, he'll keep me clean."

While she is out of the room my grandmother takes me aside. "Out of your sight," she says, "Don't let her out of your sight."

Somewhere near the Fourth of July, the Tomato Queen returns to her hometown. She drives slowly, pausing on the outskirts to brush her hair, freshen her lipstick, to suck in the long deep breath that will glue her together. She eases her mother's Chevrolet into town, holding herself as if she expects the streets to be lined with well-wishers waving, a band of trombones and tubas waiting to play a certain pomp and circumstance.

We stop before we get too far, slide into a small parking place and I wait while Mama goes into a store, returning with a small brown paper bag tucked into her purse. We circle the family home, the house that was ours for generations—until Aunt Sue hung herself off the front porch for all the neighbors to see and my grandmother thought it best to relocate.

Mama stares up at the porch and says, "Some things are funny, aren't they?" Then we drive back into town and she walks down the street saying hello to every person she passes, acting as if they owe her some great greeting, as if she is still the Tomato Queen and this is still her day.

"A bath," she says to the attendant at the old Roman baths, "A great big bath."

The woman leads us down the hall to a room with a heavy wooden door. "You have an hour," she says, turning on the tub. Mama ushers me into the narrow room. The water is running.

"How much does it hold?" I ask.

"A thousand gallons," Mama says.

As wide as the tub and only a little longer, the room has a small space for the steps that lead into the water. There is a narrow chair and a thin cot dressed in a clean white sheet and that's all.

"Sometimes, it's just too hard, it's just too much," she says, sitting on the narrow chair. She takes off her shoes, reaches up under her dress and starts to roll down her stockings.

I sit on the cot and watch.

She smiles.

I am watching Mama, more than watching, looking.

"I'm so glad to be home. Missed you," she says, unzipping her dress, sliding it off her shoulders. "Thought about you three times a day."

She escapes her underthings and I look away. I've been looking too hard, looking instead of watching, looking instead of not noticing.

Her body continuously unfolds, a voluminous and voluptuous twisting, turning monument to the possibilities of shape, to the forms flesh can take. A body. A real body.

"Are you getting shy?" she asks. "Getting too old for your ma?"

My face goes blank, all feeling falls out of it. She reaches over and begins to unbutton my summer shirt, the one my grandmother pressed so stiff that it is sharp, painful in places. I raise my hand and take over the unbuttoning. I undress with the awkwardness of a stranger, wondering if this is the way things are supposed to be, if this is simply how it is done, wondering if my discomfort is my own peculiarity. I have no way of knowing.

Mama turns off the tub.

The Tomato Queen pulls her blond hair back, piles it high on her head and pins it there where it won't get wet. Strays trail down her neck. Her neck is damp, perspiration mixed with perfume, a sweet fruit, a strong liquor, the place you want to bury yourself, to drink. I kiss her neck and, with my lips pressed to her skin, inhale. Her neck seeps sweat. Teardrops afraid to escape her eyes sneak out the back and slip down her spine only to find her ass crack and be sucked back in.

Slowly, she descends the steps into the water. Her body, round, truly a pear, a plum and then some. The most beautiful woman, front and back. Still the Tomato Queen.

She sighs, sweeps her arms wide, and splashes. "Heaven," she says.

I slip out of my underwear, leave everything folded on the chair and sit for a minute on the cot; naked, totally naked, so naked.

"You know," my mother says. "This town is where I met your father. Right here in this park, at a party for the Strawberry Festival. He towered like a tree."

She smiles. She's back. We will leave, we'll go home to our house and summer will start again. In my memory it is always summer. None of this will ever have happened. The bath will wash us, will clean us, erase everything and we will begin again.

I plunge in and swim to my mother.

"Your father loved it here. This was the one tub he could fit into. From the time he was ten or twelve he was just too big. He loved baths. Liked to soak."

My father was a giant, a true giant, seven feet eleven inches. It ran in his family. After he died, my aunt took me into her attic and showed me piles of clothing from the nineteen hundreds, all of it larger than life. "Always save the clothes of a big man," she said. "Their hearts don't last long, so big they wear themselves out. But save the clothes because every now and then there's a new one, and it's not like you can just go down to the store and outfit 'em."

"Why did you marry him?" I ask my mother.

"I always liked men," she says, as though that's an answer.

She leaves the bath, pulls the bottle from her purse and pours herself a glass. "Bathtub gin," she says carrying the glass back into the water with her.

In the water, she turns pink, she turns red. She lies back clutching the bar that goes the whole way around and like a ballet dancer doing her exercises, she opens and closes her legs. She teases me, making waves.

"Did I ever show you what having you did to me?"

I shake my head. She shows me her breasts. "I'm bagged out," she says, cupping them, holding them up, pointing them, aiming them at me like missiles. "Bombs away," she says. "You stretched me all out."

"I'm sorry," I say, horrified.

"Nothing to apologize for. It's my own damn fault."

She reaches for the bottle she's left by the side of the tub, refills her glass and drinks quickly.

"I'm frightened," she suddenly says. Her face has lost its color. She goes white, deathly white. "Give me a hug."

I go to her. Swim there. She pulls me against her. My cheek, my mouth, is at her breast. She flattens me against it and sees my embarrassment rise under the water.

Mama smiles and hugs me hard.

"Go ahead," she says, holding my head in her hands, turning it so that my lips are at her nipple. "If it belongs to anyone, it belongs to you." She moves my head back and forth over it. The softest skin, not skin but a strange fabric, a rare silk. My lips are sealed.

She rubs her finger over my mouth, "Open," she says. "Open up. It's only me, it's your Mama. Taste, just taste."

Like butter, only it doesn't melt. A tender saucer that pulls tight under my tongue, ridges and goose bumps.

She reaches for my hand. I try to pull away. "No."

"Yes," she says pulling harder on the arm, leading it toward the place between her legs.

"No," I say, more desperately.

My hand goes through a dark curtain, parting velvet drapes. My fingers slip between the lips of a second, secret mouth. My mother makes a sound, a gutteral ahhh. I try to pull my hand out but she pushes it back in. Pushes it in and then pulls it out; pushes and pulls, in and out, in, out.

"It's your home," she says, one hand at the back of my neck, holding my head against her still, the other on my hand, keeping me there, her leg wrapped around my leg.

"It's your home," she says again. "You lived there before you lived anywhere else. You're not afraid of going home, are you?" she asks.

It grows slick, greasy with something wetter than water. My hand is inside my mother, in a place I never knew was there. Deeper. She takes three fingers and threads them into her. Perfume and juices, the cavern grows. She moves the hand in and out. My fingers are swallowed.

She grabs my arm at the wrist. "Fist," she says. "Make a fist, curl your paw." It doesn't go at first. Too large. "Push," she says. And I do. "Harder," she says. My knuckles round the edge of the bone and pop in. My fist is inside her. I turn it around, a screwdriver, a drill. I feel the walls, the meat she's made of, dark and thick. My fist is in and almost out and then in again. Her fingers dig into my bicep, she's controlling me. "Go," she says, deeply, desperately. "Go. More." She is pushing and pulling. I'm rocking, fighting. Buried in my mother I'm boxing. Boxing Mama, punching her out, afraid my hand will come off, afraid the contractions of her womb will amputate me at the wrist. My shoulder is stretching, nearly popping out and I can't stop, that much is clear. Whatever I do, I can't stop. She is filled with fury and frustration and there is no way of saying no.

She keeps my mouth at her breast. "Suck," she says, "bite it. It's yours." Harder and harder. Never enough.

And then with no warning, the teeth of this strange mouth bite my hand. Her head goes back and she bellows like I've killed her and I cry out too because she's hurting me and I don't know what's happening. I'm scared and I want my hand back and I want my mother back and I want to be out of this place.

It's over. As suddenly as it started. Mama holds up a hand, "Stop," she says. "Stop," she whispers in my ear. "It's enough." She puts her hand on my shoulder and tries to push me away but my fist is still inside her and suddenly I'm an intruder, a thief. I am doing something wrong. I takes me a minute, more than a minute. I've gone deaf, I don't catch on right away, I keep pulling and pushing and boxing, punching her insides, going the rounds, giving it my best. I'm doing my job, doing all I can.

"Stop," she says again loudly, the echo off the tile makes it sound like a shot.

I stop.

She reaches between her legs, plucks my hand out and lets it drop like some discarded thing. I've failed. I turn full front toward her and begin to rub her, to poke at her with my skinny stub. She laughs and pushes me away, "Now you're just all excited. All riled up." She laughs as though it's funny. She gives me a kiss on the lips and climbs out of the tub, wrapping a towel around herself. She lies back on the cot, hand over her eyes and sighs, breathes heavily, deeply.

I'm staring, wondering what I've done wrong.

"Don't ogle," she says without even looking at me. "Swim some, get your flippers wet."

I am still so small a boy that for me this tub is a pool. I take off, circling, turning laps and somersaults. I make myself relax, lose the cat-o'-nine-tails that stood between us.

A knock at the door. "Hour's up."

Shriveled, I climb out of the water. My mother gets up, wraps me in a towel and I sit on the edge of the cot, resting while she dresses. I suck water from the towel and try not to look while she loads herself back into her costume.

"Don't worry," she says. "It's not to worry about. It's not you. It's not new."

She pulls herself together and leaves me to dress alone.

"Are you ready for lunch?" she asks as we step out of the bathhouse into the steamy July afternoon. "Let's have ice cream, ice cream all around. Six courses: milk shakes, ice cream sandwiches, spumoni salad, strawberry shortcake, pie à la mode and hot fudge sundaes."

The motel is cheaper than the inn. "Widow's got to watch her wallet." Mama pours herself a fresh glass as soon as we're safely in the room. "My medication," she calls it. "I am a woman who needs her medication. Three times a day in Charlottesville, can you believe that, three times every day." She holds the glass out to me, "Here, take a taste, it won't kill you."

I shake my head.

"Between the sugar in the ice cream and this," Mama, says, tapping the side of her glass, "I'll be lucky not to go into a coma." She lies down on the bed. "A little nap. Just a little nap and we'll be all refreshed. Then we'll have dinner, Tom Turkey." She puts her head on the pillow and is asleep. In the bathroom I wash my hand and arm up to the elbow. Soap and water. Soap and water. I wash until I am burning red, until the skin is raw, until it can get no cleaner without being taken off, boiled and hung up to dry like Grandma's laundry.

My mother lies face down on the white chenille bedspread, her fingers reading the braille rose, the dit-dit-da dashing of Morse code, like a somnambulist. My eyes grow heavy and I lie next to her. Her arm hooked around me. Mama and her boy in a close knot. In the safety of her sleep, I sleep. When I wake she is in the bathroom with the door closed behind her. I can hear the whining of the hot and cold taps as much water is poured. Finally she emerges, renewed, her face portrait-pink, her dinner dress white silk, always white. She says it allows her to glow, allows her color to come out, her light to shine. I sit up. She comes at me with a wet comb. I stand and she tucks my shirt in, efficiently and expertly dipping her hands into my pants, tugging my tails all the way down.

"Did you sleep?" she asks. "Dream a pleasant dream?" She speaks as if singing, as if writing herself little lyrics, little lines.

I shake my head.

She seems fine, like herself, like she's always been, exactly as I remembered her. Me, it must be me, my stomach turns. It was I who slipped through God's graces and did such a terrible thing. My hand beats, pulses, throbs with the reminder and yet she seems without symptoms. I want to lift her dress, to snake my fingers, my eyes, into what lies in that lost location, searching to see if, beneath its protective costume, its mask, it is truly unaffected, unamused, or whether it is indeed weeping, seeping from the events. She acts as if everything is as it always has been, as if she is still my mother and I, her son.

We drive to the grand country inn, sneak up the stairs and then descend for dinner, sweep down the steps playing the game of paying guests. Everywhere there are men and women of opportunity and affluence, heroes and heroines who come here as George Washington did, to soak themselves, to let the waters work their wonders. Behind them trail the grandchildren; little girls with flowered dresses and boys in jackets and ties. Angry and ashamed, I tuck my shirt in tighter, sweep my hair over to the side.

As we go toward the dining room I feel the appetite of a carnivore rise, I smell juices dripping, can nearly suck the greasy grizzle, the bittersweet droppings of so many meats. It is as though I've been kept from my feed for lengths of days and nights although I quite clearly remember the glazed ham from the night before, the pineapple chunks, bright red cherries. But now the night before is the year before, the lifetime before, so much time has passed, so much has happened. I go into the dining room growling with the full hunger of a man.

Mama orders for me. When my plate arrives I can't hold my knife, can't grip it without crying, "my hand, my hand." Mama shushes me. Crippled, I will have to learn to write with a pencil between my teeth, a lick of lead steered by my tongue.

Mama clucks, then leans over and cuts everything into pieces.

"Can you manage now?" she asks, handing the fork back to me.

I nod. Flavor. Food comes alive in my mouth, on my tongue, more alive than I. The dull flesh of the turkey, stringy, as though one could shred a bird, pull him apart string by string, the taut berry tang of cranberry compote, stewed and soaked in lemon and sugar, a hearty woody walnut stuffing with simmered mushrooms, carrots, celery and mixed nuts, the high-rise biscuit filled with steam. I dip myself into the food, as though I've never eaten before, never truly tasted.

And since that night, I have not taken the most pilgrim holiday, the Thanksgiving meal, without conjuring the acts of that day, that out-of-season afternoon, that simmering July, without wondering exactly what it is one gives thanks for. Thanks that my life, my mortal soul was spared, that in her merciless need, she didn't duck me under, dip me down below the water line, and hold my head there while I sucked her, sucked water, drowning me in her desire.

I fall far in love with my food, bewildered by my appetite, curious that I am able to eat at all, to enjoy. But I do enjoy, pure pleasure in each fork raised to my mouth. I am eating and loving it. I look around at the other people. Right there at the table, I am growing, turning more complex. I push some things down and let others come to the surface. There is no point to certain things. I am different from these people and will always be different. I love Mama and I hate them. I hate Mama and I love them. I love all of them and Mama and I hate myself. I hate myself. I am a bad boy.

A man appears at the table. A big man, a large man with a belly and a moustache, Santa Claus's brother.

"Can you bear for me to introduce myself?" he asks in long, drawn-out tones.

Mama looks up, blotting her lips with a napkin.

"I'm Verell Reed from Lynchburg, Virginia. I'm an insurance salesman. This hotel is something I insure."

Mama introduces herself, shaking the man's hand, "And this," she says introducing me, "is my boy."

"And you're a fine boy. Why don't I buy you a hot fudge sundae. It's not turkey dinner without dessert."

Mama and I look at each other. "No ice cream," we say simultaneously. He looks at us like we're crazy. I look away.

"Whatever you do, no ice cream," Mama says again.

I scream. You scream. We all scream.

"Join us for coffee," she says to the man. "Brandy," she calls to the waiter. My shoes are off. Under the table, my feet, my toes are rubbing the wooden floor. Everything is sensation. Mama dips her nose into the brandy glass. They talk. I don't listen to what they say. I am exhausted, broken off, floating. I am a boy, still a boy. Tired boy. Stunned boy. A boy who has just killed some part of himself.

The band begins to play. People start to dance.

"Shall we?" Verell ask my mother.

Her moment, her element. "Of course," she says.

Verell turns, puts his hand out to me. "And you," he says. "Do you dance as well?"

I don't answer.

"Like a prince," Mama says. "He dances like a prince." And they each take a hand and the three of us go onto the floor and I'm between them with my stocking feet on Verell's shoes and Mama's dress pressed against me. Like the middle of an Oreo, I am the cream. Verell presses closer to Mama and she's leaning into him, and soon there is no room for me. Verell and Mama take off, dancing, and I go back and put my head down on the table. I watch them through my water glass;

small and far away like the wind-up couple on a music box. I close my eyes, I hear the music, the band is in my head. I sleep.

Someone is half-carrying me. We are in the parking lot.

"I could drive you back to your motel or we could go up to my room," Verell says. "I could get a cot for the kid."

"We'll be fine. It was a lovely evening, lovely to meet you, lovely to dance."

He kisses Mama on the cheek, tries to kiss her on the lips but she turns away, closes the car door, locks it. Verell blows drunken kisses as we back away.

"Alone at last," she says. "How horrible. How horrible that was. Are you sleeping? Are you in the land of dreamy dreams?"

"No."

I am awake. It is very dark, our motel is down the road ahead of us, the flaming orange "Vacancy" sign like a beacon drawing us home.

"Can you make it in all right?"

"Ummhumm." I trip over the curb, fall down. Mama laughs, thinks it is a joke. I tear my shirt and skin my palms, only I don't know it yet, don't know it until we get inside, into the light.

There is one bed, one big bed. I am beyond worry, care. I have no fear that what happened before will repeat itself. I strip down to my underwear and lie on the bed. The pillow is deep. I don't know who I am or where I am. The light in the bathroom is off. Mama, dressed in a nightgown, moves towards me, a ghost. She is in the bed and I am awake, suddenly awake, fully alert.

Her arm hooks around me. "Sleep tight," she whispers.

No sleep, no rest. No slumber.

Mama and her boy in a close knot. Mama's arms at rest around me. In my arm there is a tingling, a clear memory of her on my fist, Mama fitted around me and me pushing harder and harder into her, against her. I reach beneath the blankets, and touch myself with my other hand. I lie awake until the sun comes up and then sleep in the seeming safety of early light until Mama kisses me, wakes me for breakfast and disappears into the bathroom.

The sheets are peeled back and in the middle of the pit where Mama had lain there is a bright blush of red, a thick streak of blood.

"Blood," I scream. "There's blood."

She is in the bathroom. I hear the whining of the hot and cold taps. My fault. All my fault.

"My curse," Mama says through the bathroom door. "It's my curse."

And then the door opens and she appears, fully dressed, made for the day. "Did you sleep? Dream a pleasant dream?" She asks again, still speaking as if singing. She is fine, like herself, like she has always been. Were it not for my sore hand, I would think it had not happened at all. I would think that it was something that had leapt out of me, a bit of my imagination. Me. It must be me. My stomach turns.

"Today," she says, "I'll go with the ladies and you go with the men. I need to be taken care of."

I don't respond, I have nothing to say.

"You look a little pale, do you need some lipstick?"

Her hand dips under her dress, her legs bow slightly, she pulls out fingers dipped in rust. She paints blood across my lips.

At breakfast I can't eat. The carnivore from the night before has vanished, withered and returned to its cage.

"We should go home. Grandma will wonder where we've been, what we're doing," I say, wanting a way out.

"This afternoon," Mama says. "After the baths."

It couldn't happen again. I wouldn't allow it. I would do something, I didn't know what.

Back to the park by the inn, the baths, the bubbling springs. This time at the other bathhouse, the one divided into male and female. I am relieved. I am taking a bath without Mama.

"Otis will be out for the boy," the woman behind the desk tells Mama.

"Be good," Mama says, going through the door marked "Women." "See you in an hour or so."

"Otis will show you the way," the woman behind the desk says, introducing me to a man dressed like a baker, all in white. "His ma's next door," the woman tells Otis. Otis blinks. He is skinny and bald, not a twig of hair on him. On his arm is a green tattoo—a woman in a grass skirt. Except for the tattoo, everything, including his shoes, is white.

I follow him through a door. Naked men. I've never seen naked men before. It is worse than I could have imagined. I want Mama, I don't care what she makes me do.

"Put your clothes in here," Otis says, showing me a locker. "I'll get your bath."

Naked, everyone except Otis is naked. I am a boy, a small boy, a baby boy, clean and white. Dark monsters. I look at them, at the mats of hair from where they come, the bellies that drop down over them. I hope it will never happen to me. The way I am. I want to be the way I am for the rest of my life.

Otis takes me to my tub. It is a regular bath, narrow and long. I lie in the water; it is warm. I can see other men in their baths, men in the middle of the room being pounded on by men like Otis, men in white, who plunge their hands into flesh and knead it like dough. The men lie there taking it, blank-faced. Their eyes are closed. It is best not to watch. I shut my eyes.

Otis comes for me. "Can't have you shrivel up, what would your ma say." I climb out of the tub and he wraps me in a sheet, makes me into a mummy and takes me down the hall to an empty room filled with cots. "Pick one," Otis says. "Take a rest. Don't worry, I won't forget you."

I lay on the cot. Because I didn't sleep the night before, because the bath was so warm, because I have been so afraid and now am alone, I relax, I fall into a deep sleep.

A man comes up behind me, touches me. At first, because I think it is the same as what I saw in the other room, I do not say anything. I keep my eyes closed as though I am still sleeping. He rubs his hands over me, taking the sheet down. He touches and pretends not to touch. He is over me and he is on me. I am being laid upon. Poof, like a sofa cushion. I can't breathe. I try to turn my head but can't. There is something bristly on my neck, feathers or pins, bristle. There is so much of him, he is so large, that he pours out over me, over the edge of the cot. I am trying to keep my head up, to keep my head from being pressed into the pillow. It is all I can do. If I could breathe, I would scream. His arms are on either side of me, they are thick and hairy—there is no tattoo. He is on me. I can feel the heat of his cock, his thick and ready worm. I hold myself, clenched closed and tight. He is kissing the back of my neck, humping my ass. I cannot breathe. I faint. I feel myself falling away.

I don't remember more. Otis has me by the shoulders, shaking me, waving something strong under my nose. "Don't tell your ma, kid, whatever you do, don't tell your ma. I must have left you in for too long. Did you have anything to eat today? Did you have breakfast? Here, eat this." A candy bar, chocolate and caramel and nuts. He holds a glass of water for me. "Drink," he says. "Drink some more, swallow. Haven't ever had a kid go out on me like that before. You really scared me. Scared me." Otis helps me dress and I sit in the office with him until he is sure I won't faint again, won't fall out from under, then he lets me go. I run. I run out of the building and into the park. It is a sunny day. A bright and sunny day. The sun is high. There is a pool in the middle of the park. There are children in the pool. I watch them. I run up and down the length of the fence that goes around the pool. I am running and barking like a dog.

Mama comes. She comes out of the bathhouse looking radiant. She buys us ice cream and we sit on a bench looking at the pool, the park, and back at the bath house.

A man comes out, a big man with a moustache, Verell Reed. Mama waves. He looks at us, flushes red, then turns and hurries away. I begin to cry. The ice cream falls off the cone.

"Don't worry," Mama says. "There's always more, there's always more where that came from."

I am crying, weeping, wailing. People are beginning to watch, to wonder. Mama tells me to stop. I can't stop. There is no going back. Mama takes me to the car and we drive back to Grandma's house. I cry the whole way home.

"Stop," Mama says. "Stop, you're driving me over. Stop, boy, stop. You're driving me."

Mama is dead.

The telephone rings, Grandma answers it, listens then hangs up, turns to me and says, "She went over, off the road at the panoramic view, by the steakhouse. She's dead."

A bomb has been dropped. We're all dead only I don't know it yet. There is nothing left. I am alone, all alone. She has left me here with this woman who will keep me only because it would be more embarrassing not to.

The howling begins. A wail. A siren that never goes off, only grows distant and then more near, a siren that warbles within me, deafening me. And when they ask, I tell them I am an orphan raised from birth by my grandmother, my mother's mother. Orphan.

THE PATIENT

I had a rambling apartment in Brooklyn and I fucked my girlfriend Jody in every part of it. So did a lot of other people. One time, I came home, she was going at it with this saggy old dyke that had a cane. The dyke was on her knees and her flesh hung off her in folds. She had her mouth buried in Jody's bush. Communing there. She had one hand on Jody's ass and the other resting on a cane that she held out to the side.

When I came closer, Jody looked at me and smiled, her tiny perfect teeth like miniature Chiclets dancing in her lovely face. Jody winked at me, then pushed The Crone's face out of her crotch and said to her: "Millicent, this is my boyfriend Rob."

Millicent's fleshy mouth was sparkling with Jody's girl dew as she grinned up at me. And her gnarled hand, the one resting on the cane's carved head, did this weird squeezing motion. It was the most revolting thing I've ever seen in my life.

I got a hard-on right away.

"You don't mind, baby, do you?" Jody said, tilting her head and opening her eyes wide at me.

I just grunted, went to stand behind Jody, rubbed against her bare ass and sniffed at the back of her neck.

By now, Jody had brought The Crone's face back into her crotch. With one hand she reached back and unzipped me.

"That's my boy," Jody said, taking my cock and wedging it into her ass.

Jody was exceptional in many ways. Not least of these her ability to climax from being fucked in the ass. Even without clit stimulation. Of course, in this instance, she had a lot of that going on. That Crone's tongue was like some weird reptile's, darting rapidly, blue and hard. It must have worked wonders though. Or I did. Jody came so violently, she fell forward onto the floor, causing me to lose my balance and land right on top of The Crone.

And so, I fucked The Crone too. It was one of the most horrible things I ever experienced. I don't think she'd had anything in there, including a tampon, in a good decade. The woman had to be pushing sixty. She was dry as a bone as I wedged my way in.

Jody managed to get over her waves of coming and was sitting up now. She rubbed her hand between her legs, then reached down and applied this moisture onto The Crone's snatch. This facilitated things a great deal. And for some reason, caused The Crone to start laughing. The whole flesh sack of her started trembling with this laughter. Which made me shoot into her. Hard. Seeing silver spots in front of my eyes.

I don't know what happened then. I probably went and scrubbed my cock with a Brillo pad. And Jody did God knows what. She had this way with all these horrible people she fucked. She'd make them feel glad for getting used like disposable sets of genitals. Glad for never even getting acknowledged by Jody if and when she ran into them somewhere. She was that kind of girl.

She was leggy with no tits and red hair that hugged her little head. She had an acrobat's body and a nympho's insatiability. But she wasn't quite a nympho. She was a doctor. Or at least, on her way to being one.

Some weeks, she shot speed and studied those neuropsych tomes for days on end. She had such focus. Pausing only to jerk off and suck her thumb. I wasn't allowed to fuck her during these jags. Then though, when she'd passed some test with flying colors, she'd go on a fuck binge. She'd take me along to sex clubs where she'd sit in these rooms sucking her thumb and playing with herself and looking twelve.

Everyone went nuts for her. Men, women, *anything*, tried to fuck her. But she'd just sit there jerking off and watching. She made me suck dicks and fuck monstrous women. She had a dog lick me once. She tied me up. She rammed zucchinis up my ass. She beat me.

She was incredible and I loved her.

The thing that ruined everything had to do with the dyke Crone with the cane.

Somehow, and I don't know how, Jody ran into that old Crone again. God only knows where she'd found her. Some mental clinic at Bellevue on rounds or something. I don't know. But Jody actually ran into her and it transpired The Crone was knocked up. That's right. That old bag had a baby in her and I'd had something to do with it. Well. I'd had everything to do with it. Turns out I was the only guy that'd been up that disused love canal since 1963.

Now you'll get what I'm doing here. When I tell you the rest of it.

So Jody comes back one day and tells me this story. Now Jody, for all her charms, was psycho, so I just thought she'd shot too much speed or something. There was no way that Crone could be pregnant. Just impossible. And I put it out of my mind. Until one day I come home from work and The Crone is in there. In *my* apartment. Lying on *my* bed, wearing only white cotton briefs. She had her large feet propped up on some pillows and Jody was all kitted up in this sexy outfit, solicitously leaning over The Crone. And, you guessed it, that Crone was very obviously knocked up. It was so fucking hideous. Worse even than fucking her. Her nipples were the size of dinner plates and blue veins stood out and throbbed like gorged flower stems.

I mean fuck that, right. I was a nice Jewish boy from Chicago. I made good grades in high school. I loved my high school girlfriend but we broke up right before college. I dated a few different women at Princeton, but none of them moved me very much. Then, once I had a BFA, I got a job in Manhattan working as assistant to Frederico Malodorio, the Italian painter. I started to meet some strange women. And then Jody. She was the daughter of two prominent psychiatrists. She'd dropped out of Vassar but then finally finished up premed at Columbia and now was at Cornell. Right away I could tell she had a few screws loose, but I'd never met anyone like her. And I just went with it. Now, we'd been together a year and it was stormy but good. Good until this whole Crone thing happened.

Jody didn't even ask. She just moved The Crone into my apartment. The Crone's girlfriend had kicked her out or something. If you believe a thing like that could even have a girlfriend. And I had to go along with it. I loved Jody.

So in the day I'd go off and work for Frederico. Everything's cool, I'm meeting all these people, women are coming on to me, men are coming on to me, the world is pouring itself over me like honey.

And at night, I go home to my girl and her Crone. At this point, I'm not sure Jody's even showing up at med school. She's stopped shooting speed and even smoking cigarettes, like it's her body that's carrying the thing. She's gone all macrobiotic and she and The Crone sit around reading natural childbirth guides and going to Lamaze classes. Forget about Jody coming out to dinner or a club or something, never mind letting me fuck her.

But that was the thing with Jody. I couldn't say no to her. Even when she's got this knocked-up ninety-year-old lesbian living in my apartment and she's barely talking to me, I love her. I love her with every fiber of my being.

Things kind of degenerated then. The Crone's about to have the kid and Jody's all worried that we don't have enough money to get all the baby things she'll need. Every time I come home from work, she's sold off something else. First it's my mother's engagement ring. I don't even know how she found it. My mother had sent it to me because I was getting ready to pop the question to Jody. That is, before The Crone moved in. Then it's the stereo and VCR and pretty soon she's sold off all the normal furniture and amassed all this baby stuff. Like the whole apartment has become a nursery. I start to think maybe this is too much. No one ever made me feel the way Jody did, but enough's enough.

One day I come home, ready to rip Jody out of there and force her to go outside with me and talk. But The Crone's nowhere in sight and Jody's all kitted up in her red thigh-high stiletto boots and a white bustier with a string of pearls around her neck. And she's on the bed and she opens her arms wide and says, "Baby, I've missed you."

I just melted. I mean, just like that. Like all this horrible weird stuff hadn't happened. Like she was just my girl, my beautiful crazy Jody. I loved the way her tits failed to fill out her bustier. I loved the way the thong in the back separated her moon-crescent butt cheeks. I loved how wet she was when I stuck my fingers inside her. Her whole body arched as I bit her nipple through the bustier. She started ripping my pants off then, frantic, possessed.

I ram myself into her and it's the best feeling I've ever had in my life.

"Baby, I've missed you," I whisper at her, looking in her eyes and gently sliding in and out of her.

"I know," she says.

Things start to build. We haven't done this in so long. I've watched her fawn over that Crone for MONTHS now. It's all welling up in me, like this enormous balloon.

I pull out of her. She peels off one of her boots and flips me over onto my stomach.

"Take this, my love," she says, sticking the heel of the boot in my ass. I come just as the thing rips me. But it's not enough. I need more of her. More and more. I eat her. I devour her. She comes like 590 times.

Even when The Crone gets home later that night, slagging her huge belly in front of her, I almost don't mind. I almost feel warmly toward her and the little being that's kicking up a storm inside her huge old stomach.

And then, two days later, Jody leaves me.

I come home from work. All the nursery furniture's gone. Everything's gone and there's this fucking note. The Crone's gone into labor and they're going to the hospital. Then, they're going to live on their own. With the baby. I shouldn't try to find them. They'll find me. When the time's right.

And that's what did me in. She fucking left me. I loved her. And she left me.

So I guess I lost it a little. I guess I turned up on the maternity ward at the hospital looking for them, trying to figure out which one was the kid. You know how they have that glass partition and all the happy parents stand there gazing through at their little shrively offspring. So I get in there and I'm looking through the glass, trying to pick out which one is the kid, right, trying to stake it out, half expecting to see it with red glowing eyes, like Rosemary's fucking baby or something.

I've got the Colt .45 in my gym bag. Some freak who buys a lot of Frederico's paintings, he's like a gun smuggler always showing off about it. Bringing Frederico these fucking unbelievable weapons that Frederico just leaves lying around like chick magnets. So I just took one.

So I'm standing in the maternity ward with this Colt .45 in the gym bag. I want to make this big. And I want Jody to see. I want her to pay attention to this.

I unzip my gym bag and take the thing out. All these people start shrieking like you hear in disaster movies. High-pitched porcine squeals. Even if I wasn't 100 percent sure about doing it, the sound of those squeals would have decided me. I wedge the black muzzle against my temple and pull the trigger.

So next thing I know, right, I'm awake. I don't remember at first. I'm just in this white room. There's tubes in my arms and a tent over my bed. But it all comes flooding back pretty quickly. And then there are eight million doctors swarming around me. Marveling over me. The bullet traversed my frontal lobe and went out my right temple, but I'm fine. I'm better than I ever was, actually. They tell me I've in effect lobotomized myself. And, I understand perfectly that this should be disastrous. I should be upset. But I'm at peace. I see more of Jody than I ever did. She's a resident now. Neuropsych. I'm her patient.

As for the kid, thank God, it's a boy.

Because I know better than most, girls are trouble.

BUCKLE BUNNIES

"Charlie used to be able to call up Cocksucker any time of day and say, 'Cocksucker, come over here and suck my cock,' " a cowboy named Jason told me. "Cocksucker really liked Charlie," he added fondly. "She liked him a lot."

This is a story about women in rodeo. It's not about the women who rope calves or race horses around barrels, or these days, get tossed off bulls for a living. That's another story altogether. This is a story about the women who follow rodeo, or more specifically, the women who follow rodeo cowboys.

There's Nasty Wendy, TJ, Tammy, and Angie. There's a girl called Fisheyes, whom the cowboys told me I would know on sight. In Canada, there's someone called Motorcross, for no reason that anybody remembers. There's Hoe Down, who's handy with a MasterCard, and Dawn, who will spend a week's paycheck on a bullrider, if he asks her to. There's a little woman in Montana named Andrea, whom a cowboy can always go home with at the end of the night, if he hasn't found anyone better. And there are the famous Clarksville, Texas, girls: Peterbelly, Blondysocks, Grapenuts, Copenhagen, Tiny Tim, Hammerhead, Skoals-a-Little, and Cocksucker, who likes Charlie a lot.

Buckle Bunnies like cowboys enough to screw random ones rapaciously, often several at a time, and then provide breakfast, laundry services, telephones, and medical attention the next morning. They

like cowboys enough to pay their rodeo entry fees, which can run anywhere from $50 to $500, depending on the prestige of the event.

Buckle Bunnies travel. They hang out behind the bucking chutes at
every rodeo with six packs and ice packs, waiting for the cowboys to
finish tempting death in the ring. They stand in pairs at country bars,
laughing crazily, as if standing with a girlfriend in a strange bar is the
most fun a person can have in this life. They fill arenas with their tight
jeans, their pink blouses with the geometric holes cut out of the backs,
and their Loni Anderson hair. When the rodeo is over the bullriders
limp out of the ring with the adrenaline rush of firing-squad survivors,
grabbing beers and girls. And every night the grabbed girls shriek and
laugh, as if all of this attention is a big fat surprise.

"If you're a top cowboy," Jason said, "getting laid is never a
problem."

"What if you're not a top cowboy?"

"It's still not a problem. It's just that the top cowboys have more
selection."

A cowboy's trophy belt buckle is engraved with every kind of necessary
proof. "Champion Bullrider," it might read, "San Antonio Stock Show
and Rodeo, 1993." It's the shape of a shield and a little bigger than a
nice bar of soap. Since it's a hideous offense to wear a buckle that you
didn't earn yourself, it's a pretty safe way to tell quickly who matters
and who doesn't.

A cowboy will pass through a crowd with one hand casually on his
buckle, touching it and shifting it, like it's a satellite dish emitting and
receiving information. Which, of course, it is. The buckle is conve-
niently portable, a trophy that only comes off when the jeans come off,
at which point its work is done, anyhow. Girls in bars kneel or squat
in front of guys to read the buckles closely, a gesture rich with promise
for later. In a sport without any protection, a buckle is the only point
of invulnerability on a cowboy's body. And in a community where divorce and desertion are epidemic, a buckle is the only token of real
worth.

One morning, bored in San Antonio, I called sixty-eight local pawn
shops and had this conversation sixty-eight times: "Hi. Do you have
any rodeo belt buckles in stock?"

"No, ma'am, we sure don't."

"How about wedding rings?"

"Yes, ma'am, we've got hundreds of wedding rings."

It means something to be given a belt buckle. Wives get belt buckles. Sweethearts get belt buckles. Mothers get belt buckles. Buckle Bunnies, generally, only get cowboys. But a buckle can redeem a woman, too. Many rodeo wives and girlfriends are ex–Buckle Bunnies, promoted out of trashhood to a moral high ground from which they can scorn the whores below. And many Buckle Bunnies are ex–rodeo wives, who lost their marriages and their standing and are back in the bars, scanning the buckles for a different future.

I once asked a bullrider named Mel to describe the perfect wife. "Tall, blond, long legs," he said, "great job, great cook, great mother." Then I asked him to describe a typical Buckle Bunny. He said, "That's a piece of trash. You put it outside your window when you're done with it, and someone else will pick it up." (Incidentally, when asked to describe the perfect husband, Mel said, "Great attitude. Not a woman hater." Luckily for Mel, there are no height or salary requirements for men.)

A woman involved with rodeo cowboys can either be the wife who gets cheated on or the woman who has one-night stands with married guys. And while it may seem like a choice between nothing and not much, the distinction between Buckle Bunny and buckle holder means everything. Still, not everyone gets it.

Several cowboys told me proudly, "Bunnies aren't after the buckles. They're after what's under the buckles."

Hey, guys? Bullshit. It's the buckle, stupid.

I could have used a buckle myself, because the Bunnies didn't want to talk to me. I was only in Texas for a few days before word got around that I was asking folks about getting around. It's a small world for a big state. I was in Uvalde, interviewing a candidate in a bar when a woman came running over. "Don't talk to her!" she yelled, pointing at me. "She's doing a story about Buckle Bunnies!" Then she ran back out onto the dance floor. Her friend watched, then turned to me. "A few more drinks and she'll be taking her shirt off," she said sadly, then walked away. She wouldn't give me her name.

"You only came over because someone told you I was a Buckle Bunny," hissed a girl in the same bar.

I had some trouble denying this convincingly.

She went on. "Well, you can write whatever you want, but I think there's enough wrong with the world that we don't have to worry about other people's business. And if a girl wants to run around, or die of a disease, then that's her business. And I don't care what people think about me."

Well, I do. And she hated me. Finding a woman who wants to talk about her experiences as a Buckle Bunny is like finding a Frenchman who wants to talk about his experiences as a Nazi collaborator.

But guess what? Getting the cowboys to talk was no problem at all. In San Antonio, I met Kirby, a bareback rider who wanted nothing more out of life than to set me straight. "We don't call them Buckle Bunnies anymore," he said. "That's a '70s expression. These days, we call them good old dirty-legged rodeo whores."

Kirby had some swell stories. He sought me out one night in Cowboy Corner to tell me his favorite Buckle Bunny moment. It was about this girl in Somerville, Texas, who everyone tried to screw, and how he chased her down a road and caught her finally, and they screwed in the middle of the highway until a car came and scared her and she ran off into a barbed wire fence and cut her titties all up. Kirby was a million laughs.

I changed my approach. "I'm doing a story about Buckle Bunnies," I started telling women, dropping the little Texas two-step of innuendo and evasion. "Can you tell me anything about them?"

They were delighted to talk. Every woman had an alibi for why she herself was legitimately at the rodeo. Either she was a cowboy's wife or girlfriend, or a civic volunteer, or a former barrel racer, or the daughter of an old bullrider, or a rodeo queen from 1985. And while she may only date cowboys and while she may have traveled a great distance to get there that night, she certainly was no Buckle Bunny herself.

When I asked women if they would point out who in the room was a Buckle Bunny, it turned into a cross fire of gossip, a farce of indictments from across the bar. Two unattached girls told me heatedly that you can always tell the Buckle Bunnies because they're the ones that never have boyfriends. Cheryl, a heavily made-up girl in a rodeo parking lot, told me you can always tell Buckle Bunnies because they're the ones all dressed up fancy to walk around in cowshit. Vicki, in a hot pink shirt so small it might have been a necklace, said, "You can always tell a Buckle Bunny by the way she dresses."

Vicki also told me that she and her friend Christy were not themselves Buckle Bunnies, but they play them as extras in the movie *8 Seconds*. Shannon in Houston said she thought Buckle Bunnies were slutty out of insecurity, and when I didn't respond she said, "Don't you think so? I mean, to sleep with someone? You don't think so?"

Two women in San Antonio wouldn't give me their names: One, because she's a rodeo official; the other, because she's the ex-wife of a well-known bullrider. The ex-wife, after a half hour, admitted that five years ago she'd been "the biggest Buckle Bunny on the face of the earth." When I asked her to define the expression, she said, "A Buckle Bunny doesn't care about a guy's name or anything except that he's a top cowboy. She'll fuck him for one night, and never see him again."

"Was that you five years ago?" I asked, and she froze, like a perjurer trapped on the stand.

"No," she said finally. "See, I knew all those guys."

I asked Vicki if women in rodeo ever get hurt or raped. She said, "It doesn't happen." Doesn't happen? "Well, if you're stupid enough to go to a motel with guys you don't know, then you're a Buckle Bunny and you get what you deserve."

The next day, I called the local Planned Parenthood to ask about women's issues in cowboy country. "This is not cowboy country," someone named JoAnn told me. "That's a misconception about San Antonio." Then Little Miss Conception went on to say that it did sound to her like a girl who goes home with strangers gets what she deserves.

Then I called Joyce at the battered women's shelter, and she said they get more victims of truckers than victims of cowboys. Then I called the courthouse to ask about divorce rates, and Mr. Garcia told me he thought rodeo marriages break up so often because cowboys have sex with their horses.

Then I called my sister to complain that the only thing a woman can be in Texas is somebody's good girl or somebody's bad girl. "Or somebody's governor," she added.

Then I called a friend in Philadelphia and she told me to watch what

I wrote, unless I wanted to become the Salmon Rushdie of rodeo. She called my story "The San-Antonic Verses."

On my last night in San Antonio, I went to a place called Midnight Rodeo—one of those strange Texas bars big as Kmart, sunk in some epic parking lot. I met Tonya, who was born on an Austin ranch, but now worked in the city. She was smart and funny and her hair wasn't big. I asked her about cowboys, and she told it straight. "None of them are worth a shit," she said. "They can't keep a job. They cheat on their wives. They're never home. They're lazy, and you can't trust them. None of them are worth one shit."

As a visual aid, good old dirty-legged Kirby came over just then. He was staggeringly drunk, and he wanted to talk to me some more about girls. "I got a beautiful girl I'll probably marry someday," he said. "Sometimes I like being nice to girls, like, 'Hey, how ya' doing, nice to meet you.' Other times, I just go around like, 'Fuck you, bitch! Suck my fucking dick!' "

I was writing all of this down. "You're going to make someone a great husband someday," I said.

Kirby considered this. Then he howled, "Hey! I'm young, I'm dumb, and I'm havin' fun!" Suddenly, he noticed my new friend Tonya. "Wanna dance?" he asked her.

She looked up at him and smiled slowly. "Okay," she said. "Sure."

Later, I drove to Schertz to drink at the Blue Bonnet Palace, a great big place with a great big idea: Live Bullriding! Inside the bar! I sat with the rodeo wives and watched the bulls circle that small ring like sharks. Kids hung on the fences, swinging like bait. Oddly, nobody was killed. Bulls are scary. So are rodeo wives.

An arch-blond named Lola told me about how she, an innocent, was deceived by Nasty Wendy, a legendary Buckle Bunny. "For a whole year I thought she was my friend," Lola said. "I didn't know she was a whore. I even tried to warn her that there are a lot of whores in this business, and to be careful to stay away from girls like that, but she fooled me."

Lola was full of shit. Lola's been around rodeo for years. I'd been in Texas three days, and I already knew all about Nasty Wendy, who is famous for only sleeping with the current top fifteen bullriders in the country. The National Finals Rodeo Bulletin is known as Wendy's black book. She's a legend, for Christ's sake.

Jennifer, a twenty-year-old rodeo wife, told me, "Sometimes I'll be in a bar with my husband, Beau, and some girl I've never seen before will run over and hug him and say, 'Hi, Beau, remember me from Denver?' But he doesn't even know those girls. They just think they know him because they recognize his name."

Jennifer seemed happy with this answer.

Later, I was interviewing a bullrider named Ronnie, when the bartender asked him, "Do you think all women should be treated with respect?"

"Every woman should be treated with respect," Ronnie said.

"What about Buckle Bunnies?" I asked.

"That's different. Buckle Bunnies don't count."

Hell, who wants not to count? Sluts? Whores? Trash? Who wants to sign up for that mailing list? For all the cowboy talk about the freedom of the lifestyle, rodeo is basically a small town on the move, a road show of the same bulls, the same cowboys, the same bars, the same girls. It's a circus, and everyone knows you don't see the world when you run away with the circus. You just see the inside of the same grimy circus tent from Beaumont to Buffalo and back.

In a community where the only liberal thing around is the use of makeup, it's not surprising that no woman is ready to stand up and say it loud, I'm a dirty-legged rodeo whore, and I'm proud. Which is a shame, because they subsidize the whole show. Without their cash and ass, the sport could not exist as it does, and if Buckle Bunnies ever unionized, the changes would come fast and hard.

But there's no danger of this. The ethic of rodeo forbids boat-rocking from any angle, and the urge to conform shows up in weird ways. One night in Houston, the announcer asked the 58,000 spectators, "Is anyone here not from Texas?" A dead silence fell over the Astrodome. It was exactly as if he'd asked, "Who here likes taking it up the ass?" If there were any among us who were guilty, we weren't talking. I sure didn't volunteer. I may be from out of town, but I'm not stupid. When in Houston, Ich bin eine Texan.

A bullrider named Will said to me one night, "Buckle Bunnies get a bad rap. But when you're a thousand miles from home and broke and hurt, and it's two-thirty A.M. in Iowa, and the bar is closing, they're pretty nice to have around."

A kind statement, sure, but this is the same Will who described his girl-selecting process to me in scientific detail, finishing it up by saying that if he's still solo at closing time, "It's time to change weight class." He pointed to a chubby girl across the bar and said, "If I really needed a place to stay tonight, that would be my target, right there."

"So go talk to her," I said.

"You don't want to get one too early," his friend explained. "Then you gotta buy her a beer."

The older guys seemed capable of greater generosity. Mike, who's thirty-seven and still riding bulls against all advice, calls the dedicated Bunnies "campaigners" and "solid sons-of-bucks." He told me about being rescued in Canada by a girl when his friends had left him, broke and broken-ribbed, after a rodeo. She took him home, and the next morning her mother came into the bedroom to ask how they wanted their eggs. Mother and daughter took care of Mike for a week, and then lent him the money to fly back to Midland, Texas. They still send a Christmas card every year. He said campaigners will do anything for anyone, and it's not all about sex. It's about something weirder than that, about some fascination with providing the most macho guys on earth with the only brand of nurturing they will accept: a one-night marriage.

Will went with me to Houston, to make sure I got into the Chute Club, the bar under the Astrodome where the big-name Buckle Bunnies would absolutely be hanging around. A pretty, pregnant woman called Will over. While they talked, I read a note on the bulletin board. "Jerome Davis," it said. "We are here. Where are you? Meet us at the Chute Club entrance one hour after the rodeo is over. Love, Tiffany, Cindy, Linda, Pat, and Kelly. Think you can handle this?"

Will kissed the pregnant woman, and came back over. "That was Wendy," he said under his breath. Nasty Wendy, of the National Finals Rodeo top fifteen. I felt like I'd seen God.

Around midnight, Wendy and a handful of the most legendary Buckle Bunnies in Texas invited me to play poker with them at the Holiday Inn bar. I can't relate much of what happened because my permission to be there was a fragile thing, hinging on my emphatic promises of no names and no questions. I also can't remember a lot since we were drinking pretty seriously.

Someone made a toast, "To bulls that buck and girls that . . . dance good."

I told a joke, "How come Texas never floated away into the Gulf of Mexico? Because Oklahoma sucks so much."

I had a spectacular losing streak. When I ran out of money, Wendy paid my ante and TJ kept dealing me in. The place was packed with cowboys, but it was all women at the table, with their smart bets, cigarettes, and inside jokes.

The Holiday Inn campaigners were wonderfully content, the only women I met around rodeo who weren't nervous about something. By late night, the rodeo wives were all at home, worrying about their marriages, and the young bunnies were in scattered hotel rooms working hard. The campaigners were left in the calm company of their own people. And if a cowboy stopped by the card table to say hello, he would sit on the edge of someone's chair and get a warm, wifely kiss. He would watch the poker game for a while. Then one of the most famous Buckle Bunnies in Texas might lean forward and show him her cards, easily, comfortably, as if she held no secrets in that hand at all.

PLACEDO JUNCTION

Where we lived, "Where to tonight?" didn't have many answers. Home was a mud field, an oil camp where derricks were trees and the miles between houses meant talk to your own self for someone to talk to.

Mother said how many days you managed to get through sane in that heat was a mark of how strong you were getting to be. Or worn down.

Nothing had a shine in Placedo. Nothing but Earl's, that is, a roadhouse whose neon made nighttime a darkness you needn't be lonely because of.

Earl's unopened was dank and boarded and shuttered but Earl's with the lights on was where you wanted to be. If you'd never been farther than just up the road or done more than get through a day, then "Earl's" blinking red in a circle of blood-colored gravel caused your heart to beat faster.

Pulling into Earl's meant Mother checked her lips in the mirror on the back of the visor, said "Look at who's talking," when Eugene told her it looked as if who she cared how she looked to was some man other than that sweet-faced husband who'd driven her there.

Mother just laughed. She said slicked-back hair and python boots so high in the heel my father had to stoop when he danced took the How-do-I-look? prize.

They did like to dance, and I liked to watch them on a Saturday night, Eugene looking bored and tight and Mother looking dazed from how she had to wait for signs from Eugene's hands, my father being a slow smooth dancer with a snakelike style that made it seem his feet were hardly moving. But they were.

Mother wore slippers that had to be kicked off to dance in, open-toed, low-vamped red things her younger sister Lona asked to borrow and her older sister Martha called "sin shoes."

There wasn't much sin in Placedo. Martha said a woman was a fool to be tempted, everyone watching to see if she was, when she was, and by whom.

Earl's made it hard not to be. "That long-backed oil field worker at the end of the bar," Lona said, "the one with a plain gold band stuffed down in the bottom of his pocket and 'No place to go but back home' in his eyes? The one who was lifting his glass up and smiling at you? That oil field worker looked a whole lot better than a book on a couch and a ceiling you knew every corrugated inch of."

Lona said romance was just a handful of dimes, some cowboy with just enough paycheck to buy you a beer, just enough style to roll you a smoke and light it on the side of his thumb, a rodeo rider in a hand-tooled belt that read "Sonny," on his way up to Austin who wanted to know what a sweet thing like you could be doing in a bad place like Earl's.

It wasn't really that bad. Smoke and drink and the perfume of women with men they didn't belong with made Earl's off limits to some and a magnet to others. Mother said the women looked lovely because of how wanted they were hoping to be and the men looked better.

Martha didn't buy it. She said nights you reached out and steadied yourself at the bar, nights Earl helped you into your truck and pointed which direction your home was, added your name to that pact Earl had signed with the devil when he opened a roadhouse. She said Mother and Eugene shouldn't take their daughter to a place where the stories were lies and the smoke wasn't only tobacco.

Eugene and Mother got angry. Eugene said Earl was a friend who gave a man credit when he didn't have any money and held out a Zippo for a woman when nobody noticed that she needed a light. Mother said taking her daughter to Earl's was a damned sight better than leaving her alone with a dog on a chain for a friend and protection. She said,

"Thank God for something at the end of the day, even if all that something happens to be is a roadhouse called Earl's."

Martha took it back. She had to since all that she had in this life was her family. Mother said Martha unloved was a genuine waste but Lona unloved was just one more roughneck with cellophane flowers and a box full of candy and a grin on his face delayed by an engine burned out from how fast he'd been driving there to give her those things.

Long bare legs hiked up on the dash of a truck pulled over in the dark—you could make a bet were Lona's. And somebody's husband was with her. Or a boy raised to be sinless who wasn't anymore. No one was not good enough. Mother said if Lona couldn't love you then nobody could. "All it takes is a match held out to her Lucky. A Stetson lifted up above a genuine smile."

On a bad day, Lona said women love men and men let them. Good days, close in the evening and kind in the morning, a good-bye kiss she wouldn't be able to say wasn't love was enough.

It had to be enough. Mother said you never got used to no sound in Placedo, to no one knocking on your door but a stranger, the driver of a car left idling who was looking for some place you'd never heard of, a stranger you'd gladly give a glass of iced tea to and directions, if you could, and a sandwich and a chair in the shade and your own life story, if that stranger was willing to listen.

In the place where we lived, small pleasures were worth what in some other place greater pleasures would have been. Some big place like Houston. Or Nuevo Laredo.

My father used to go to Nuevo Laredo. But he didn't go by the time that I knew him. And if he did, he wouldn't take his wife or his daughter. He said north of the border was always much safer than south. Over the border meant you had to watch what you ate and take care where you ate it if a hard rubber tube down your throat and a case of the shakes and the sweats on a narrow white cot in the critical ward at the Holy Mary convent clinic wasn't quite your notion of a good time night on the town.

But if ptomaine didn't matter, if sober was something you weren't able to recall what it felt like to be and your taste buds were fried from the smoke and the weed and the worms at the bottom of too many bottles of Tomo Tequila, then my father had a long list of late-night places he said he'd be pleased to recommend—and you could say that he sent you—dives with a room overhead you could rent for an hour—for whatever reason—back street cantinas where the man behind the bar cut first class anjeo with grain and spiced his tamales so a patron never guessed there was greyhound mixed with the beef.

Eugene said, that dog you laid down the bulk of your paycheck on just a few weeks ago at the dog track, that one-time first-place runner that had given up sprinting for loping on arthritic haunches might well be the meat of a red-hot tamale you were peeling the corn husk back on—that is, if you ate in those places Eugene recommended.

Higher aspirations in Nuevo Laredo were a gold tipped Havana boated over from Cuba and a shot of Jalisco mescal from the wild blue agave to wash down a plate of frijoles borrachos. But you had to have luck with frijoles borrachos. Not much business made a cantina owner cut costs, made a cook scrape back in the pot what another man left in his plate, some cowboy with serious appetite loss and loose gray skin and a cough he hadn't been able to kick so that whoever bought his portion of chili and beans got a little bit more than he paid for. Or more than a little. Eugene said not even Jesus in fourteen carat on a chain around your neck, not even the foot of a rabbit you'd tied to the band of your Stetson made a difference when things stopped going your way in Nuevo Laredo.

Whether it was dog or it was King Ranch grain-fed beef in your enchiladas molé depended on whether the run you were on was a good one or not. Sandbagged cold in an alley with your pockets turned out and your belt and boots stripped off meant luck wasn't yours anymore. But the nails of a perfumed cantina dancer sunk into the curve of your spine as she whispered, "Enamorado," meant you had just enough luck left to make it back over the Cordova Bridge and stay on that side of the Rio Granda del Norte where nothing bad happened.

Eugene said you had to think real hard before crossing that border again, certified King Ranch steak being bound to be better than a greyhound tamale you only had a fifty-fifty chance of surviving.

Earl's of Placedo was safer, he said, people you'd known all your life and beer that was bottled and plates of those ribs Earl swore up and down on a Bible were cut from the side of a top grade longhorn he guaranteed he knew who the breeder of was, ribs in a sauce that was sweeter or hotter depending on how things were going with Earl.

Hard times, Earl dumped in Tabasco. Good times, he dumped in molasses so if you liked it hot, you might find yourself wishing some small bit of trouble would land on his doorstep. Not much. Just a little, since Earl in a funk that he couldn't pull out of was something you didn't want to see. Not if you'd already seen it. Not if you'd been around when his wife ran off with his partner and all of his Guadeloupe National savings.

Earl in the red, Earl in debt to the Lone Star brewery and Southwest Power and Light and the ranch those prime slabs of rib were trucked down from meant Earl's, as you knew it, was over, for a time, the juke box strapped to the back of a repossess truck and the lights turned off when you got there.

Earl said the only way out of a mess like the mess he was in was through hard work and patience and acts of contrition he made himself say, Earl being Placedo's only real Catholic, one with no church to go to since what we had for a church was whatever preacher on the Gulf Coast Evangelist circuit might set up a tent in a field and stay until cash in the donation basket had piled high enough to move on.

All the Catholics that Earl ever talked to were crawlers. Mother explained, when I asked her, that a crawler was a man on his knees on his way down south to a pilgrimage church that he had to pass through Placedo to get to, a Mexican mostly, making his way to a black ash Madonna that was rumored to sew up your wounds, if you dropped a drop of the blood from your knees on the hem of her skirt, a hand-embroidered robe that was stiff as a board from how much blood there was on it.

Earl took a bucket of water and sprinkled the crawler to cool him, walked by his side for a bit of the way, asking questions if the crawler spoke English, crossing himself if he didn't.

Mother said that was a sight. Earl Bodel and a crawler with a two-by-four cross tied onto his back. She said it looked from a distance like Earl was out walking his dog so if you'd been driving that interstate road we were on, and you'd come across Earl and a crawler, you probably would have taken your foot off the pedal, taken your sunglasses off and turned your head around to see what the hell what you'd seen really was.

Earl doing his best to get back on his feet was the roadhouse locked and pads tied onto his knees, not for a crawl but for an all night burning of candles he told us were blessed by a Monterrey Padre and sent

through the mails, candles with saints painted on them, bone-thin Seb-
astions that were run through with arrows, and a brown-skinned Mary
with rhinestone tears glued onto her cheeks that had streamed one
evening, had rolled, Earl swore, in a copious way, down the pale white
beeswax stain of her skin, a sign, according to Earl, that God wanted
Earl's back open. Right away. To make people happy.

Next day, Earl took a loan out and opened for business.

Mother said a sign like that must have had a little something to do
with the Toma Tequila, but Eugene said whatever lifted Earl Bodel
from the dumps was okay by him since the lights turned out when you
pulled up in front meant no place to go and no one to go there with
but those with a surname the same as your own.

Nights when Earl's wasn't open, our family had to drive back home
and make a party out of just who we were, my mother Leda Marie and
my father Eugene, me, and Aunt Martha and Lona.

It wasn't much of a party. My father, pitching a ball to himself in the
dark, said a brother-in-law around the place wouldn't cause any pain—
some fellow a fellow could talk to while Mother was talking with Martha and Lona, whispering in a swing on the porch so a husband felt
lonely and a daughter had to sit very close if she wanted to hear all
the gossip.

You had to scrounge for your gossip in Placedo Junction. Small
things happened. Mother said awful was better than nothing at all.
Third-hand got you through an evening, something someone in some
other town you'd never even been to was said to have done.

The rest of Placedo had Lona to gossip about.

Martha said, "What would they do without Lona?"

Mother said not even half of those circulating stories had a basis
in fact.

Lona was Baby to Mother and Martha. But Eugene said Lona wasn't
getting any younger.

"Come forty or fifty," he said, "that face, on its way between lovely
and gone, won't look quite as good in the flame of a Zippo. Over the
hill means out of the picture, means no one can see you. Over the hill
means you better find yourself some man to hold onto, a good man,
not one of those roughnecks you like to laugh in the low light of
Earl's with."

Lona said good was a hard thing to find in Placedo.

Eugene had a damned fine idea where to look, he told her. If she cared to.

"I'll bet he means Earl's," Mother said. "But behind, not in front of the bar."

Lona just laughed. "Leg to leg on a stool at that bar," she said, "is a small-time thrill that takes a woman's mind off how lonely her life would have been without someplace like it. But who'd want to live there? Earl's is a roadhouse you go to that you can come back from. Not stay in. If a woman married Earl, she'd know every inch of Earl's ceiling. Then where would she go to forget it?"

Eugene said Earl Bodel needed someone to help get his spirits back up, and word had it that a woman he knew named Lona was in charge of the lifted-up-spirits concession in Placedo Texas. At least among the male population.

Lona kept right on brushing and braiding my hair. She told Eugene that Earl wasn't really her type.

Eugene didn't know there was such a thing, he said, a fellow who wasn't her type.

My aunt's aim wasn't good and she missed Eugene with the brush when she threw it. But he reached out and caught it in the mitt of his hand so that Lona had to chase him down to get it back, trip him and land on top of his stretched out body and pound him, laughing, and screaming.

Martha shook her head. She said neighbors, if there'd been any neighbors to hear us, would have called us heathens for the sound of how raucous we were.

Mother just waited it out. She thought nothing of it. She was used to her sister going after her husband, pinning him down or backing him up against a wall so that just to get away my father had to twist Lona's arm behind her back until she begged him for mercy, until finally, she cried.

That was all that she wanted. Lona had to cross that line now and then between not quite enough and a good deal too much, Mother said. After that she was fine, except for how heavy the breathing she did was.

Eugene didn't go back to pitching a ball to himself. My father hooked the heel of his boot on the back of Mother's chair and rested his hands on her shoulders. Mother said, "What is it, honey?" since Eugene hardly ever came close on a night when the sisters were talking.

But he didn't say anything. Nobody did. We all just sat in the dark with the yard lights off, listening to the pumps in the field until Martha told Lona it was time to go home and let the Banderas side of the family grab a little shut-eye.

Eugene checked the air in Martha's tires and Mother said, "Lock all the doors. Don't forget to drive with your high beams on. Watch out for Lona."

There wasn't any danger. Eugene said, "Nothing to fear" was the alternate side of the "Nothing to do" coin.

After the sisters were gone, it was quiet, so a girl in her bed got to hear her mother and father in a swing on the porch say things she might not have heard if they'd known their daughter wasn't sleeping.

Mother told Eugene that Martha had a hard on for Earl. When Eugene said, "Bull," Mother swore on the head of her daughter. She'd watched it develop, she said, the blush when Earl's name was brought into the story, how tongue-tied she was when she saw him. But Earl wasn't looking at Martha since he was too busy looking at Lona, watching to see whether Lona might want anything, a dusted off seat at the bar, or a beer, or a light for a link in the chain of her Luckies. Mother said why Earl couldn't see Martha was a mystery that she couldn't fathom.

Eugene said it wasn't a mystery. All Mother had to do was take a look at the two of her sisters.

That's when Mother said lovely doesn't matter. And ugly doesn't either. She said, "One arm withered makes the other arm stronger."

Eugene didn't know about that, he said, but one thing he did know. And that was that Martha in a union with Earl was a heart-stopping thought. Sun tea. Limeade. No smoking and the neon sign and the lights turned out before nine so that nowhere to go would be all she wrote in a town where a nicotine fit was diversion and a man had to make something up just to say something happened.

When he suggested, he said, if Mother wanted life to go on as she knew it, was just to forget about sisters and give her husband that kiss he'd been wanting all night.

But she wouldn't do it. She said she had Eugene, and Lona had cowboys, but Martha needed someone to be with on nights when a guard dog asleep on the porch of a house you passed in the dark made you feel it was you locked out and not the neighbors locked in.

Martha growing up beside Leda and Lona was an unfair thing, Mother said. Boy after long-backed fired-up boy pulled up to the yard with a rubber in his wallet he was praying was all that would stand between him and one of Martha's two sisters. Mother said all Martha got on those nights was a pat on the back and a "How you doing, Martha," but Leda and Lona, in the cab of a truck with the engine turned off and the soft white light of a Placedo moon up above, got to see what a tattooed snake looked like that could strike when a boy flexed the muscle in an arm he had dared them to put their sweet little fingertips on.

Eugene said he never had heard about the boys with the snakes on their arms and why hadn't Mother told him that story.

She said, "Hush, Eugene." She said if he'd help to fix things up between Martha and Earl, she'd give him that kiss he'd been wanting.

I couldn't hear anymore after that, except the creak of the swing on the porch and what sounded like Eugene's boots coming off, a rustle and a whisper that might have been nothing but a breeze just over from the coast making noise in the branches of a chinaberry tree.

Everything was quiet, and dark where we were, so if you'd been driving that interstate oil field access road, and you'd caught our house in the beam of your headlights, you might not have known we were there. You probably would have kept on driving. Right past us. Like most people did. North. Up to Houston. Or south. To Nuevo Laredo.

HYENA

I saw a giraffe with three tick birds perched in its mane. Every time I tried to take a picture, one of them flirted its tail to the other side, so they were never all three facing in the same direction, as if such order were to them distasteful. I submitted and lowered the camera. They switched about like a chorus line and regarded me with heads cocked this way and that.

The giraffe raised its head as if it were on a string and chomped thoughtfully in my direction. I had sworn to take no more giraffe pictures with my limited film. Film was hard to get in Kenya, and, in the first two months of a semester in wildlife management, I'd taken five rolls just of giraffes feeding. But I couldn't resist photographing the tick birds. They hopped through the mane like crickets in grass. I don't know if they knew that their tree was alive and moving, but the giraffe seemed to lower its head with extra care, for the visitors.

I saw two lion cubs abandoned in a tree, one on top of the other. The larger one, with wisps of mane already starting under his ears, draped his shoulder over the other cub, and they peered out with heads together, massive paws flopped over the crotch of the tree. Pale but complacent, they blinked their gold eyes in dapples of sunlight through the leaves. Perhaps the pride had gone to hunt, leaving their treasure, like pirates, in an old tree. As our van drove nearer, the heads stretched out straight over the monster paws and the cubs tensed together. Then we were past, and I looked back to see them relaxed again, all ears.

The van slowed, then stopped, for a hyena in the road. It was a spotted hyena, the kind people think of when they hear the word "hyena"—a dirty, matted creature, dripping with blood. It must have made a good kill. The prey must have been large enough for the hyena to thrust its whole head in, up to the blocklike shoulders.

This must be why the hyena has such a snake of a neck—so it can delve deep into a dying animal and eat the best parts before thieves chase it away. Hyenas always go first for the softest parts, like entrails, although they have jaws stronger than a lion's, and can eat bones.

This hyena's belly bulged over its legs, and it sat in the road, as if musing, making no attempt to clean off the blood. The slurs that human beings cast at the species fall as useless as gossip about Greek gods. The hyena sat there despite all our encouragement to it to move, and, long past the point when a lion would have slunk peevishly away, we had to slither over a ditch to pass by.

As we drove away, I saw other hyenas stretched flat on the savanna. They were all dipped in blood, but every stain was different. One could see which animal had gnawed at a leg, cheek pressed to bloody flank, or which had held a piece to its chest and embraced it there as it chewed. The prey animal, a wildebeest or a zebra, like one of the human shadows of Hiroshima, was left only in negative, fragmented about the savanna in ghostly prints of blood.

The deathbed was almost clean. A crowd of vultures pounced on and squabbled over pieces of skin ripped free when the hyenas pulled off their parts, and a few insects had already stripped clots of blood from the soaked grass. Nothing else was left.

Spotted hyenas are the sharks of the savanna, superpredators and astounding recyclers of garbage. They hunt in large, giggling groups, running alongside their prey and eating chunks of its flesh until it slows down through loss of blood, or shock, or sheer hopelessness, and then the hyenas grab for the stomach and pull the animal to a halt with its own entrails or let it stumble into the loops and whorls of its own body. They eat the prey whole and cough back, like owls, the indigestible parts, such as hair and hooves.

Hyenas in the wild can roam dozens of miles a day. They leave their young in small dens and trot or lope across the savanna, head down or held high and rear tucked under, until they've found a hare or a pregnant gazelle or a nicely rotted piece of flesh. But when the herds begin to migrate the hyenas leave their dens to follow them, and, passing over hills, through rifts and acacia stands, and along dry riverbeds, they reach the open plains of the Serengeti, where wildebeest beyond count mill and groan in clouds of dust.

I once saw a family of hyenas playing on an elephant skull. They rolled on their backs, biting gently at each other's legs. Two cubs squeezed under and then out of the elephant's mandible. A female turned on her side, paws in the air, and broke off a piece of the skull as if eating a biscuit in bed. Hyenas almost never kill humans—only now and then taking a piece from the cheek of a sleeping man, and that probably because some villagers used to put out their dead for hyenas, flies, and any vultures in the area. As the man jumps up— perhaps he is a messenger between villages or someone searching for a bridge—the hyena instantly, peaceably, retreats.

Africa is like no other place on earth, and there is no better place to watch animals. They roam sun-dazed on the savanna by the million, sniffing up the scent of dried grass, swishing their tails, eyes often half closed. Sometimes they ignore human beings, sometimes they stare, but always there is something to look at: impalas dancing together in a mock fight, giraffes slow-swinging across the horizon. In the distance, vervet monkeys hop through branches. An ostrich runs with tail rampant, all the while flapping its wings in agitation, like a maiden aunt caught in a shower. A baboon nurses its toe. A lion quietly chuffs to itself.

I had wanted to go to Africa since my childhood, in Connecticut. Before I was born, my eyes lost their attachment to each other, the instinctive knowledge of how to swivel together, how to analyze data in tandem. The vision of one eye is only slightly cloudy, but it withdraws from cooperation with the other. My eyes do not work like two halves of a whole, and I have no perception of depth, so human faces blend into their background and are unreadable. The unreadable is frightening. When I was a child, friendly voices could dig deep and sharp without warning: without depth perception, there is no warning.

I had to learn about emotions, which are subtle and often masked, from animals, who signal theirs so much more clearly, with mane and tail and the position of the body. Human beings were a hazard.

There was only one thing that my eyes took in with ease. As the school bus crossed the marshes on a small cement bridge, we could see down the river toward a bend of trees. In the swamp that ran alongside it grew cattails and rushes, as naturally gold as they were tall. They were semi-translucent. Each blade glowed separately in the morning sun as if lit within. Together in their bending, high-feathered swamp, they bowed under the weightlessness of light. Sometimes there was mist rising from the water, and altogether it was the only masterpiece I ever saw in my suburban town. I don't know why I needed to see those rushes so badly, or how I knew Africa would be the same, but it was.

I had never wanted to work anywhere except in Africa, but after I graduated from college a wildlife-reserve director from Israel told me that he needed someone to set up a breeding site for endangered animals and I decided to go. When I got there, I was told that the project had been postponed and was asked if I'd mind taking a job as a volunteer at another reserve, cleaning enclosures. The reserve was dedicated to Biblical animals, many of them predators from the Israeli wild—hyenas, wolves, foxes, and one unmated leopard—attackers of kibbutz livestock. It was something to do, with animals, so I trudged off every day in the hundred-and-fourteen-degree heat with half a sandwich and a water canteen. I was being groomed for the job I'd initially been offered, but for the moment I sifted maggots for the lizards and snakes, and cleaned the fox, cat, hyena, wolf, and leopard corrals.

As the days got hotter, my fellow-workers and I carried gallon jugs of water in our wheelbarrows, poured it over our heads, and drank the rest until our stomachs were too full for food. It became a steady rhythm: sift dung, pour, drink, sift. We worked in pairs among the larger animals for safety, but toward the end of the month I was allowed to feed a young hyena and clean his cage. Efa had been taken from his parents as a cub because his mother rejected him. Also, he was a cross between a North African and an Israeli striped hyena, and nobody wanted him to confuse the gene pool further by mating. He was a beautiful animal. A mane trickled down sloped shoulders like a froth of leftover baby hair; he looked strangely helpless, as if weighed down by the tangled strands, and his back rounded to a dispirited slump. Even though he had a hyena's posture, he was like a German shepherd, a little dirty, but graceful, and so strong he didn't seem to have any muscles. His stripes twisted a bit at the ends and shimmered over the coat like feathers at rest. With his bat face and massed shoulders, he would have been at home in the sky, poised in a great leap, or swooping for prey. But here he was given aged meat, and he often left even that to rot before he ate it.

He had been, they said, an adorable cub, crying "*Maaaaaa!*" to Shlomi, the gentlest of the workers and the one who reared him, and he followed Shlomi everywhere. Then he grew too big to run loose, and he started biting at people, so they put him in a corral—a square of desert surrounded by an electrified fence with a large water basin perched in the center.

Efa was bored and lonely. He flipped the basin over every day, attacking it as if it were prey. When we fed him in the morning, there was nowhere to put his water. He knocked over everything, so we had no choice: we had to put him in a holding cage outside his corral while we built a concrete pool that he couldn't move. This was worse. Locked in a cage, he rebelled. He refused to eat, and every box we gave him for shade was torn to pieces. After a few days, I walked by and saw him standing defiant in the cage, his shade box in splinters and his water overturned again. "*Maaaaaaaa! Mmaaaaa!*" he croaked at me. I made a note to return and water him when I'd finished with the others.

I stopped to talk to the leopard, who was in heat. This was my first chance to get near her; when she was not hormonally sedated, she lunged at passersby, swatting her claws through the chicken wire.

"You're so beautiful."

She purred, and rubbed against the mesh. The men said you could stroke her like a house cat when she was in these moods. I wanted to touch her, a leopard from the oases of Israel's last deserts, but I stayed away, in case she changed her mind, and squatted out of reach to talk to her. I didn't want to force her to defend herself.

It might have been the attention I gave the leopard, but Efa was in a frenzy of "*Mmmaaaaaaaa*"'s when I returned to his cage. He crouched like a baby, begging for something. I filled a water tray and unlatched the door that opened into a corridor running between the cage and the corral, then I closed it. If only I'd just squirted the hose into the cage, but instead I unlatched the cage door and bent over to put the dish down, talking to him. The mind, I found, is strange. It shut off during the attack, while my body continued to act, without thought or even sight. I don't remember him sinking his teeth into my arm, though I heard a little grating noise as his teeth chewed into the bone.

Everything was black and slow and exploding in my stomach. Vision returned gradually, like an ancient black-and-white television pulling dots and flashes to the center for a picture. I saw at a remove the hyena inside my right arm, and my other arm banging him on the head. My body, in the absence of a mind, had decided that this was the best thing to do. And scream. Scream in a thin angry hysteria that didn't sound like me. Where was everyone? My mind was so calm and remote that I frightened myself, but my stomach twisted. I hit harder, remembering the others he'd nipped. He'd always let go.

Efa blinked and surged back, jerking me forward. I stumbled out of my sandals into the sand, thinking, with fresh anxiety, I'll burn my feet. I tried to kick him between the legs, but it was awkward, and he was pulling me down by the arm, down and back into the cage. When I came back from Africa the first time, I took a class in self-defense so I'd feel safer with all the soldiers, guerrilla warriors, and policemen when I returned. I remembered the move I'd vowed to use on any attacker: a stab and grab at the jugular, to snap it inside the skin. But the hyena has callused skin on its throat, thick and rough, like eczema. I lost hope and felt the slowness of this death to be the worst insult. Hyenas don't kill fast, and I could end up in the sand watching my entrails get pulled through a cut in my stomach and eaten like spaghetti, with tugs and jerks. I started to get mad, an unfamiliar feeling creeping in to add an acid burn to the chill of my stomach. Another removal from myself. I never let myself get mad. I want peace. I tried to pinch his nostrils so he'd let go of my arm to breathe, but he shook his head, pulling me deeper into the cage.

I think it was then that he took out the first piece from my arm and swallowed it without breathing, because a terror of movement settled in me at that moment and lasted for months. He moved up the arm, and all the time those black, blank eyes evaluated me, like a shark's, calm and almost friendly. By this time, my right arm was a mangled mess of flesh, pushed-out globs of fat, and flashes of bone two inches long, but my slow TV mind, watching, saw it as whole, just trapped in the hyena's mouth, in a tug-of-war like the one I used to play with my dogs—only it was my arm now instead of a sock. It didn't hurt. It never did.

The hyena looked up at me with those indescribable eyes and surged back again, nearly pulling me onto his face. I remembered self-defense class and the first lesson: "Poke the cockroach in the eyes." All the women had squealed, except me. "Ooooh, I could *never* do that." Ha, I'd thought. Anyone who wants to kill me has no right to live. I'd poke him in the eyes.

I looked at those eyes with my fingers poised to jab. It was for my family and my friends that I stuck my fingers in his eyes. I just wanted to stop watching myself get eaten, either be dead and at peace or be gone, but other lives were connected to mine. I'm not sure if I did more than touch them gently before he let go and whipped past me to cower against the door to the outside, the Negev desert.

Events like this teach you yourself. We all think we know what we would do, hero or coward, strong or weak. I expected strength, and the memory of my tin-whistle scream curdles my blood, but I am proud of the stupid thing I did next. He cowered and whimpered and essentially apologized, still with those blank ummoving eyes, and I stood still for a second. My arm felt light and shrunken, as if half of it were gone, but I didn't look. From the corridor, I had a choice of two doors: the one through which I'd entered, leading back to the desert, and the one opening onto the corral. I didn't think I could bend over him and unlatch the door to the desert. He'd just reach up and clamp onto my stomach. And I didn't want to open the door to the corral, or he'd drag me in and be able to attack the men if they ever came to help me. My body, still in control, made the good hand grab the bad elbow, and I beat him with my own arm, as if I had ripped it free to use as a club. "No!" I shouted. "No, no!" *Lo lo lo,* in Hebrew. I might even have said "Bad boy," but I hope not. It was the beating that damaged my hand permanently. I must have hit him hard enough to crush a ligament, because there is a lump on my hand to this day, five years later, but he didn't even blink. He came around behind me and grabbed my right leg, and again there was no pain—just the feeling that he and I were playing tug-of-war with my body—but I was afraid to pull too hard on the leg. He pulled the leg up, stretching me out in a line from the door, where I clung with the good hand to the mesh, like a dancer at the barre. It felt almost good, as if the whole thing were nearer to being over. In three moves I didn't feel, he took out most of the calf.

I opened the door to the desert and he ran out, with a quick shove that staggered me. I couldn't move the right leg, just crutched myself along on it into the Negev. He waited for me. The cold in my stomach was stabbing my breath away. The hyena and I were bonded now. Even if someone did come to help, there was still something left to finish between us. I was marked—his. I saw, in color, that he was going to knock me over, and I thought, in black-and-white, No, don't, you'll hurt my leg, I should keep it still.

A workman stood by a shed uphill, leaning on a tool in the sand. He watched me walk toward the office, with the hyena ahead and looking back at me. He was the only spectator I noticed, though I was told later, in the hospital, that some tourists, there to see the animals, were screaming for help, and three—or was it five?—soldiers had had their machine guns aimed at us throughout the whole thing. Israeli soldiers carry their arms everywhere when they're in uniform; but they must have been afraid to shoot. I don't know. Stories get told afterward. I didn't see anyone except the workman, looking on impassively, and the leopard, pacing inside her fence, roaring a little, with the peace of her heat gone as suddenly as it had appeared.

As I walked, the black-and-white faded, and color washed back in. I saw the blood for the first time. It was in my hair, had soaked into my clothes all the way to the skin, and was drying in a trickle from arm and legs. Each step left a cold puddle of blood around the right foot. I held up the arm and fumbled for the pressure point. The hyena trotted ahead of me as if he were afraid to be alone in the desert but was all right with me. Every now and then, he looked back, as if thinking about finishing me off—once again a predator, calm and competent, silver, and splashed with blood. But the men ran up shouting, and I stopped, and snapped, sorry even then for sounding like a bitch, "Get Efa and bring around the van."

Shlomi ran up and grabbed my good left arm, hustling me forward. Not so fast, I wanted to say, but I didn't. Every step felt more wrong, and I dragged back against moving until he almost shoved me forward.

In the van, blood sloshed around my feet and I tried to find the pressure point of the groin but gave up. I held up the arm instead, and pretended I knew what I was doing. Shlomi stopped to open the reserve gate, and then again to close it. As he got back in, I lost feeling in my right leg.

We drove for what seemed like a long time, then turned into a kibbutz and roared past lines of women planting pineapples, past a cement yard, and then he was running me into a clinic past gasping women. And I wanted to apologize. I never cut in line. Shlomi pulled me forward while I stiffened up. Damn it, I want to be carried, I've done enough by myself, I remember thinking. But I made it to the examining table and Shlomi yelled for a doctor in Hebrew. A woman came in and told him there was no doctor—only nurses. They stopped telling me what was happening. Hands shaking, she yanked me forward and stuck my arm under a faucet. Hey. She turned on the water and it fell onto the bone and a minor nerve, full force. That was a sensation I wish I couldn't remember. No pain, but a tremendous feeling of wrongness. My insides were out.

She tried to get my leg into the sink, pulling at the ankle, and the shrivelled arm twitched in the air for balance. I tensed, so she couldn't; I wished later that I'd let her, because it was weeks before the dried blood and dirt peeled off. She told me to get on a stretcher, and then she poured hydrogen peroxide into the trenches in my leg. It foamed with a roar that spat froth in the air. That felt wrong, too, Shlomi grabbed the sink for support. I told him it didn't hurt. He wasn't listening. I was starting to feel better. Someone was making the decisions.

"Don't worry, Shlomi. I never wanted to dance ballet."

"No, I don't know, the leg is very bad."

Like all Israelis, he could make a statement of fact sound like an accusation. I knew it was bad, I just didn't see the need to dwell on it when I was so very surprised to be alive. The nurse picked up a towel and started wiping off the blood and dirt with brisk, scratchy strokes, and I cramped in the stomach again, worrying about infection. And what were we waiting for? We waited awhile, and then she gave me antishock injections.

"I'm not in shock." I said, and meant it. I thought I was thinking more clearly than she was. Shlomi told me that we were waiting for an ambulance. He was gray, with sick, inturned eyes, the way I must have looked while the attack was happening. But I was over it, and he was just beginning. He and the nurse did not share my pleasure. In fact, the seemed taken aback at my jokes, so I stopped talking.

I had a new terror, but it was peaceful compared with the other, so I lay back. Fly home, microsurgery, I can spare the leg if something has to go, but I have to have the hand for graduate school. Helicopters, international flights, nerve damage.

The ambulance came. The nurse and Shlomi looked as bloodless as I felt. They pushed me around, telling me to get onto the gurney, and I tried to make them let go so I could just roll onto it instead of jumping down from the table. They did, and wheeled me out in state through a crowd of horrified kibbutzniks. They showed no excitement over it; pain is too real to Isrealis.

I am sure Efa crawled out to greet me with no intention to kill. He had cried to me like an infant in distress, hunched over and rounded. His ruff lay flat and soft and his tail hung down. He attacked me, I think, in a moment of thirst-induced delirium and loneliness. If he had wanted to eat or to attack, he could have taken my arm in a snap: one sharp jab and jerk, and the wrist would have been gone before I even noticed. If he had wanted to kill me, he could have leaped for my stomach as soon as he had pulled me down by the arm.

Cheetahs often catch hold of their prey's nose and run alongside it. As the victim stumbles and falls, or staggers, or tries to run, the cheetah holds tight, closing mouth and nostrils in one stapled hold, or—with larger prey—biting into the throat to cut off air. Leopards like to leap down from trees for a quick crack of the back. Lions improvise. Each has its own specialty. Some leap up from behind, like a terrestrial leopard; some try a daring front leap, risking hooves and horns to bite into neck or face.

Hyenas are far more efficient. They catch hold of flesh, not with small nips and throwing of weight but by smoothly and quickly trans-ferring chunks of it from prey to throat. Food slips instantly from toothhold to stomach. Like human infants nursing, they seem to swal-low without pausing for breath, as if food and air travelled in separate channels. They are the only predators adapted to eating bone. Their dung is white with it.

I heard a story of a young boy in Nairobi who was watching over a herd of goats and fell asleep leaning on his stick. A hyena appeared and opened the boy's stomach with one quick rip. For the hyena it might have been play, this trying on of assault. But he won, as he was bound to do. I was told that someone took the boy to a doctor and he died a while later. He could have lived; we don't need all our intestines, and the hyena had probably left enough behind. But maybe they didn't have the right antibiotics or sterile dressings. I would have liked to ask him what he saw in the hyena's eyes.

In the ambulance, the driver chatted for a bit, then said, "Don't close your eyes. If you feel faint, tell me and I'll stop right away."

To do what, watch me? I didn't tell him that I'd been exhausted for months—I'd got parasites in Africa—and always shut my eyes when I had the chance. I closed them now, and he asked me questions with an anxiety that warmed my heart. I love to be taken care of. It was good to be strapped down and bandaged, all decisions out of my hands after the hard ones, the life-and-death ones. It was also, I learned, a good thing to have the wounds hidden. Once they were open to the air, my stomach clenched with pain and that made life temporarily not worth living. The arm, I finally noticed, was curled up on itself, like paper shrivelling inward in a fire, but heavy instead of too light.

We arrived at the hospital with a screech and a yank and a curse. The doors were stuck, but the driver pushed, and ran me in. Then he left with a wave of farewell. I waited and waited. A doctor came in and plowed my arm in search of a vein with blood, going deep under the muscle, to attach a saline drip. My nails were white, like things soaked in formaldehyde, and I was freezing. Bled white, I was. Nothing left to fill a test tube.

I asked the doctor to talk with the reserve's veterinarian before he did anything. Hyena bites are violently infectious. The animals' mouths are full of bacteria from rotten meat. He shrugged. But when Shlomi told him to wait for the vet he did. The vet told him to clean the holes out and leave them open for now, because the infection could kill me.

"The infection will probably take the leg anyway," the doctor told me. "The chances are fifty-fifty that we'll have to amputate."

I looked down at the leg before they began cutting out the dirtier shreds of flesh and paring the whole surface of the wound. The holes were impossibly wide, more than twice the size of the hyena's face. I know now that skin and muscle are stretched over bone like canvas over a canoe. One thinks of skin as irrevocably bonded to flesh, and all as one entity. But skin is attached to flesh only with the lightest of bonds, and, once it has been ripped, the body gives way naturally, pulling the flesh back to its scaffolding of bone. The invisible woman, I thought, as the chill took me; I can see right through my leg.

I couldn't see all of it because of my bad eyesight, and the leg was still covered with blood-stuck sand, but it was strange the way the leg went down normally, then cut in to the bone, along the bone, and then out again to a normal ankle, except for a small gash on the side with fat poking out. I couldn't yet see the other hole. It was lower down, starting halfway past the one I could see, and continuing around the back of the leg to the other side, so almost the whole leg was girdled around. I still don't know how blood got to that stranded wall of flesh.

The doctor worked on the leg for an hour, clipping pieces of flesh out of the wounds with little scissor snips, as if my leg were a piece of cloth that he was carefully tailoring with dull tools. I asked for a large dose of anesthetic, not because I felt any pain—I never felt any, really— but because I could feel the scissors scissoring away the flesh and I couldn't breathe. Between bouts of cutting, I kept joking, happy it was over, or might be over, and people crowded into the room to watch. No sterilization? Who cares? I was alive. They pumped saline into me so fast that my arm swelled and I had to go to the bathroom. For the first time, I realized how my life had changed. There is, after all, no simple dichotomy: intact and alive versus torn and dead.

They sent some of the people out and stuck a bedpan under the sheet. With one wrist locked to the I.V. and the other paralyzed, I couldn't wipe. Warrior to newborn babe in an hour. Someone brought me my sandals. They were dirty and covered with dried blood, like small dead animals.

*   *   *

I had expected the hyena bite in Africa, not in Israel. I had expected the price I paid for Africa to be high. The need that had driven me since I was eight years old had made me willing to risk anything, even death, to be in Africa watching animals. Anyone who works with animals expects to get hurt. You are a guest in their life—any intrusion is a threat to them. It is their separateness that makes them worthy of respect.

After the hospital, I went back to America for physical therapy and treatment of the parasites, which burned a path in my stomach for the next six months. Before I left, people from the reserve asked me to stand near Efa's cage. They wanted to know if his animosity was specific to me. He looked at me, again with those friendly blank eyes, and then rose up against the wire with a crash so loud that I thought he was breaking through. For one second, I saw his face coming toward me, mouth open, and I hopped back. They told me they were going to send him to a zoo where the keepers wouldn't have to go into the cage, but I heard later that a veterinarian came and put Efa to sleep. ("Forever asleep," the workers said.) Shlomi was there.

Back in America, too ill for school, I read about animals on my own. Then I went to graduate school, but I found the statistical and analytical approach to animals too reductive. So I gave it up. But I couldn't return to Africa. Five years after the hyena bite, I went back. Without a job, or any scientific purpose, I backpacked between Tanzania and Kenya, seeing the savanna in short bursts of safaris and hired cars and *matatu* buses.

Africa smells of nothing but dust, and that dust lingers with sweetness in the nose and like powder on the skin. It comes from everywhere, even the greenest grass, and its fingers into clothing like minuscule parasites. Shirts blossom red or brown, sometimes yellow, with dust; when clapped they puff into a cloud of color, like a dandelion blown adrift. With the wind in my face and the dust drifting over me, I have never felt so clean.

In spite of its color, the dust is translucent. African sunsets are famous. People say the dust rises into the atmosphere and reflects the sun's light. I think the particles rise, with their own separate colors, and the sun shines through them, heat through translucent splendor.

I believe that, even if you pass through quickly, there are landscapes that are particularly yours. Thousands of explorers returned home with shards of Africa embedded in their lungs. Breathe deeply enough, and you become part of that world, filled to the brim and clogged with its clays and dust.

In the Kenyan highlands, the nights are always cool, and there are so many stars that a book can be read by their light if there's no moon. Eyes sparkle in the light. At night, they reflect it back in small round circles. Snakes are tiny pinpricks in the grass, hares in a field sparkle like fireflies as they turn their heads to look at the car. Mice eyes are like snakes', but closer together. As we drive by, antelope flash one eye and then the other at us, white orbs of light in gray shadows. If you sit in the open mouth of your tent before the fire, the eyes of the hyenas shine green and gold, low down to the ground, and they look at you. People in Africa usually put their garbage pits too close to their camps, so we ate our dinner next to baboons screaming over a cabbage leaf, or hyenas snarling over bones. I hadn't told anyone here about the hyena bite. I liked to watch the hyenas rushing in and out of the pit, squabbling and rolling over each other, but still very friendly, trotting away flank to flank and stopping to look at me. An animal trainer told me that once you've been bitten badly enough to limp, even if the limp is almost imperceptible the animals will know, and from then on you are prey, not master.

Driving away from my tent camp in Africa, I came upon a den of hyenas. The first one stood like a statue on the great pan of rock, the kind I loved to play on as a child, full of towers and caves and little ledges, with the rock smooth underfoot. It was a silvery animal, very serious, like a young sentinel, and it wasn't until we saw the mother that we realized it was a hyena. Three generations lived in the den. Babies rolled in balls under the mother's feet and she pricked her ears at us and stepped clear, to watch with the sentinel. Water pooled in a curve before her, rocking the flashes of light in the wind, decadent somehow against the dried grasses. We moved and she made a noise and they disappeared—the babies first, then the mother, then another adult, who had been sleeping in the grass. The sentinel walked to the shaded side of the rock and stared at us from there.

I had almost died, eaten alive, and I was glad to be alive. The scars had healed. Three long dents ran around the arm and the leg, blurred with spider tracks of canine punctures. The one war wound, the bump that grew where I hit the hyena, still hurt, but I was back in Africa.

YSRAEL

1.

We were on our way to the colmado for an errand, a beer for my tío, when Rafa stood still and tilted his head, as if listening to a message I couldn't hear, something beamed in from afar. We were close to the colmado; you could hear the music and the gentle clop of drunken voices. I was nine that summer, but my brother was twelve, and he was the one who wanted to see Ysrael, who looked out towards Barbacoa and said, We should pay that kid a visit.

2.

Mami shipped me and Rafa out to the campo every summer. She worked long hours at the chocolate factory and didn't have the time or the energy to look after us during the months school was out. Rafa and I stayed with our tíos, in a small wooden house just outside Ocoa; rosebushes blazed around the yard like compass points and the mango trees spread out deep blankets of shade where we could rest and play dominos, but the campo was nothing like our barrio in Santo Domingo. In the campo there was nothing to do, no one to see. You didn't get television or electricity and Rafa, who was older and expected more, woke up every morning pissy and dissatisfied. He looked out on the patio in his shorts and looked out over the mountains, at the mists that gathered like water, at the brucal trees that blazed like fires on the mountain. This, he said, is shit.

Worse than shit, I said.

Yeah, he said, and when I get home, I'm going to go crazy—chinga all my girls and then chinga everyone else's. I won't stop dancing either. I'm going to be like those guys in the record books who dance four or five days straight.

Tío Miguel had chores for us (mostly we chopped wood for the smokehouse and brought water up from the river) but we finished these as easy as we threw off our shirts, the rest of the day punching us in the face. We caught jaivas in the streams and spent hours walking across the valley to see girls who were never there; we set traps for jurones we never caught and toughened up our roosters with pails of cold water. We worked hard at keeping busy.

I didn't mind these summers, wouldn't forget them the way Rafa would. Back home in the Capital, Rafa had his own friends, a bunch of tígueres who liked to knock down our neighbors and who scrawled *chocha* and *toto* on walls and curbs. Back in the Capital he rarely said anything to me except Shut up, pendejo. Unless, of course, he was mad and then he had about five hundred routines he liked to lay on me. Most of them had to do with my complexion, my hair, the size of my lips. It's the Haitian, he'd say to his buddies. Hey Señor Haitian, Mami found you on the border and only took you in because she felt sorry for *you*.

If I was stupid enough to mouth off to him—about the hair that was growing on his back or the time the tip of his pinga had swollen to the size of a lemon—he pounded the hell out of me and then I would run as far as I could. In the Capital Rafa and I fought so much that our neighbors took to smashing broomsticks over us to break it up, but in the campo it wasn't like that. In the campo we were friends.

The summer I was nine, Rafa shot whole afternoons talking about whatever chica he was getting with—not that the campo girls gave up ass like the girls back in the Capital but kissing them, he told me, was pretty much the same. He'd take the campo girls down to the dams to swim and if he was lucky they let him put it in their mouths or in their asses. He'd done La Muda that way for almost a month before her parents heard about it and barred her from leaving the house forever.

He wore the same outfit when he went to see these girls, a shirt and pants that my father had sent him from the States last Christmas. I always followed Rafa, trying to convince him to let me tag along.

Go home, he'd say. I'll be back in a few hours.

I'll walk you.

I don't need you to walk me anywhere. Just wait for me.

If I kept on he'd punch me in the shoulder and walk on until what was left of him was the color of his shirt filling in the spaces between the leaves. Something inside of me would sag like a sail. I would yell his name and he'd hurry on, the ferns and branches and flower pods trembling in his wake.

Later, while we were in bed listening to the rats on the zinc roof he might tell me what he'd done. I'd hear about tetas and chochas and leche and he'd talk without looking over at me. There was a girl he'd gone to see, half-Haitian, but he ended up with her sister. Another who believed she wouldn't get pregnant if she drank a Coca-Cola afterwards. And one who was pregnant and didn't give a damn about anything. His hands were behind his head and his feet were crossed at the ankles. He was handsome and spoke out of the corner of his mouth. I was too young to understand most of what he said, but I listened to him anyway, in case these things might be useful in the future.

3.

Ysrael was a different story. Even on this side of Ocoa people had heard of him, how when he was a baby a pig had eaten his face off, skinned it like an orange. He was something to talk about, a name that set the kids to screaming, worse than el Cuco or la Vieja Calusa.

I'd seen Ysrael my first time the year before, right after the dams were finished. I was in town, farting around, when a single-prop plane swept in across the sky. A door opened on the fuselage and a man began to kick out tall bundles that exploded into thousands of leaflets as soon as the wind got to them. They came down as slow as butterfly blossoms and were posters of wrestlers, not politicians, and that's when us kids started shouting at each other. Usually the planes only covered Ocoa, but if extras had been printed the nearby towns would also get leaflets, especially if the match or the election was a big one. The paper would cling to the trees for weeks.

I spotted Ysrael in an alley, stooping over a stack of leaflets that had not come undone from its thin cord. He was wearing his mask.

What are you doing? I said.

What do you think I'm doing? he answered.

He picked up the bundle and ran down the alley. Some other boys saw him and wheeled around, howling but, coño, could he run.

That's Ysrael. I was told. He's *ugly* and he's got a cousin around here but we don't like him either. And that face of his would make you *sick*!

I told my brother later when I got home, and he sat up in his bed. Could you see under the mask?

Not really.

That's something we got to check out.

I hear it's bad.

The night before we went to look for him my brother couldn't sleep. He kicked at the mosquito netting and I could hear the mesh tearing just a little. My tío was yukking it up with his buddies in the yard. One of Tío's roosters had won big the day before and he was thinking of taking it to the Capital.

People around here don't bet worth a damn, he was saying. Your average campesino only bets big when he feels lucky and how many of them feel lucky?

You're feeling lucky right now.

You're damn right about that. That's why I have to find myself some big spenders.

I wonder how much of Ysrael's face is gone, Rafa said.

He has his eyes.

That's a lot, he assured me. You'd think eyes would be the first thing a pig would go for. Eyes are soft. And salty.

How do you know that?

I licked one, he said.

Maybe his ears.

And his nose. Anything that sticks out.

Everyone had a different opinion on the damage. Tío said it wasn't bad but the father was very sensitive about anyone taunting his oldest son, which explained the mask. Tía said that if we were to look on his face we would be sad for the rest of our lives. That's why the poor boy's mother spends her day in church. I had never been sad more than a few hours and the thought of that sensation lasting a lifetime scared the hell out of me. My brother kept pinching my face during the night, like I was a mango. The cheeks, he said. And the chin. But the forehead would be a lot harder. The skin's tight.

All right, I said. Ya.

The next morning the roosters were screaming. Rafa dumped the ponchera in the weeds and then collected our shoes from the patio, careful not to step on the pile of cacao beans Tía had set out to dry. Rafa went into the smokehouse and emerged with his knife and two oranges. He peeled them and handed me mine. When we heard Tía coughing in the house, we started on our way. I kept expecting Rafa to send me home and the longer he went without speaking, the more excited I became. Twice I put my hands over my mouth to stop from laughing. We went slow, grabbing saplings and fence posts to keep from tumbling down the rough brambled slope. Smoke was rising from the fields that had been burned the night before, and the trees that had not exploded or collapsed stood in the black ash like spears. At the bottom of the hill we followed the road that would take us to Ocoa. I was carrying the two Coca-Cola empties Tío had hidden in the chicken coop.

We joined two women, our neighbors, who were waiting by the colmado on their way to mass.

I put the bottles on the counter. Chicho folded up yesterday's *El Nacional*. When he put fresh Cokes next to the empties, I said, We want the refund.

Chico put his elbows on the counter and looked me over. Are you supposed to be doing that?

Yes, I said.

You better be giving this money back to your tío, he said. I stared at the pastelitos and chicharrón he kept under a flyspecked glass. He slapped the coins onto the counter. I'm going to stay out of this, he said. What you do with this money is your own concern. I'm just a businessman.

How much of this do we need? I asked Rafa.

All of it.

Can't we buy something to eat?

Save it for a drink. You'll be real thirsty later.

Maybe we should eat.

Don't be stupid.

How about if I just bought us some gum?

Give me that money, he said.

OK, I said. I was just asking.

Then stop. Rafa was looking up the road, distracted; I knew that expression better than anyone. He was scheming. Every now and then he glanced over at the two women, who were conversing loudly, their arms crossed over their big chests.When the first autobus trundled to a stop and the women got on, Rafa watched their asses bucking under their dresses. The cobrador leaned out from the passenger door and said, Well? And Rafa said, Beat it, baldy.

What are we waiting for? I said. That one had air-conditioning.

I want a younger cobrador, Rafa said, still looking down the road. I went to the counter and tapped my finger on the glass case. Chicho handed me a pastelito and after putting it in my pocket, I slid him a coin. Business is business, Chicho announced but my brother didn't bother to look. He was flagging down the next autobus.

Get to the back, Rafa said. He framed himself in the main door, his toes out in the air, his hands curled up on the top lip of the door. He stood next to the cobrador, who was a year or two younger than he was. This boy tried to get Rafa to sit down but Rafa shook his head with that not-a-chance-grin of his and before there could be an argument the driver shifted into gear, blasting the radio. *"La chica de la novela"* was still on the charts. Can you believe that? the man next to me said. They play that vaina a hundred times a day.

I lowered myself stiffly into my seat but the pastelito had already put a grease stain on my pants. Coño, I said and took out the pastelito and finished it in four bites. Rafa wasn't watching. Each time the autobus stopped he was hopping down and helping people bring on their packages. When a row filled he lowered the swingdown center seat for whoever was next. The cobrador, a thin boy with an Afro, was trying to keep up with him and the driver was too busy with his radio to notice what was happening. Two people paid Rafa—all of which Rafa gave to the cobrador, who was himself busy making change.

You have to watch out for stains like that, the man next to me said. He had big teeth and wore a clean fedora. His arms were ropy with muscles.

These things are too greasy, I said.

Let me help. He spit in his fingers and started to rub at the stain but then he was pinching at the tip of my pinga through the fabric of my shorts. He was smiling. I shoved him against his seat. He looked to see if anybody had noticed.

You pato, I said.

The man kept smiling.

You low-down pinga-sucking pato, I said. The man squeezed my bicep, quietly, hard, the way my friends would sneak me in church. I whimpered.

You should watch your mouth, he said.

I got up and went over to the door. Rafa slapped the roof and as the driver slowed the cobrador said, You two haven't paid.

Sure we did, Rafa said, pushing me down into the dusty street. I gave you the money for those two people there and I gave you our fare too. His voice was tired, as if he got into these discussions all the time.

No you didn't.

Fuck you I did. You got the fares. Why don't you count and see?

Don't even try it. The cobrador put his hand on Rafa but Rafa wasn't having it. He yelled up to the driver, Tell your boy to learn how to count.

We crossed the road and went down into a field of guineo; the cobrador was shouting after us and we stayed in the field until we heard the driver say, Forget them.

Rafa took off his shirt and fanned himself and that's when I started to cry.

He watched for a moment. You, he said, are a pussy.

I'm sorry.

What the hell's the matter with you? We didn't do anything wrong.

I'll be OK in a second. I sawed my forearm across my nose.

He took a look around, drawing in the lay of the land. If you can't stop crying, I'll leave you. He headed towards a shack that was rusting in the sun.

I watched him disappear. From the shack you could hear voices, as bright as chrome. Columns of ants had found a pile of meatless chicken bones at my feet and were industriously carting away the crumbling marrow. I could have gone home, which was what I usually did when Rafa acted up, but we were far—eight, nine miles away.

I caught up with him beyond the shack. We walked about a mile; my head felt cold and hollow.

Are you done?

Yes, I said.

Are you always going to be a pussy?

I wouldn't have raised my head if God himself had appeared in the sky and pissed down on us.

Rafa spit. You have to get tougher. Crying all the time. Do you think our papi's crying? Do you think that's what he's been doing the last six years? He turned from me. His feet were crackling through the weeds, breaking stems.

Rafa stopped a schoolboy in a blue and tan uniform, who pointed us down a road. Rafa spoke to a young mother, whose baby was hacking like a miner. A little farther, she said and when he smiled she looked the other way. We went too far and a farmer with a machete showed us the easiest loop back. Rafa stopped when he saw Ysrael standing in the center of a field. He was flying a kite and despite the string he seemed almost unconnected to the distant wedge of black that finned back and forth in the sky. Here we go, Rafa said. I was embarrassed. What the hell were we supposed to do?

Stay close, he said. And get ready to run. He passed me his knife, then trotted down towards the field.

4.

The summer before, I pegged Ysrael with a rock and the way it bounced off his back I knew I'd clocked a shoulder blade.

You did it! You fucking did it! the other boys yelled.

He'd been running from us and he arched in pain and one of the other boys nearly caught him but he recovered and took off. He's faster than a mongoose, someone said, but in truth he was even faster than that. We laughed and went back to our baseball games and forgot him until he came to town again and then we dropped what we were doing and chased him. Show us your face, we cried. Let's see it just once.

5.

He was about a foot bigger than either of us and looked like he'd been fattened on that supergrain the farmers around Ocoa were giving their stock, a new product which kept my tío up at night, muttering jealously, Proxyl Feed Nine, Proxyl Feed Nine. Ysrael's sandals were of stiff leather and his clothes were Northamerican. I looked over at Rafa but my brother seemed unperturbed.

Listen up, Rafa said. My hermanito's not feeling too well. Can you show us where a colmado is? I want to get him a drink.

There's a faucet up the road, Ysrael said. His voice was odd and full of spit. His mask was handsewn from thin blue cotton fabric and you couldn't help but see the scar tissue that circled his left eye, a red waxy crescent, and the saliva that trickled down his neck.

We're not from around here. We can't drink the water.

Ysrael spooled in his string. The kite wheeled but he righted it with a yank.

Not bad, I said.

We can't drink the water around here. It would kill us. And he's already sick.

I smiled and tried to act sick, which wasn't too difficult; I was covered with dust. I saw Ysrael looking us over.

The water here is probably better than up in the mountains, he said.

Help us out, Rafa said in a low voice.

Ysrael pointed down a path. Just go that way, you'll find it.

Are you sure?

I've lived here all my life.

I could hear the plastic kite flapping in the wind; the string was coming in fast. Rafa huffed and started on his way. We made a long circle and by then Ysrael had his kite in hand—the kite was no handmade local job. It had been manufactured abroad.

We couldn't find it, Rafa said.

How stupid are you?

Where did you get that? I asked.

Nueva York, he said. From my father.

No shit! Our father's there too! I shouted.

I looked at Rafa, who, for an instant, frowned. Our father only sent us letters and an occasional shirt or pair of jeans at Christmas.

What the hell are you wearing that mask for anyway? Rafa asked.

I'm sick, Ysrael said.

It must be hot.

Not for me.

Don't you take it off?

Not until I get better. I'm going to have an operation soon.

You better watch out for that, Rafa said. Those doctors will kill you faster than the Guardia.

They're American doctors.

Rafa sniggered. You're lying.

I saw them last spring. They want me to go next year.

They're lying to you. They probably just felt sorry.

Do you want me to show you where the colmado is or not?

Sure.

Follow me, he said, wiping the spit on his neck. At the colmado he stood off while Rafa bought me the cola. The owner was playing dominos with the beer deliveryman and didn't bother to look up, though he put a hand in the air for Ysrael. He had that lean look of every colmado owner I'd ever met. On the way back to the road I left the bottle with Rafa to finish and caught up with Ysrael, who was ahead of us. Are you still into wrestling? I asked.

He turned to me and something rippled under the mask. How did you know that?

I heard, I said. Do they have wrestling in the States?

I hope so.

Are you a wrestler?

I'm a great wrestler. I almost went to fight in the Capital.

My brother laughed, swigging on the bottle.

You want to try it, pendejo?

Not right now.

I didn't think so.

I tapped his arm. The planes haven't dropped anything this year.

It's still too early. The first Sunday of August is when it starts.

How do you know?

I'm from around here, he said. The mask twitched. I realized he was smiling and then my brother brought his arm around and smashed the bottle on top of his head. It exploded, the thick bottom spinning away like a crazed eyeglass and I said, Holy fucking shit. Ysrael stumbled once and slammed into a fence post that had been sunk into the side of the road. Glass crumbled off his mask. He spun towards me, then fell down on his stomach. Rafa kicked him in the side. Ysrael seemed not to notice. He had his hands flat in the dirt and was concentrating on pushing himself up. Roll him on his back, my brother said and we did, pushing like crazy. Rafa took off his mask and threw it spinning into the grass.

His left ear was a nub and you could see the thick veined slab of his tongue through a hole in his cheek. He had no lips. His head was tipped back and his eyes had gone white and the cords were out on his neck. He'd been an infant when the pig had come into the house. The damage looked old but I still jumped back and said, Please Rafa, let's go! Rafa crouched and using only two of his fingers, turned Ysrael's head from side to side.

6.

We went back to the colmado where the owner and the deliveryman were now arguing, the dominos chattering under their hands. We kept walking and after one hour, maybe two, we saw an autobus. We boarded and went right to the back. Rafa crossed his arms and watched the fields and roadside shacks scroll past, the dust and smoke and people almost frozen by our speed.

Ysrael will be OK, I said.

Don't bet on it.

They're going to fix him.

A muscle fluttered between his jawbone and his ear. Yunior, he said tiredly. They aren't going to do shit to him.

How do you know?

I know, he said.

I put my feet on the back of the chair in front of me, pushing on an old lady, who looked at me. She was wearing a baseball cap and one of her eyes was milky. The autobus was heading for Ocoa, not for home.

Rafa signaled for a stop. Get ready to run, he whispered.

I said, OK.

ME & MICHELANGELO

The Italian writer Tobino once wrote a story about a sculptor in Pietrasanta who developed "a mystical mania to carve angels from white marble." The reader can see the narrator shrug when he says, "Pietrasanta is an enchanted city," as if the Tuscan town was the cause of the affliction. I was sitting in the window of our apartment looking out over the terra-cotta roofs, watching a woman shaking a yellow rug out a distant window, and wishing for a little of Tobino's sculptor's mania.

A pancake of clouds covered the gray horizon; a light breeze flowed over and cooled my bare feet. Soon I would stroll to the Bar Michelangelo for a morning vino, another attempt at reading a local newspaper, and a day of conversation with young marble sculptors from around the world. Shirley slipped into the bedroom; she had been listening to an Italian language tape in the kitchen. She wrapped her arms around me from behind, and lay her head on my shoulder. To illustrate my developing aesthetic sensitivity I said, "Look at all the shades of terra-cotta red on the roofs down there."

"Which building?"

"Any of them."

Shirley pointed down to the roof of a large building beneath us, in front of which sat a few teenagers in shiny blue bomber jackets. "You mean that building?"

"I wasn't looking at any building in particular," I said, "but the red of the terra-cotta roofs."

"That building is a methadone clinic. Those are heroin addicts," said Shirley. "It's why our rent is cheap. Sometimes they climb in the windows and rob the people who live here."

She said something to me I didn't catch and left the room. I climbed out of the window and followed her into the long dark hallway that led to the kitchen. On the walls were velvet paintings of the Tuscan countryside, rolling hills covered with vineyards and old stone farmhouses.

The long windows were open in the kitchen. On the checkerboard tablecloth on the table was a wooden cutting board, covered in fresh vegetables of yellow and green and white. A plastic bag spilled open with yellow pasta. A pale blue kettle squealed and rocked on the stove. Shirley had a cookbook open on her raised knee.

"What are you doing?" I said.

"I've been invited on a date to go to a marble quarry. I'm preparing a dish for lunch."

"Oh?" I said. "Anyone I know?"

"Savan."

"The French sculptor?" I said. "He just wants to sleep with you."

"No shit."

"Don't be sarcastic."

"When are you going to get it through your skull: I only want to be with you."

"But then," I said, "why are we never together?"

"You never ask me out on a date."

"But Shirley," I said. "We live together. Do I really need to ask you on a date?"

"Yes," said Shirley. "It might help."

"I don't know what to do with you."

"Do you want me to tell you what to do with me?"

I was about to answer, when Shirley cut me off.

"You might start with lots of gentle kisses behind my ears. And it wouldn't hurt if you brought home a bottle of Champagne sometime. And maybe if you came up with some romantic things to do once in a while. Take me away from the studio to Pisa or Florence or some little Italian town. Take me to the wall above the piazza and whisper in my ear. Hold me in the Bar Michelangelo and kiss me. We're living in the most romantic country in the world, anywhere in Italy will make my heart flutter. With the smallest effort you could have me swooning all over you instead of being such a bitch."

There was a young Italian man who would clomp across the piazza and whinny like a horse if it was going to rain the next day. His name was Paulo; he was simple and had a long and toothy face. The old Italians at the Bar Michelangelo would smile at him and nod among themselves. He was always clean and well dressed; his white shirt was pressed and his dark pants ironed and his black shoes shined. He sat at the Bar Michelangelo with his hands folded in his lap at his own table, and Gabriella would bring him a drink, and he would wait with a look of blank expectation. And then lightning would strike, his face would grow dark and disturbed, and he'd set off on his ritual gallop.

As Shirley and I arrived in the piazza, Paulo took off from his seat at the Bar Michelangelo. The French sculptor Savan walked over to us from the bar as we watched Paulo circle the piazza and said, "You will see; tomorrow it will rain. This horse man is a true artist." Savan was graceful enough to bow out of his marble quarry date with Shirley. I complimented him on the *David* tattoo on his shoulder and he told me he had tattooed it himself, and offered to put any of Michelangelo's works permanently on my body. He then patted me on the arm and said, "I think it is good you and Shirley are alone." Savan went back to his chair at the Bar Michelangelo and opened the local newspaper. The waitress Gabriella came around and took his order.

Shirley stared blankly at me, and I finally grabbed her hand and pulled her across the piazza. She stutter-stepped behind me, and slowly walked, and by the time we were across the piazza she had her arm around me. I still held her hand, and ran my fingers over its delicate bones. We walked down the Via Mazzini, past the expensive Italian clothing and antique shops and all the markets toward the green bronze sculpture of the Roman warrior by the Colombian sculptor Fernando Botero in the center of the rotary. We saw the orange bus we wanted pulling out of the station, and ran to catch it. It started to pull away quickly but the driver saw my waving arm as I ran behind the bus down the road.

"Well, we caught the clap," I said, as we made our way down the rocking aisle.

CLAP was the acronym of the local bus line.

The bus line ran under the honor system. Riders were supposed to buy a ticket and punch it on the bus. We never bought a ticket, so every ride I sat feeling guilty in the back, but at the same time ready to be an ignorant *straniero*. Shirley said she didn't mind riding free, pointing out that in Ireland writers don't pay taxes. "The world owes artists a living, or at least a boost now and then," said Shirley. "We don't destroy anything, we try not to hurt anyone, and we want the world to be seen as beautiful."

We were in the Apuan Alps outside of Pietrasanta.

Shirley and I walked down the rocking bus and stood behind the driver. Shirley seemed to know where we were heading. She craned her neck sideways in the bus to look up at the peaks. An old Italian woman with a mustache smiled at me and nodded, her arms around a bag of groceries.

"*Per favore, signore,*" said Shirley to the driver.

The bus left us next to a chestnut tree. Around us were mountains, but they couldn't be seen from the road. Shirley and I walked up a nearby dirt road. I took the picnic pack off her back and put it on mine; she went into the woods and came back with a walking stick.

A truck rumbled down the road at us; we had to step off into the trees. The driver, a young blond Italian, waved to Shirley from his cab. His cab was walled in vivid blue fur, he had a string of small colorful flags hanging from the inside of the windshield. On the flatbed behind sat two hunks of white-striped blue marble the size of a VW bus. They weren't tied down. His air brakes wheezed.

We came out above the trees. Above us rose the plain of a mountain, covered with rubble. Chunks of all sizes flowed from the clouds. A road wound back and forth up the field of stone. Tiny trucks moved at the top of the mountain, and minuscule men moved around. An explosion sent a tremor through the ground at my feet. Shirley hugged me and said, "Isn't it beautiful here?"

"Should we be here if they're blasting?"

Shirley ignored me, and made her way up the field of stone, skipping from rock to rock, her arms out and wavering like a tightrope walker. I looked up at the workers at the top of the quarry, and saw a plume of smoke rising from the explosion.

"This marble is called *bardiglio*," said Shirley from atop a large boulder.

"You mean all this gray stone is marble?"

"Every single piece. And the best thing is, it's free."

It didn't look like marble. The stones on the back of the truck looked like marble, with their freshly blasted sides of clear, glassy stone. The stone under my feet was weathered, dark, and bland. Shirley was racing up the hillside, so I followed. The air was cool and fresh; even at the bottom of the mountainside of rubble there was altitude and solitude. It was like walking on the moon. After a time I could look back and see all the way to the coast, but then I had to turn and race after Shirley again.

I hopped and skipped as best I could, but it was difficult with a wobbly pack on my back. Shirley raced ahead like a mountain goat. She had stripped to a tank top, and wrapped her sweater around her waist. Shirley looked at home on the field of stone; she stopped now and again to look down and wave me upward. At one point she yelled, "We have to find you the perfect stone!" Her voice echoed across the mountainside.

"Wait!" I yelled. "I'll be up in a minute."

Shouldering the pack, I quickly picked my way upward. I had to spend a lot of time looking at my feet, rather than at the view. The quiet was broken by another blast from the quarry above. The hillside was steeper, the climbing became work, and every step was heavy. Shirley continued to float upward. I was sweating. I swore at myself for climbing after this crazy woman. I talked to myself as I marched upward about the idiocy of being out on a barren marble hillside. The sun slipped behind some clouds, and it was quickly cooler and darker.

"Shirley!" I yelled up the mountainside. "There's a million tons of marble here. Why do we have to climb to the top to find the perfect stone?"

Shirley yelled back, "Find a stone that talks to you!"

I drove up the hillside, driven by fury. When marble started talking to me, I was heading home. The American expat sculptor Peter Wagner had warned me everyone who stayed in Pietrasanta went insane; perhaps it started with a casual chat with a block of marble. Up top, I could see quarry men waving down to Shirley. I suspected they had binoculars, and could see a blue-eyed, raven-haired, braless woman in a tank top scrambling up the stones to them with an ecstatic smile on her face.

Despite myself, I looked at the stones beneath my feet, wondering how one might signal to me. A stone might quiver slightly. But all the stones looked the same. Some were big, some were small, all were immobile and silent.

Another explosion rocked the hillside, perhaps the quarry men were celebrating the arrival of Shirley in their midst. I stood on the edge of a large stone, bent my neck back and watched a cloud of smoke rise above the mountainside and into the white sky. Shirley was now dancing from stone to stone, as if she had the lead in a ballet.

"Shirley!" I yelled up the hillside.

The workmen above were waving to her, and Shirley was clearly heading for the top. I charged up over the boulders, the pack bouncing on my shoulders, my thighs driving downward into the stone. I skipped, jumped, and scrambled. "Shirley!" I yelled. "Shirley, wait!" For a time, it all came together. The pack stabilized, my feet were the feet of a mountain goat, and I could have closed my eyes. Instead, I raised my eyes from the stones flashing by beneath my feet to look up the mountainside for Shirley. When I looked back at my feet, they were in midair between stones, waiting for further instructions. When I hesitated, they locked, and I flew forward, landing in a gap between two boulders.

I lay there, out of sight of the world. My hands were scraped, my elbows and knees were bruised; the pack had whacked me in the back of the head. Stone surrounded me, and I thought I heard the large boulder to my left say, "This guy's a jackass." Another explosion rocked the hillside. Rubble dribbled into a crack between two smaller stones. The weight on my back was a comfort, a hand saying, "Stay down, my friend, don't move; she will give up and go away soon."

From up above and far away I heard a voice crying, "I found it! I found a stone!"

"So have I," I said.

"It's a beauty!" cried Shirley. "Where are you hiding?"

The words *beauty* and *hiding* echoed around above me. I didn't feel like shouting or moving. My elbows were beginning to ache as the thrill of throwing myself against stone wore off. I stared at the boring, gray stone, and closed my eyes. Shirley yelled up above on the desolate plain of rubble about the stone she had found, and eventually curiosity raised me from my grave. I wondered: Among a million stones, what could be the attraction of any one?

"I've found it," Shirley said.

She was right above me, blocking the sun.

"Are you all right?"

"I'm fine," I said without moving from my facedown position. "I was just chatting with these two fellows."

"You fell?"

"Yes."

"But you're all right?"

"Yes."

"Good," said Shirley. "Because I found a wonderful stone."

Shirley sat down; I could see her feet dangling into my pit.

"I'm curious," I said. "What makes this stone so special?"

Shirley reached down and started to wrestle with the pack. She undid the straps and pulled it off me. "It spoke to me," said Shirley.

"Does it really talk to you, or is that a figure of speech?"

"I'll tell you if you get up out of there."

So I rolled over, groaning for drama, and Shirley gave me her hand and I stepped from the stone pit.

"Where is it?" I said.

"Up there," said Shirley, pointing back up the hillside.

"Why didn't you carry it down?"

"It's too heavy for me," said Shirley. "That's why I brought you along."

"I'm just a coolie?"

"Yes," said Shirley. "If you couldn't find your own stone, you should at least carry mine."

Shirley sat down and opened the backpack. She removed a jug of red Chianti, saying, "At least you didn't break this." She took out a covered bowl of pasta, a round loaf of brown bread, mozzarella and pecorino cheese, plates, utensils, place mats, and napkins. The bowl and the bottle had been wrapped in towels, which she set out on a large slab for us to sit on, and then she set a rock table. A blast sent a shudder from the hillside. Shirley handed me the bottle of Chianti, and I rubbed my fingers over the old label. She explained that Peter Wagner had given her the bottle of Chianti. "He has a whole cellar of old Chianti bottles," said Shirley. "When he first came here to learn to sculpt, he did odd jobs to survive, and some restaurant was being torn down in Forte Dei Marmi, and they told him he could have whatever Chianti he could remove from the cellar. He took twelve cases." Shirley told me Peter Wagner was a graduate of the Rhode Island School of Design who was making a name for himself in SoHo in the early 1980s with conceptual sculptures and installations, but woke up one morning and just decided to quit "making ugly art." He left for Pietrasanta a couple of months later with a plane ticket and a couple of hundred dollars.

Looking up from the Chianti bottle and across the horizon, I saw a tiny ship making its way up the Italian coast. I dug a Swiss Army knife from the backpack, and I pulled out the cork. Shirley took a delicate sip from the bottle and closed her eyes.

"Wonderful," said Shirley. "Now we make a proper toast. Here's to you as you begin your sculpting career." Shirley took a sip and handed me the bottle and cut slices of pecorino. I swallowed and put the bottle between my knees. I took a bite of the sharp cheese and said, "How did you know I was going to start carving?"

Shirley ignored my question and said, "See if you can create a new fish."

"A new fish?" I said.

"Think about the forms of Henry Moore and Jean Arp," said Shirley. "In their day, those were new fish; now everyone knows about those forms. Go around to the studios and you see dozens of artists doing versions of Moore's and Arp's shapes. People call those copies 'Smoores' and 'Swarps.' "

"What's the difference between a Smoore and a Swarp?"

"A Smoore is any work that looks like one of Henry Moore's blobs, and a Swarp is any blob with a hole with in it."

"You're not showing much respect for the masters."

"I have a lot of respect for Moore and Arp," said Shirley. "What they did in their day was interesting. I have no respect for all the artists here who imitate old work. You have to make a new fish to earn my respect."

"But what's a new fish?"

"Imagine there is no such thing as a fish in the world," said Shirley. "Imagine if you invented the first fish. Everyone would be amazed."

"You're making it all sound a bit simplistic."

Shirley shrugged and said, "I don't think it *is* that complicated. There are a lot of people in the world who ruin art for everyone by making it all too complicated and confusing just so they can feel superior."

There was a blast from the quarry above. I had another drink from the bottle of Chianti, and was light-headed. I suddenly wanted to put my hands on marble. It was as if it was someone else who had been dithering. We finished lunch, and Shirley led me by hand up the hillside to her stone. It was bigger than a shoe box, and one side was covered in mud, the other in crystals.

"Why didn't you at least pick a clean one?"

"I like the dirt," said Shirley. "I won't carve all the dirt off. I want the stone to retain some sense of its origins."

Hoisting the stone up and cradling it in my arms, we started picking our way down the mountainside. Shirley wore the lightened pack. The sun was straight across, descending into the glass ocean, above which the sky was clear and blue.

"We're lucky," said Shirley. "I hope you know that much."

The church bells rang up from the riverside town of Seravezza. They tolled on and on. We had been to Seravezza, seen the World War I monument in the center of town with its machine gun pockmarks from World War II. The monument was of a naked man throwing down a large stone. We had sat by the river and had an espresso, under date palm trees, and watched the aquamarine river.

I walked faster than Shirley, perhaps because I was watching my feet, and she was admiring the view. At the bottom of the mountainside, I turned and waited for her to float down to me. As I watched her make her way down the mountainside, I thought about the sculpture Shirley had recently shown me. I was glad it was good. I needed her to be talented; otherwise we'd be two fools. Shirley had picked up hammer and chisel upon arrival in Pietrasanta and carved a nude female figure in a block of *statuario,* leaving a large section of the block raw stone. She made no model, she had no lessons; she simply banged out the sculpture. She learned Pietrasanta style: by watching and imitating other sculptors. Questions in Pietrasanta were a last resort for novice sculptors. When Shirley got to where I was sitting she said, "You didn't have to rush ahead."

"I want to get my hands on a hammer and chisel."

We stood in the road, waiting for the CLAP bus. Shirley finally rummaged in her backpack for the bus schedule. We studied it for some time, pondered the significance of the dots and stars and asterisks and their asociated fine print at the bottom of the schedule. "Maybe today is a *festa*," said Shirley, folding the schedule. We stood, looking down the road toward Seravezza, and then I turned and began to walk toward Pietrasanta with Shirley's stone. I hadn't gone too far when Shirley yelled behind me. She had been following, but at a distance. We were at least two miles from town, and the sun was setting. The western sky was turning orange.

She was off the side of the road, in rubble and tall weeds and rusting metal machines. All I could see was the top of her head, and her hand waving me over urgently. I slowly walked back to her; I wanted to get back to the piazza.

"What is it, Shirley?"

"Come see what I found."

Shirley was spitting on stones when I walked into the weeds. I asked her why she was spitting on stones at the end of the day by the side of the road, and she said, "So I can see what kind of marble I've found. I think this is statuario." Shirley was pointing to a small stone near her foot. It didn't look like much in the shadows.

"Statuario?"

"I think so," said Shirley. "If you want to carry it back you could make your first sculpture out of it."

Putting down Shirley's bardiglio, I moved past her and picked up the anonymous white chunk of stone. It was muddy, but Shirley spit on it again and wiped off the spot with her sleeve. "See how it looks translucent?" said Shirley. "It's statuario."

We both turned around in the road to look up at the peak of Mount Altissimo. A few kilometers north of Pietrasanta in the Apuan Alps, Monte Altissimo had always been Olympus to the marble carvers of Pietrasanta; Michelangelo went to extraordinary lengths to obtain pure white statuario marble from caves he cut into the peak of this cathedral of craggy, weathered stone.

Sergio was in his studio on Via Teatro just off the Pietrasanta piazza, and waved us in from the street. Shirley asked him if I could work at her table until he closed, and he smiled and went back to his own carving. Sergio was short and thick, with black hair and brown eyes. He was in his late thirties, and had inherited the studio a year before from his father, who had taught him the skills of an *artegiano* while warning him not to try to survive as a studio owner.

Shirley took a chisel and used it to tighten a large wooden vise on my stone. She handed me plastic safety goggles, and went to get a hammer from her locker. My stone was mute. It sat there. It didn't give me a hint what to do with it. Sergio had eight *studenti di marmi* at a time in his studio; each worked at their own wooden table. Everything was covered with white marble dust as if there had been a snowstorm. Shirley's white nude was on a shelf; a large yellow abstract occupied Sophia's table. At the table of an Israeli sculptor named Ari there was a copy of one of Michelangelo's hands emerging from black marble. Shirley came back with the hammer and said, "This is what you swing over your head in mighty blows, Michelangelo."

I took the hammer and tentatively swung it through the air. "Maybe we should start tomorrow," I said. "We shouldn't keep Sergio here."

"Take this," said Shirley, handing me a red chisel that looked like a railroad spike. "This is called a *subbia*. It's for removing chunks of stone, for roughing out the form."

Standing with the subbia in my left hand, the tip against the stone, I raised the hammer in my right. And I held that position for a while, thinking how I had always believed an artist should be able to see something trapped in the stone waiting to be released and granted life by genius. I saw nothing but a dirty stone under the tip of the subbia and was paralyzed. I was about to put down the hammer when Shirley said, "Just hit the hammer to the subbia to the marble."

With my first blow I grazed the subbia, and smacked the thumb of my left hand. I put down the chisel and hopped around the room. Sergio stopped his own carving, came over, and slapped me heartily on the back. He grabbed my injured thumb in his hand and yanked it about, smiling and chattering in Italian. After a while he slowed and I understood he was saying something like, "And now you are one of us." He raised my thumb in the air, and Shirley kissed me on the cheek.

My second blow, the hammer hit the subbia hit the marble. The subbia dribbled across the surface of the stone leaving the faintest of scratches, a tiny lightning bolt through the dirt. I had not even dented the stone. My first thought: *Marble is hard*. I took a moment and looked around again at the sculptures of the students on the tables, and I realized something had changed: I had a place in the marble sculpting world now; I was beneath the bottom. I was that scratch, that ancient riverbed as seen from the moon. A hierarchy was formed with my scratch at sea level and Michelangelo atop Monte Altissimo.

The stone was now my stone; I owned it. I wasn't in any way proud of the dribbly scratch, but I did feel a bonding going on, a sense of a future opening up between me and the dirty little stone. The stone wasn't going anywhere, so I left it and went over to watch the studio owner Sergio. He was carving the profile of a Madonna in relief, with her hands held in prayer, and her head bowed. His hands with hammer and chisel waved over the stone, as if he was in the midst of casting a spell. He was humming, and he danced around behind his table. Behind him, on the wall, a dozen of the same Madonna.

Looking back at my stone, I realized I had to come up with some idea for a sculpture. I stared at the marble hard, tried to see some hidden form. I closed my eyes and waited for inspiration to hit, some dream image to float before my eyes. Back in our apartment, late at night, I had come up with a number of ideas for sculptures, but now with the stone in front of me my mind was blank.

In order to look productive, I aimlessly made lines across the face of the stone. They looked like my original lightning bolt, but deeper. It gave me some small satisfaction that I could make these rows of wobbly lines across the stone, but it was the satisfaction of action, of the feel of the hammer in my hand, of the sight of the specks of dust falling.

Shirley took the subbia from me and said, "Use the right tool. The subbia is for removing chunks of stone. If you want to carve a line, use the *gradino*." Shirley placed a chisel in my hand. The chisel gave satisfaction; I was able to make straight lines. Using the chisel was using a tiny snowplow; it shaved off the stone smoothly. As I weighed the power of the hammer in my hand, I fished for an idea. Any shape out of the universe of shapes was available; not a single shape came to mind. My hand kept swinging the hammer; marble dust drifted to the floor.

Time passed; I whacked.

I was no longer hoping to make anything; the goal was to swing the hammer until Sergio closed his studio. Shirley left for the Bar Michelangelo. Sergio's tapping was a metronome, and I synchronized with him and the two of us worked our stones in harmony. I picked up the subbia again, and hit the stone harder. Since I had no hopes I was going to be able to come up with a sculpture, I enjoyed destroying my stone. The goal was to reduce the stone to chips and dust. My hand tightened on the subbia. I gave the hammer a little more handle. A few chips bounced off the wall. It crossed my mind that I might even look like I knew what I was doing to the stone.

As I would come to discover for myself, stone carving is demanding work. In the initial stages of a new marble sculpture, it is aggressive and violent. Stone does not give way to a caress. The stone yields with a shudder that echoes through the bones of the body, which are themselves stone, constructed of the same calcium as the marble. At the end of the day the hands are crabbed, the joints swollen, the spine crooked and stiff. There is little more primitive than this struggle of flesh wielding tools against stone, and the pains that come with the creative demolition. Sculptors pull muscles, pinch nerves, develop repetitve-motion disease, slip disks, and are constantly whacking thumbs into a pulp of bruised bone and tattered tissue. But beyond the daily pain is the always present risk of serious disfigurement or disablement. Stone is weighed by the ton, and those tons sometimes fall on fingers or toes or even legs. But the daily demand on the whole body that only marble sculpture as an art calls for, the daily bodily drain and pains, are rarely discussed at the Bar Michelangelo; there is a culture of stoicism.

My arm was a piston; it was on automatic. That first afternoon I finally took chisel to stone, I bashed my thumb a couple more times. And then although I wasn't looking for anything, there was the bas-relief of a Roman nose in my stone. The nose was an accident; I had dug around in one place for too long. As I carved out this newly discovered nose, I remembered a story my mother once told me. She said that when I was a child, I had turned to her as we walked across a field and asked, "Is it okay if I see things in the clouds?" There was an unspoken bias in my ambitious family against *seeing things in the clouds*, against seeing *anything* other than the concrete realities.

After seeing the Roman nose in the stone on that day I first took chisel to stone, I couldn't sculpt fast enough. Shirley returned from the

Bar Michelangelo and handed me a chisel, and I carved a mouth. I decided I could carve this mouth, as I could vaguely see it in my mind already carved. The lips went smoothly; I even surprised myself with what I thought was some delicate carving. The stone was now soft as flesh, and I thought of a conversation I'd had with the German sculptor Markus on one of my first nights in the Pietrasanta piazza. "How long have you carved marble?" I asked.

"This I must tell you now," said Markus, grabbing his empty glass of Chianti and almost angrily pointing at me. "Stone is now not so hard as before when I do not carve marble."

I said, "I suppose it gets easier the more you do it."

"No, this is not my meaning," said Markus. "This is not what I say to you. It is the stone that is not so hard now, the stone."

Taking off my safety goggles that first afternoon in Sergio's studio, I found they were covered in dust. I had been sculpting half blind. I stood up straight; my back cracked. I felt as if I was returning to Tuscany, to the studio, and wondered how one applied for citizenship in the world I had just visited while sculpting. I enjoyed *that* world much more than *this* world.

Sergio had set down his tools; he smiled at me and said, *"Va bene?"*

I said, *"Va bene. Grazie, Sergio."*

What I had carved, what I had uncovered, what was staring up from the small chunk of Michelangelo's statuario, was clearly a god. An ancient god, murderously enraged with me for leaving him buried for decades. Sergio turned off the lights and we left the studio and walked through the drizzle down the dark and narrow Via Teatro toward the lights of the piazza.

AZURE

My mother, also known as Helen, appeared at my classroom door this morning, her dark glasses propped over her regular ones. "Excuse me, Azure, will you come with me?" she said. The teacher had been talking about I don't know what, and I was writing a note to my boyfriend Bir, who is also the king's youngest son, telling him to meet me after school to go to the Annapurna Coffee Shop. But I just picked up my books and stuffed a wad of notes in my pocket, and Ms. Grafton did this accusing squint while she kept talking—blah, blah, blah. She should be used to this by now. It's the third time this year I've had to leave school. I stay out for a few weeks and then come back when Helen realizes there is nothing else for me to do.

Helen's shoes clicked ahead of me down the empty hall, her green dress swishing, and I sneezed at the door in the bright sunlight. She told Ganesh, our driver, to shake a leg, and he dropped his cigarette, stubbing it out as he got into the Jeep. Helen says if we lived in England, where she is from, she would definitely drive herself. But living in Kathmandu, driving is enough to give any normal person a coronary.

"Sweetheart," Helen said. A cigarette dangled from the corner of her mouth as she twisted around in the front seat to look at me. "I'm sorry. You know this isn't because of you. I wanted to tell you this weekend, but I realized after you left the house this morning that I needed you to help me with the party tonight. At least this way, they can blame

your crazy mother." She blew smoke out her window as we passed a
crowd of students in the park listening to a man with a megaphone.
She took hold of my knee. "I just couldn't stand to think of you another
minute with all that embassy trash, corrupting all that's good in you.
And we need to get ready to go to Tokyo in a few weeks. Do you forgive me?"

I squeezed her hand, and she let go of me and faced forward again.
"The teachers are mostly dolts anyway," I said and tapped the glass
with my knuckle. Two boys on a rusty bike teetered next to us, staring
in until Ganesh cut them off, veering out of the traffic down a side road.

Helen said she was going to take my brother, Sonam, who is fourteen
and a year older than me, out of school too, but she would tell him
when he got home, because she wanted the day to be just for us.

We were getting out of the car at the house when another car appeared at the open gate—a Yak and Yeti Hotel car—and Helen motioned it in. The driver opened the door for the couple in back, and
they slid out, smoothing the damp creases in their clothes as they
stood. "Well, hiii, you must be Helen," the woman said, touching her
blonde, curled-back hair with her fingertips. She gave a toothy smile,
but her face made me think of pancake makeup. The man rubbed a
soiled handkerchief over his forehead and smiled weakly. Stomach
problems, I decided. Helen introduced me and asked if I didn't want
to rest as she led them to the little annex she uses as her shop.

Upstairs, at the edge of the ballroom, I kicked off my shoes and ran,
sliding across the long diamonds of sunlight on the parquet out to the
balcony, where I caught myself on the railing. On the roof next door,
the maid lifted wet clumps out of a plastic basin and unfurled the saris
down the dry brick walls, securing them with rocks. We used to live
in a much nicer house, but three years ago Helen was offered a price
she couldn't refuse. She needed the cash, and at the time she wasn't
talking to my father, Nima. They're divorced but they still do business
together. This house, like our other one, used to be a *rhana* palace, but
we think it must have been used just for entertaining, or for a mistress,
because it has so few rooms—just a maid's room and the kitchen
downstairs, and upstairs a big ballroom with a room behind it where
we sleep.

I changed into a leotard and shorts and put on my Walkman. Bir and
I mostly listen to The Cure and harder British stuff, music that churns

you like a wave breaking and spits you out the other side, sputtering and wanting more. I danced around the half-packed suitcases on the sandy floor and up onto the bed. When the song stopped, I took off the Walkman, walked over my hands, and went into the big room to practice Newari dance.

Since I was tiny, I have been taking lessons with Helen at the Hotel Vajra. The idea is to isolate and control different parts of your body, sending all your *prahna*—your life energy—toward that foot or set of fingers or neck or whatever. "Seduce without sex, without losing control of yourself," Shiva says, which is the kind of thing he has always said to Helen and is just beginning to say to me. Before I could walk, I can remember watching Helen dance, moving above me with her eyes wide open but not seeing, her silver *dhorje* swinging from her neck, her hair pinned up, and her shirt patchy with sweat.

Helen's slippers tapped lightly as she came across the floor, and I opened my eyes. She was smiling, with her arms crossed.

"Let's go to the Solti for lunch and a sauna," she said.

"You sold something?" I asked.

"Clever girl! The tapestry from Bhutan that we've had for a year. Fifteen hundred dollars."

"Hooray!" I did a little spin.

The Solti is one of the nicest hotels in Kathmandu. We took the sauna first, which gets the demons out and makes you feel like a baby you are so clean—as if your skin was made of lettuce or a very thin dough wrapping. We had chicken sandwiches on homemade bread, green salad with vinaigrette, mango sherbet, iced tea. Then we fell asleep in the sun. Before we left, we had our nails painted and bought a French *Vogue* that filled the car with too much perfume and made it smell like another country on the way home.

Sonam's bike was outside when we got there, but Helen didn't notice, so I went upstairs ahead of her to see if I could find him. He was bouncing a basketball on the balcony, still in his school clothes with his tie loosened and his shirt untucked. Before I could say anything, Helen came up behind me.

"You're not planning on continuing that, I hope," she said.

Sonam caught the ball and pushed his bangs back from his eyes. "There's no other flat surface to bounce on."

"You know how it irritates me when you talk back," she said.

He bounced the ball once. "Can I just—"

"Go outside," Helen said, pressing tighter on my shoulders. Sonam shook his head and walked in through another door on the balcony, holding the ball. "Stop. Wait. Actually, I need you two right now to help with this party for Frederick."

Frederick is an American Buddhist who lives out in Boudha with his family. He translates books for some of the holiest Tibetan lamas and has written his own, all of which we have at our house. I was looking forward to seeing his daughters, Leslie and Angela, and finding out what people said about me at school after I left.

"First of all, tell Maya that memsahib wants all the tables dusted and the pillows beaten. Then we have to roll back the rugs," Helen said. She has us do all her translating even though she used to speak Nepali. "Then I want you two to go buy *raaxi*, soda, and some spicy *kaajaa*."

Sonam changed his clothes and we walked up to the little bazaar at the crossroads, past the bicycle repair and the sari shop, where a pantless baby played on the mat in front of the stacks of bolted cloth. Sonam wanted to buy chocolate, but I told him we had to get Helen's liquor and snacks first and see how much was left over. In the end, we bought Chinese candies from a jar instead.

At home, we helped Helen arrange the cane chairs outside and set out the bottles and bowls of hot peanuts on a table. Sonam was tossing peanuts higher and higher in the air and catching them in his mouth when he bumped into the table.

Helen spun around. "You better not cause any trouble tonight," she said.

"Why do you always think I will? I don't," he said.

"You're stubborn, you don't listen, and you don't use common sense most of the time," Helen said. She was stirring her drink with a ballpoint pen.

Sonam dropped the peanuts he was holding back into the bowl and walked into the house.

"Your grimy hands," Helen said, picking off the top peanuts and throwing them into the bushes.

Frederick and his family arrived first, bringing ice cream from Nirula's, except our refrigerator is broken, so we ate the ice cream right away out of glasses—Helen had sold the bowls. Others began to arrive, by car and scooter, and Sonam and I took Leslie and Angela upstairs. We left the grown-ups talking with their faces tilted to the last of the sun, showing the veins on their necks. Helen motioned me over and whispered to put away the little ancient bronze statue she had just bought.

Our house is actually an extension of the annex, because most things in it, including the house itself, are for sale so that we can move abroad for the summer and make a clean slate of it when we come back. *If* we come back. Helen says Nepal has been driving her batty ever since the students started protesting. She says that if people knew what was good for them, they would go back to the days of the *rhana* regime, that this country was never made for democracy, and democracy is a joke anyway, if you look at America these days. "At least people have a sense of God here," Helen says. We ourselves are Buddhists, which is why my parents met. Helen came overland via Turkey, and when her British friends went home, she stayed—first because of her teacher, then because of Nima, my father, whose family had a store down on Freak Street then. He had escaped from Tibet to Kathmandu with his mother when he was a kid after his father was killed by the Chinese. He and Helen named me for the blue sky over Tibet and because a cloudless sky is also the symbol of a clear and peaceful mind. Now we only see Helen's teacher a few times a year, but we make offerings at our shrine every morning at the far end of the ballroom. I do it if Helen forgets.

The four of us played freeze tag on the wood floor and Sonam skidded into Maya, who was sweeping, and held onto her waist. He said she had to play now. "O.K., little boy," she said—even though she's only a few years older than he is—and darted after him. Leslie had just made a dash, unfreezing all of us, when Helen called from downstairs. "Azure, is everything ready? Can we come up?"

"Two minutes," I yelled back. "Sonam, light the candles and I'll do the mosquito coils. Leslie, Angela, you two straighten the pillows." I sent Maya down with the small bag of trash and heard Helen say, "Memsahib really does hate to wait." But it was in English, so maybe Maya didn't understand.

Alastair, who is about forty, caught me by the elbow on my way out and called me "little sister" in Nepali, asking me to come talk to him. Later, I told him.

"Promise?" he said, still holding on.

"Promise," I said, and he winked and let go.

We kids went into the kitchen, and I wanted Maya to make us some food. She said she would, but there was only a little bit of rice left. Not even onions or garlic. It was dark, and I was sure the stores would be closed.

"Why don't you have any food?" Leslie asked. I told her that since we were leaving the country soon and the fridge was broken, we had been eating out a lot.

"Not even lentils?" Leslie asked. I said I wished she would drop it.

Maya said she had a little food in her room and came back with a bunch of small, sweet bananas and a couple of packets of biscuits. We sat down on the little stools and divvied them up while Maya brewed black tea.

"This sucks," Sonam said, peeling his second banana. "I am definitely moving back in with Dad." They get along much better than Sonam and Helen do. But Nima has a new wife and baby, and also—though I don't remind him—Sonam has to go to Tokyo with us in order to get the paintings out. Each person is allowed three artifacts going through customs, and a second painting can be concealed behind the first between layers of silk backing. My father supplies the paintings from his Tibetan art and relics store on King's Road, and Helen transports them to auction houses in Europe or Japan, where she can get prices sometimes five times more than what the tourists in Kathmandu will pay.

"I think we should go dance," I said when we'd eaten everything.

Sonam was playing an invisible guitar on the landing and singing Buddy Holly's "Roller Coaster" when Helen came out with Frederick and stopped behind the doorway at the top of the stairs. I grabbed Sonam to shush him, and he scrambled downstairs. Frederick and Helen started to kiss. Leslie looked up at them and at me, and I put a finger to my lips and motioned for her to take Angela down. I've seen Helen kiss him before, but never with his daughters standing there. Frederick used to come over to our house a lot a few years ago, and I asked Helen about it then. She said that he and his wife, Sherry, had a special arrangement in their marriage so that they would never feel claustrophobic. I was hidden in the shadows, but when Helen made a humming noise, I used it as a cover to move out.

The three others were outside drinking Cokes and bouncing a tennis ball between them. I leaned against the house and closed my eyes.

"Azure," Sonam said. "Play with us." He lobbed the ball to me, so that I had to squint up at the night to see it. It fell right in my hands. The music still twirled out over us.

"Me," Leslie said, and I smashed the ball down so that it scattered pebbles as it bounced. "Jeez," she said going back into the dusty grass to find it. I felt sick of them all of a sudden. The burning end of Maya's cigarette made little orange arcs in the air as she sat smoking on the step to the darkened kitchen, and I went to sit with her.

Maya handed me the pack and called me naughty. I tapped one out and cupped my hands as she struck the match. The little yellow-blue flame lit up our faces. We have the same color skin. She's been at our house just three weeks, and Helen says maybe she'll bring her to Japan with us. I exhaled. They were Khukri cigarettes, the Nepali brand that's just a little tobacco and a lot of filler leaf mixed in. Bir says that I of all people should smoke imports, but I like Khukris. They make me calm.

"My mother's horny," I said in English, but Maya smiled.

"It's a horny party. Come here," she said in Nepali.

We walked over to the wall.

On the balcony, Alastair and this woman, Tsering, were making out. Mashing face, Bir calls it, maybe from his brother who went to school in England. Through the windows, we could see people dancing, and there was a woman's high-pitched "Ooh, that's awful."

Alastair leaned away from Tsering, and she shook her hair over her shoulders. He put his hands under the front of her blouse. They laughed, and I shivered. "Old people," Maya said, smiling. We went back to the step and sat down. Maya crushed her cigarette under her flip-flop and said she should go upstairs. I told her I'd go with her, but I saw Sonam climbing the trellis up the wall to the bedroom and went to lean against it so it wouldn't fall over.

"Thanks," he said and disappeared into the dark room. A flashlight beam waved around, and when Sonam came out he dropped two jackets and scooted down, with his guitar in one hand. Reaching the bottom, he handed the jackets to Leslie, who was rebraiding Angela's hair.

Upstairs, Frederick and Sherry danced cheek to cheek. Alastair and Tsering were talking inside now, and Alastair grabbed my hand and asked me to dance, but Helen called me over.

I sat down next to her, and she put her arm around me, enclosing me in the cloud of her breath. "You know all these people, don't you?" And she introduced me to Jacques and his new wife Sylvie, and Bob, Christine, Art, Heidi, Tom. I knew most of them by face anyway.

"Are you having a good time?" she asked.

"Yes," I said and moved away a little.

"Would you ask Sonam to see if he can find one more bottle of *raaxi* and some 7-Up? We're nearly out."

I nodded.

"Good. And I wish you'd stay up here."

"I'll just tell Sonam first."

Sonam said no when I asked, picking up the song he had been playing for Leslie and Angela.

"Please do it," I said.

"She's a witch," he said.

"You're just stupid if you don't. I promise it will make her happy." He groaned and asked me to put his guitar in the house. Leslie said she and Angela were coming with me, and when they came into the room their parents pulled them into a circle to dance. Helen was laughing on the couch, speaking slurry French. And Christine and Art each took one of my hands. They danced very American—all wavy legs and arms—and I can't really dance like that, but the house felt warm suddenly, filled up with light, and the mosquitoes and moths, even with the coils, were having their own party around the lamps, with all the doors to the balcony open. It would be impossible to sleep later. I danced in spite of myself, feeling good, jumping up and down with my hair flapping around me. I saw Maya out of the corner of my eye emptying ashtrays and picking up plastic cups. Just beyond the doorway, she finished someone's drink.

Sonam's face was shiny and pink when he returned, so I knew he'd sped the whole way, and I watched him go to Helen on the couch, pushing back his hair, and present the bottles. I wondered how far he'd had to go to find a store that was open. She motioned for him to put them on the coffee table and said, "Go away now. That's enough."

"I tell you," she said to Tom. "Someone is going to Swiss boarding school next year. He causes me no end of grief."

I followed Sonam to the top of the stairs. He punched his fist into his hand and trod little circles, sucking in short, catching breaths.

"Fuck," he said. I stood by the wall. He rubbed his eyes suddenly with his fists and leaned over the marble railing resting his head in his arms. "Fuck," he said again.

"Hey," I said, putting my hand on his back. His shirt was damp. "You know she's drunk."

"Even when she's not," he said with his head still down. "I just thought—I'm so stupid." Looking at him, I noticed I was pulling on my hair over and over. He turned away.

"Do you want a Coke?" I asked.

"Yeah, where did you put my guitar?"

Sherry and Frederick walked out with their girls. Angela was in Frederick's arms. "Good night, you two," Sherry said. I stood up.

"Bye, Azure. Bye, Sonam," Leslie said, looking back up the stairs. "See you soon."

I lifted a hand.

The party wound down after that. I gave Sonam a sweater, and he went outside. Helen took me by the hand as she said good-bye to people and then rested her arm heavily on my shoulder. "That last bottle nearly did us in. It was just a step away from kerosene," she said. Alastair hugged her and planted a wet kiss on my cheek. He smelled of deodorant and sweat. Tsering laughed, and Helen did too. I looped my arm around her waist and smiled with my lips closed.

Everybody was gone. I flicked off the music, and Helen collapsed on the couch and closed her eyes. "Azure, will you please turn down these lights and find me some aspirin?" she said. I did, and Sonam tiptoed past her to the back room.

I brought in the coils and closed the doors. "Such a good girl," Helen said, and I sat down on the couch with her. "Come here." She pulled me to her, putting a cushion on her lap, and I lay down, but the cicadas' trilling buzzed as if it were coming from inside me.

"Won't you dance for me?" Helen asked sleepily.

I jumped up.

"Can I wear one of the new dresses from Hong Kong?"

"Of course," she said, and I ran into the other room and pulled the three that were still on hangers from the open suitcase.

"Which one?" I asked, holding them up.

"Let me see," she said toeing off her shoes and drawing her feet under her. I rested the white one on the arm of the couch and tore the sheer plastic from the black ones. The long one was tight velveteen on top with a full gauzy skirt and the short one was simpler, just silk with thin straps and a skirt of petals.

"This one, please," I said, holding up the short one.

"Of course."

"Sonam, stay in the other room," I said and changed right there. The night had gotten cold and blew through a window, bringing up goosebumps on my arms, but I didn't care, and I asked Helen to zip me up.

"Beautiful," Helen said and smiled. I did a little turn and went to clip back my hair and find a cassette.

"Come help me roll out the rug," I said to Sonam, who was curled up on the bed reading a comic book with a flashlight. We moved the chairs and unrolled the white carpet. It was a perfect square to dance on. I set the tape player on the table, and Sonam moved into the shadows.

"You are a vision," Helen said, propping her chin on her hand as I stood in a corner waiting for the music to start. The tape whirred and clicked as it finished rewinding, and I dropped into the music as if into water. The white space, the air above it, was mine, an aquarium. We've been listening to the tape for years. The singer's voice is thrillingly low, and it shook through me as I dipped and drew my arms, folding in and turning out again.

"Wait, Azure," I heard Helen say. "Wait for me." And she hoisted herself up and went to one corner. I went back to the other. We started again.

Her loose white blouse and pants billowed around her like sails. Her bare feet are still smooth and white, with red toenails. She drew a moon and cut it in half. I circled her in my black dress, feeling small and light, able to sense where she would turn next. I could just see Sonam leaning back against the wall and Maya's glowing cigarette in the far doorway. How strange we must have looked to them, I thought, my big mother and me dancing as if we were truly happy.

NOW WHY COME THAT IS?

That squall. That squall: metallic and beastly, squalling, coming from the bottom of hell itself, a squall full of suffering and pleas for mercy, a squall so familiar since Percy's earliest days, from when he was a little boy feeding his daddy Malcolm's Poland China brood sows . . .

But he didn't want to hear it now, damn it, not now, no, for now Percy Terrell was deep inside a dream. He and Elvis were on the town—was it Memphis? New Orleans? Nashville?—he didn't really know, and it didn't really matter. 'Cause he was in this diner with the King after a wild night of drinking and pool—the velvet night as tangible as the sheets in which he entangled himself at this moment of the dream—at this moment when he and Elvis sat in the diner with the checkered red and white tablecloth with two blondes, one each, one for him, and one for the King; and Percy had his hand on the milky-red thigh of that big-legged gal who smiled through her smacking gum and that leg was so soft and so inviting and she smiled even bigger as Percy moved his hands up that thigh toward—

But that squalling got louder as if someone were murdering that damn hog over and over, calling Percy back to wakefulness, and Percy didn't want to wake up, not with this fine big-legged thing sitting next to him, practically begging for it, and Elvis looking on across the table through his sunglasses, his arm around his sweetie for the night.

"What's your name again, hon?"

"Evangeline," she said.

"Evangeline. What a pretty name. Yeah." Percy slid his hand a little higher. "Yeah. What's that smell?"

At that moment, the moment when the dreamer begins to lose the threads and fabric of his dream, Percy began to dwell more and more on that vile, that powerful and obnoxious odor. Was it the woman? No, hadn't smelled her before. She looked clean enough. And the squalling kept on and on and the smell of hog. Hog. Hog.

Percy sat up in the bed, wide awake. As he blinked and focused, the squalling continued, but not in the bedroom now, and presently stopped altogether. Percy swung his feet over the side of the bed and one foot landed in something warm and slick, the sensation at once comforting and sickening, ooey and gooey and warm. His bare foot slid on the Carolina blue carpet.

"Shit."

Shit. There it was, and Percy's heart almost leapt for joy. Almost. For his foot was in a turd. But he had proof. At long last, the evidence he needed.

"Rose," he called to his snoring wife, turning on the bedside lamp. "Rose." He began to shake her. "Rose, wake up. Look, honey, look. That damn bastard has been here and he's left his calling card. Wake up!"

Rose Terrell smacked her mouth absently, and frowned, the sleep so deep around her eyes. "Hmmm?"

"Look, honey, look." Percy held his soiled foot perilously close to his wife's face. "See, Rose, see it there! I wont lying. He was here. That bastard was here."

Rose barely opened one eye, briefly glanced at her husband's brown-stained foot and gleeful face, and rolled over. "Percy? Pllleeeeaaassee take a bath. You stink." Rose brought the sheet over her head, and almost as quickly began to snore.

Percy, a little dejected, removed his foot, and with a little hesitation began to wipe it clean with a tissue. Yet he was not completely deflated, no. He was not crazy, as his besoiled foot and annoyed nostrils bore witness. This proof was all he had needed, a physical sign, a residue; and with all the stubbornness his Scotch-Irish blood could muster, he was going to prove—at least to himself—that he was not mad; he was indeed being visited by a hog.

A reddish-brown rusty razorback, to be exact, an old boar hog with unpulled incisors long enough to be called tusks, kite-big, floppy ears, and massive testicles the size of a catcher's mitt. For now on six weeks this hog would appear out of nowhere, without warning or preamble, anywhere—in the living room, in the cab of his pickup, at the store, entreating Percy, staring at Percy, following Percy, and the damned fool thing of it was that nobody but Percy had—could—see it; and Percy had no idea how it came and went.

Rose Terrell had listened to Percy—who for not one minute believed the hog to be a figment of his imagination—and was absolutely unconvinced. In fact, seeing that Percy otherwise had all his faculties, she clearly assumed Percy was fooling again—like the time he swore up and down that there was a snake in the plumbing (a very bad joke), and ignored him. Percy could tell that was what she had figured, and had given up on her, had simply stopped commenting on the hog, even when it showed up and sat at his side all through breakfast. Now he knew the whole damn thing could be explained away. Something someone else could see, smell, hell, even taste. Now he just had to find out who was going to such lengths for a practical joke. Percy wasn't certain. But he'd find out in time. Got your hog right here, mister. So Percy would play along, 'cause there was no way in hell she and everybody else didn't see that damned hog.

But now, now he had evidence and substance. And though, upon reflection, he had no idea what to do next, other than clean up the mess, sitting there on the side of the bed, his foot encrusted with drying excrescence, Percy Terrell felt a glimmer of something like hope, a sense that perhaps he were not going mad.

That first night he had seen it, madness was far from his mind; the whole occurrence had simply been a matter of negligence, of chance, of curious curiosity. He had been at his desk around eight o'clock in his office at the back of the general store, deep in thought, poring over tax document after tax document, trying desperately to find a mistake his fool accountant had made, cussing at this damn new machine that Rose bought him, damn thing was supposed to be fast, digital and all, but it kept losing the figures, coming up with zero or *e*, and . . .

Percy had heard something outside his office, in the belly of the store, something clicking on the old hardwood floor. He stopped, tilted his head to give a listen. A few more clicks. "Rose? That you?" He didn't hear the clicks. "Malcolm? Percival? Philip?" Nothing, just the refrigerator going off, a car passing by outside, the buzz of the overhead light. Percy went back to work. Presently he heard it again, but closer, decidedly a *click* or a *clock* or a *cluck* sound, of something hard, yet a bit muffled against the wood. Something walking. Percy got up to inspect. Everything looked shadow-drenched and shadow-full, the ghostly beams of the emergency lights enhancing the shadowscape, making the rows of fishing rods and gun racks and boxes of mufflers and barrels of three-penny nails and the yarn section, the bubblegum machine, the pipes and monkey wrenches and shovels and baby dolls, seem about to move. Yet all was bathed in after-closing quiet, and still. Percy saw this dim world every night and he had never given it a second thought: same as it was during the day. But for some reason, this night, at this moment, he felt a little spooky.

"Who that out there?" Nothing. "Store's closed, now." By and by, Percy began to feel silly, just a tree branch knocking against the roof, and turned around to set his mind to line 27e on page 12 of whatever the hell that form was. After a bit his mind was once again stinging with the unshakable accuracy of what his accountant had cyphered true, and how much he would not be putting in T-bills this year, when he felt a presence. Someone was standing at the door. He didn't want to give in to the surprise, and his mind instantly went to the three rifles on the wall behind him, just below the flattened rattlesnake skin he had tanned himself. If they had a gun trained on him, he wouldn't be able to reach it in time. Reluctantly he looked up.

Percy actually hollered. And flung his chair back so hard that the wall shook and the bronze gubernatorial citation he had received in 1975 fell to the ground with a clank. Had it been a human being person, Percy would have been ready, but before him stood this great big ole hog, its head jerking here and there, inspecting the place, coming back every now and again to Percy, its eyes piercing and inhumanly human.

"Git!" Percy said from the chair, collecting himself, wondering how the hell a hog got in his store. "Git on, now, git." Percy sprang to his feet, now simply annoyed, annoyed that someone had obviously left the door open or it came open and this hog got in. He grabbed a broom from behind the door and waved it at the hog, no stranger to the dumb, docile nature of the creatures. "Git on, now. Git on." Wondering who it could belong to, hoping it hadn't shit in the store. Damn. Damn. Damn. The hog grunted and began to back up. In his frustration Percy hit the creature on the nose with the broom. "Git on out of here and back to where you belong!"

With that crack of the broom the hog backed up two steps and raised its head, opening its swine mouth wide, and let out a piercing, brassy bellow, a bellow of outrage and anger, loud enough to make Percy step back and almost drop the broom. And with a quickness that belied its enormous size, the hog leapt and ran, the clackety-clackety of its hoofy gallop reporting against the store's walls. Percy chased after it, but soon realized he didn't hear the hog anymore. He switched on the store lights, which momentarily rendered him blind with their glare. He didn't see the hog. He searched up and down each aisle, calling it, stopping to listen, but heard nothing. After about twenty minutes, his frustration at the boil, he got on the horn and called his sons and wife and the two men who worked in the store. "No, Dad. I don't know nothing about no hog." "Percy, I locked and checked all the doors 'fore I left. How could a hog get in there?" " 'Swhat I want to know, Ed!" When his youngest and dimmest son, Philip Malcolm, suggested, "Well, maybe he climbed in through the window," Percy just slammed the phone down, annoyed, angered, pissed-off beyond anything he could remember in recent memory. He sat at his desk, stomped his foot once, sighed, crammed all the tax forms and files into his satchel, turned out the lights, and left.

Days passed and the memory of the mystery hog began to bore Percy with the equality of its nagging and its curiosity. He went about his days with the grim, quotidian joylessness and banal glory with which he filled each day. Rising at five to feed the dogs, watching the farm reports from Greenville, eating breakfast that Rose prepared herself since Agnes didn't arrive until eight; going to open the store, checking everything; driving around the farm, checking this, maybe having a meeting in Crosstown with his lawyer or his banker or the manager of the mill, lunch most days at Nellie's Cafe, a plate of barbecue that his doctor said he should at least cut back on, with a glass of iced tea— these were his days, as empty as they were full. And even Percy, lord of York County, had dreams of going off away somewhere, maybe on safari, hunting big game. He had done that once, back in '52, and had a fairly good time in Kenya, got off a good shot at an antelope, but didn't bag a thing. These days it was too much trouble, especially since those uppity coloreds made it illegal. He'd met a man a few years back who said that they'd guarantee a big kill in one of those African countries, Percy forgot which one, but it would cost him somewhere in the neighborhood of fifty thousand American dollars, the man had said, and Percy had said, Thank you kindly, and good-bye, 'cause Malcolm Terrell didn't raise no fool. No, sir. Thank you, sir. So he figured he'd content himself with deer and coon and ducks and the occasional big fish; though, truth to tell, at fifty-eight, Percy Terrell was losing his taste for killing things, something he'd never admit to another soul. Some days just being in the woods of an autumn or in a boat under the big sky was reward in and of itself. Perhaps Percy was at a point that he could even admit it to himself.

A week and six days passed, and Percy had damn near forgotten about the hog—he remembered really, mostly, that feeling of horror that had involuntarily gripped him upon the sight of the thing. That afternoon he stopped by one of the twenty-three turkey houses he owned, a set of five over in Mill Swamp, were Ab Batts was fixing the feeding system that had been breaking with annoying frequency. This turkey house was about thirty yards long and Percy could see Ab bent over at work at the far end. Percy despised these dumb creatures, gobbling and gibbering about his feet and ankles, their heads just above knee level, the sight of their red and gelatinous waffles making him sometimes shiver with disgust. Turkeys were too dumb to walk out of the rain, but sometimes one would get its feathers riled and would peck at you. One tom turkey made him so mad once that he stomped it to death before Percy realized what he was doing, and which he later regretted 'cause the price went up that very day.

As Percy waded through the dirty white mess of jabbering poultry, kicking and shooing, he called out to Ab and Ab waved at him and went on working. As Percy got about halfway into the house, the turkeys started making more and more of a commotion, and started parting even before Percy got in their midst, bunching along the wire-mesh walls, hollering, crying even, it seemed to Percy's ears. Percy looked about, baffled and even Ab Batts jerked up, amazed at the unruly fuss. Then Ab's eyes fixed on Percy with a mild degree of consternation and puzzlement, but Percy came to see it was not he Ab had transfixed in his glare.

"Boss," yelled Ab. "What you bring a hog in here for?"

Astonished and confounded, Percy stared at Ab trying to make sure he understood what he was saying, and, as he said, "Wha—" trying to understand, he looked round about him, and directly behind him stood that same damned hog, sniffing at the turkeys, whose racket was at this point of an ear-splitting quality. And ever so briefly, in the middle of this feather frenzy, this poultry pandemonium, ever so momentarily, eye to eye with this porcine beast, this stalking ham, Percy felt that he was not in Tim's Creek, North Carolina; that he was not Percival Malcolm Terrell, first and only son of Malcolm Terrell; not chairman and chief executive officer of Terrellco, Inc., county commissioner and deacon—he was a mere blip on some otherness, some twisted reality. He didn't know where he was.

Ab rushed after the hog, and after some effort, chased it from the turkey house. " 'Tweren't your hog, I reckon," Ab laughed off the situation, walking up to Percy, who had not really moved.

"Ah . . . no." Percy rubbed his eyes, not wanting to betray himself to Ab. "No, don't know where it came from. Must a just followed me in here. Didn't even see it. Ain't that something?"

"Must a been one of Joe Richards's. He been catching the devil with his hogs. Got one of them new-fanged, fancy-dancy hog operations, over there he has, and can't keep 'em from getting out." A predicament that Ab clearly found amusing as he laughed some more.

Somehow, hearing Ab speak of the hog as a piece of a machine, a cog, an it, something that belonged to someone, and eventually on a plate, reassured Percy and filled in that momentary sense of a void; made him, oddly enough, whole again in his mind.

But that would be the last time he would feel that way for many a day, for, two days later, the hog again appeared in the back of his pickup truck while he was driving back to Tim's Creek from Crosstown. He stopped the truck and got out, worrying that the hog might vanish and convince him that he was more than a little touched. But the hog remained standing there in the bed of the truck, and Percy touched it, patted it, saying, "Whose hog are you, fella?" feeling its warm, rough, hairy flanks flinch beneath his hand, the coarseness and the solid meat. Percy laughed out loud and shook his head and drove on to Tim's Creek. He stopped at McTarr's Convenience Store in the middle of town and got out, seeing within the store Joe Batts and Tom

McShane and Teddy Miller and Woodrow Johnson, standing around the microwave counter.

"Hey, y'all," Percy said upon entering. "Anybody lost a hog?"

The men looked one to another, and all around out the window, searching with their eyes.

Woodrow took a swig of his Pepsi. "Where you see a hog, captain?"

"Out in my truck is where. Anybody heard anything about somebody losing one?"

Everyone went out to inspect the now empty truck.

"All right, now. Who took the hog out that truck?"

The men, smiling, a bit confused, watched one another, a little uneasy now.

Percy looked to see if anyone else was about. He noted a young woman filling up her compact Japanese-made piece a mess. "Hey, there. You seen anybody take a hog out this here flatbed?"

The teenager shrugged and said, "I ain't seen nothing and nobody. There wont nothing in that truck to begin with."

"There was!" Percy turned to the men, who were no longer looking him in the eye. He walked to the side of the store. Nothing. Just a lone tractor.

"All right, now." He came back before the men, who dared not look him in the face. "Where is it? There was a goddamned boar hog in this goddamned truck and I want to know which son of a bitch put it— took it—"

"Percy? You all—"

"Yes, I'm all right, goddamn it, and when I find out who—" Percy heard himself, heard himself yelling, heard how ridiculous he was sounding, him, Percy Terrell, before these men who respected and admired him, men who he knew secretly all hated and dreaded him as well. And he caught himself, the way a snake handler catches the head of an angry snake; caught himself mid-roar, and started laughing, just like that, laughing, started exerting control of the situation and of himself. He winked. "Had you going, didn't I." And he strolled past the men who were not laughing, yet, who followed him into the store where Percy went over to the drink cooler and hauled out a Pepsi and drank deeply, saying, "So, Tom, did you ever find that foaling mare the other night?"

Still a bit uneasy, Tom McShane sat down, clearly a mite rattled and said, "Ah, yeah, Percy. Yeah I did, but it was too late, they both died. Hated to lose that mare and that colt. 'Twas a colt, you know."

The men fell into commiserating and talking about this and that, and the queer spell Percy had cast over the meeting diminished by and by, though the specter of his curious behavior clung to the air like a visible question mark. And Percy, who was oh so loathe to admit it to himself, knew that he had no idea what the hell was going on; knew that in some inescapable way he was, at bottom, more than a little afraid.

The visitations stepped up after that in frequency and in their curious and unexpected nature. The hg would appear of its own accord now in the house—once when he was shaving he saw it in the mirror; once when he and Rose were in the living room watching a World War II documentary on cable ("Rose?" "Yes, Percy," she said, not looking up from her needlepoint. "Nothing." And the hog got up, during a commercial, walked out of the room and didn't return that night)— now in town—once in a meeting at the mill with John Buzkowski, the general manager, the hog walked from behind the manager's desk, with him sitting at it, and the manager saw nothing and Percy had to pretend he saw nothing; and once wile attending a court proceeding over a bankrupt furniture store he owned a percentage in, Percy swore he saw the hog walk across the front of the room and expected someone to say something, anything, to acknowledge the animal. But no one said a word, not even Percy.

Every day now, the hog was sure to show, and everywhere that Percy went the hog was sure to go. He had given up asking if anyone else had seen it. He was even no longer certain that it was an elaborate practical joke that everyone was playing on him, a joke that would suddenly come to a crescendo, a punch line, and that everyone in the whole blessed county would have an enormous, gut-wrenching, wont-that-funny-as-hell laugh over and then Percy would come out looking the good sport and the business would be finished. But nothing of the sort occurred. So Percy waited, for days and days, and he became a little resigned to his swinish companion, and had even commenced to talking to it on occasion, when they were alone, sometimes in the cab of his truck, where it would sit, as tame as any dog. And, on these queer occasions, Percy would think how sanely insane it all was, and that he himself might be, without a doubt, crazy. But one stubborn and nagging fact remained: Ab had seen it. And as long as he didn't remark upon the creature, Percy's life was going along swimmingly.

However, one day his bafflement reached a new level of strangeness. He had gone over to his son Malcolm's house, where his daughter-in-law was bad-off with the flu. Rose, who was frantic with preparing and planning for a church trip to the Holy Land next month, asked Percy to take some food Agnes had prepared over to poor ailing Maria. Malcolm and Maria Terrell had five children, three boys—Percival, Malcolm III, and Richard (after Maria's father)—and two girls—Rose and Electra—and Percy felt awful proud of his progeny, especially the second boy, who bore not only his father's name but his father's likeness, but with a sweetness the old man had never possessed. That day, as he blew the truck horn, the children all ran out of the front door to greet Granddaddy Percy and he got out of the truck and reached into his coat pockets for the treats he never forgot to bring for them—much to their mother's disquiet, she who had the unfortunate lapse of good judgment to tell him to his face that she disapproved of giving candy to her children, whereupon her husband Malcolm himself made it clear that you don't object to Percy Terrell's largess, and besides a little candy won't hurt 'em none, and so she now just grinned and beared it, the way Percy felt she should have from the beginning—but this day the children inexplicably ran to the other side of the truck. Percy walked around to discover them cooing and cuddling with the hog; little Malcolm had clambered onto its broad back, and, to Percy's amazement, rode the hog like a miniature pachyderm.

Percy stood there with a feeling like bliss and quiet resolve. "Y'all see that ole hog, do you?"

Rose, age eight, looked up as if to say, What kind of question is that? "Where'd you get him, Granddaddy? He's *big*!"

Percy lit a cigarette and watched the innocent gallivanting for the duration of his smoke, a guilty pleasure he had promised the doctor he'd quit, while promising himself he'd just cut back; he watched with a feeling of warmth at the sight of his issue's issue having fun, a feeling that he rarely felt, a feeling that he actually felt uncomfortable feeling, yet felt good feeling when they were around. Over it all, in the middle of it all, under it all, was the strange stalking porker, whose presence, for a few moments, he actually accepted, accepted as a queer reality, and at the moment, even enjoyed.

Presently, Percy took the food in to Maria, who, from her bed, asked what the children were doing out there, and Percy almost said, "Oh, they're just playing with my hog," the reality behind the word "my" pricking his brain as he thought it, suddenly aware of the connotations, the meaning of the word "my." My hog. "They're just playing."

After sitting for a few minutes with the mother of the children who would carry on his family name, his name, Percy kissed her upon the brow and ordered her to get better—she was a good-looking woman, even when she was under the weather—and returned to the playing children, now three of whom were perched on the back of the patient, ever-suffering, ever-enormous hog. Percy gently lifted his grandchildren off its back, one by one, and slapped its rump, "Go on, now. Git on." The hog didn't move. "Go on now; go on back to where you belong." Percy kicked it.

"Granddaddy! Don't!"

"Quiet now, honey. This ain't my hog. 'Sgot to go on back to where it came from."

"But Granddaddy . . ."

The hog turned around and looked at Percy with something that Percy felt to be an accusation. Without further ado or prodding, the hog trotted off in the direction of the house. Richard started to run after it, but Percy made him come back. "Leave him go, boy. Leave him go."

That night the hog left his aromatic calling card.

Having exhausted every avenue he could consciously consider short of going to a doctor—or a vet—Percy took what, for him, was a bold and unexpected step: He went to visit Tabitha McElwaine.

All the colored folks who worked for him swore up and down about Miss Tabitha, who was known throughout five counties as the best midwife and root worker around. They mentioned her name with reverence and a touch of awe: "Went to see Miss Tabitha 'bout it." As if, Percy contemplated with scorn, she was the Lord Jesus Christ Him Damn Self. When they spoke to him of her, he called them damn fools to their faces, saying they'd be better off just burning their money. "But Mr. Percy, you just don't know." "I know damn well enough that that old fool can't do nothing but make piss and deliver babies, and God can take care of that without her around!" But the colored swore by her and gave her money left and right to cure ailments and make somebody fall in love with them; to make them prosperous and to take out revenge, happily handing over hard-earned currency to that lying heifer. And if he discovered a white person doing such a thing, Percy would refuse to speak to them for years on end.

The old witch, who was about Malcolm's age, lived alone in the old McElwaine mansion that proudly stood in what was left of her grand-daddy's 208-acre spread, purchased after the Civil War. Now only five acres remained, the balance now belonging to the Terrell family, as his own father had seen to. Legend had it that his daddy had killed her daddy over it, and they had in turned killed Malcolm. But nobody could prove anything, and Percy kept the land, and they kept their hatred.

Percy stood there now, at the front door of the old Federal-style house, improbable in its competence and simple grandeur, well kept up, recently painted, red brick and white trim, fearfully large crepe myrtle bushes ringing the yard, and Percy wondered how an ex-slave could have possibly built it alone, thinking the story to be a lie in the first place. As he stood there, Percy dared not admit to himself how desperate he had to be to come to this lowliness, how perplexed and damned, and, at base, simply bored by this intrusion, this haunting; how his otherwise simple and orderly life had been thrown into chaos, and how he, Percy Terrell, was at his wit's end. How he wanted an old black woman to tell him, an old white man, what he must do to release himself. But at that time, though he knew this all to be true, he would not allow the thoughts to form in his noggin; he just moved forward with an inexorable logic, and a bitter will for exorcism. So he told him-self nothing, as he stood there knocking, knocking, repeatedly, an-noyed and calling out, finding the door to be open, and just inviting himself on in.

Grudgingly impressed again, he marveled at how finely wrought and finely attended the house's interior had been, how cavernous its halls and rooms seemed—larger than the ones at his house—fixed up like a New Orleans cathouse with lace and doilies over the velvet upholstered chairs and with ferns and potted plants aplenty, gossamer curtains, daguerreotypes of some solemn-looking Negroes staring down at him from the walls.

Without prologue he saw her straightway, on the other side of a big room, through yet another room between them, standing by a big and dark stone fireplace. She stood there, still a tall and slim woman, her head now white with gray, a red shawl over her shoulders, wearing a long blue dress that looked modern and fine; as if she'd just ordered it out of a Spiegel catalog. Percy walked down the carpet toward her.

"Nice hog," she said, not cracking a smile or moving a muscle.

"Um," Percy grunted, not wanting to acknowledge his covisitor, walking by his side, his head febrile with the fact of his being there, in her damn house, fighting with the inevitable fact of humility, of asking, of a need he for once could not solve with a credit card or the writing of a check.

He came within a yard of her and stopped; seemed his legs refused to take him any closer. The room sparkled with light from the windows, nothing haunty or frightening about it, as he had imagined it. He could have been standing in some resort hotel, somewhere far and away. "Look, Weird Sister, I got this little problem and I was wondering . . ."

"Well, Percy Terrell," she said, taking a pipe out of her pocket. "I ain't heard you call me that since 1952." She scooped and worked the pipe in a leather pouch full of tobacco.

Dismayed, Percy's eyes grew wide and even amused. "What?" He even grinned, involuntarily, so taken aback was he. " 'Weird Sister'? You remember the last time I called you that? Hell, I ain't talked to you in over thirty years."

Tabitha drew on the pipe, squinting in the cloud of sweet fog, and, blowing out the match, giving him a look as if to say, Boy you don't know your asshole from your mouth, do you? said, "I made it up, the year."

"Look," Percy said, after clearing his throat, feeling more than a little betrayed, more than a little stupid, more than a little . . . "Look, I ain't got time for this. I need—"

"Know what you need. Why you came here. Answer's no."

"Huh?"

"Can't do nothing for you."

"Wait a minute. What you mean, you 'know'?"

"Want to get rid of that damn hog a yourn, don't you?"

"Can you?"

"Oh, I can." Tabitha stopped and blew out a long stream of smoke, like a ghost's train, and looked upon him vaguely with a look of pity that quickly transformed into scorn. "But you ain't gone be willing to do what you got to do to get rid of him. So why waste my time? Can't help you." She turned to the window, clearly having said all she would say.

Percy felt his face go red. When had someone last told him flat out no? No song, no dance? Refused him anything? After he had done such a thing as to actually come to this freakish old colored bitch for help, after . . . He stood there staring at this woman who had dismissed him so rudely, and it never once occurred to him that he might plead, beg, pour out his heart, that he might say please. He just got angrier, hotter, redder. Finding his voice he finally said, shaking, "Well, why don't you just go right on to hell then, you crazy witch. You just crazy. Ain't a bit a nothing to that old foolishness you preach. Just a old charlatan. You just go right on to hell."

He watched himself storm out of the old house, wanting to break something, wanting to burn the entire abomination to the ground, vowing to himself that he'd break that old witch one day. So twisted with hate and malice and anger was he that he couldn't even frame his own thoughts, at that moment, so inarticulate with rage, such a rejected little boy that he almost came to tears. And, indeed, at the wheel of his truck, with the hog sitting quietly, peacefully beside him, driving down and away from the old house, the unfamiliar sting and pain and torment began moistening his cheek. And he did.

By the time he reached home, twilight had darkened past dusk, and, it being a Saturday night, Rose had already left for bridge and wouldn't be back until after eleven, and he simply wanted to forget this whole business, to forget the hog, forget, indeed, the feeling the mystery of the hog precipitated within him, to forget how helpless and hopeless he was feeling. He locked himself in his study, snapped on the TV, popped *The Outlaw—Josey Wales* into the VCR, and opened a fresh bottle of his old friend Jack Daniel's and took two enormous swigs before pouring four fingers neatly into a tumbler. He kicked off his shoes and loosened his belt and flopped back on the couch, before the flickering images of a West that never existed, concentrating intensely on the testosterone-deluded fantasy, and drank and drank. He had stopped drinking so much—well, during the week, now only on Fridays and Saturdays, except on special occasions, and he had stopped getting truly drunk, except on special occasions—but tonight that was exactly what he wanted, craved; he needed to erase, expunge. He lusted after what the bottle never failed to supply: power and ease and good feel-

ings. He wanted to revisit the sweet veil of haze and be-bothered noth-
ingness and the viscous warmth and head-fuzziness; he wanted to be
released from tax codes and stupid children and orders and poultry and
stocks and marriage, from maleness and the tug of gravity on his growing belly; to be released from the gray hair that he refused to dye out
of a vanity stronger than fear and the red splotches and burst veins
that would never vanish from his face and that signaled the end, years
ago, of his virility and machismo energy; to be released from the memories of that once-youth, of his escapades and all the trouble his penis
had seen and caused; away from memories of hunting and dancing and
tomfoolery: released, yes, from the hog and all it seemed to signify.
Percy drank. And drank. He swilled and slurped; he guzzled and gob-
bled, with a ferocious abandon, and with the swallowing, at his lips,
and the fuzzy now-hum of his brain, somewhere in the amber fluid of
the bottle, somewhere behind the black label, enlivened by the light of
the TV screen, he saw his father, that old demon, with his big black
hat with the huge brim, looking down upon his son with contempt.
And Percy didn't want to see his father, never ever again, knew he was
better than his father, could never be like his father, was a human
being person unlike his father, an evil freak of nature. Yes, he built it
all up from nothing; yes, he started it, murdered for it, stole and beat
for it, that son of a bitch, and left Percy with the blood, but Percy had,
had— No, he didn't want to think of Malcolm. So he drank, and drank
some more, the fire in his belly now outstepped by the fire in his brain;
he willed himself to stop seeing Malcolm, and, stumbling up and over,
switched off the VCR and turned on the CD player and fell back on
the sofa to the measured twangs and lonesome chords of Hank Williams, and sang with Hank (hell, Malcolm never could sing, never sang,
never would sing) laughing and goofy in the clouds and fumes of mash
and Benedict, Benedictine, and the deluged fretted in Antioch, O Antioch, where the glad rags had orgies of ragout in Shiloh, O, by the
door of Doomsday, yes, in Berlin where superior werewolves were sail-
ors with head colds who lost the compasses in that distance that
joint—what was its name?—of pus-filled pushovers who submit, submit, wogs and Zeus, yes, zilch, in shampoo, Zimbabwe! Gomorrah!
Dye. Die . . .

And somewhere, somehere, somethere, in the misfiring synapses
and purple blaze of effluvium that had seized his brain and body, some-

where just before passing out, Percy saw his hog sitting there by him, by the couch, and felt a little love in his heart for this friend of his, and reached out to pet him, and, forgetting he held a glass, dropped it, and his mind went to black.

The next morning found the Head Deacon and Chairman of the Board of Trustees of St. Thomas Aquinas Presbyterian Church of Tim's Creek, Percival Malcolm Terrell, sitting on the second pew along with the rest of the congregation, with a hangover that rivaled the worst hangovers of his youth—though knowing from half a century of heavy drinking that a bad hangover makes its own history. Percy felt he was indeed still drunk, for as he rose at seven after Rose banged and banged on the door to his sanctum sanctorum for him to get up and get ready for church, and as he washed and shaved and squirted drops of Visine into his eyes, and picked at his breakfast and drank four cups of coffee, the world was still tinged with a colorless aura; things were enveloped yet within a nimbus of gauze and otherness; and though he felt sick to his stomach, the alcohol had provided, at least for a spell and at a cost, a distraction from his mental confusion, had given his mind a respite from the hog that was nowhere to be seen.

Now he sat before Pastor Bergen, who could not preach to save his life, droning on and on about the faith of Zacchaeus up a tree; now he was playing the role he had part inherited and part worked for, a role so old it was capacious and well worn and comfortable, and took so little effort he had barely to think upon it to be it: He was it—he was king of his little fiefdom of mills and poultry plants and fields and social rungs, richer than most men dared hope to be, and feared, respected, paid homage unto. Why on earth should he worry about anything other than cancer and taxes? And as Bergen drew thankfully near the end of his overlong sermon, Percy felt more than a little better and the nausea seemed to abate and his mind to clear a bit and he thought of the football game he would cheer on after dinner with the kids and he realized he had not even thought of the hog all morning. As the colored light from the stained-glass windows played against the pristine whiteness of the church walls, Percy smiled to himself.

The commotion started as a low-level rumble. Whispering turned to loud talk, and somebody said, "Git it, Frank!" By the time the minister stopped in mid-sentence and stared, Percy could hear people standing, some laughing, some angry. "How'd it get in here?" And before Percy could turn all the way around, he heard a grunt at his side: There was his old friend, his familiar, his companion and seeming advocate, his own and only hog. But the thing that Percy's mind latched on to was the fact that everyone saw the hog! Percy felt released. Yet, oddly enough, the hog had stopped by his side, as if to point a finger, or a snout, at him.

"What?" Percy hollered at the hog. *What do you want from me?*"

With that the hog gave out his signature bellow and rushed toward the pulpit, around to the side and up toward the Reverend Paul Bergen. The men in the front pews, unwieldy in their Sunday-go-to-meeting best, all jumped to their feet, and the pastor let out a girlish yelp, gathered up his robe like a woman's frock and ran, being chased by this boar hog, its oversized genitalia jangling betwixt its legs, its big ears flapping like the wings of a bat, its mouth wide and frothing. As the men of the church chased after the hog, and the women screamed, and the children laughed with unbridled wildness, Percy was just thankful and amazed that everyone, *everyone*, could see the hog, at last, at long last, and he felt that the whole six-week ordeal was coming to some end, was about to affix itself to a clear and final meaning.

The men tried in utter vain to grab the hog, but it proved too ornery, too sly, and kept slipping between their legs, knocking them over and down, for it was indeed, a very large hog. At one point it actually bit Pernell Roberts on the hand, which made Pernell cuss ("God damn it!") in church, though no one bothered to scold him, for at that instant the renegade swine chomped down on the edge of tablecloth of the communion table and backed up, pulling the Eucharist, the silver pitchers full of grape juice, the little glasses, the silver platters containing bits of white bread, all crashing, clattering, tumbling down with a metal thunk and splatter. Momentarily everyone stopped; the men, the pastor, the women, the children, Percy, the hog, stopped, witnessing the spectacle as if, in that brief wrinkle in time, some clarity, some hidden codeology were to be revealed in this bedlam. But the hog brought an end to that sober oasis of reflection when it moved first its head, with its bedazzling speed, toward Percy, and then grunted derisively, giving otherworldly language to its own unquestionably blasphemous actions, and with equal speed dashed down the aisle toward the door.

Without thinking, Percy moved in front of the great mass of pork, to stop it, calling out, "Whoa!" as one would to an intelligent, malevolent, comprehending entity, "Stop," he cried. But the hog didn't stop, poking its behemoth head between Percy's spread thighs and lifting him astride its wide neck, and continuing down the way, Percy being carted along and atop, backward, yelling, through the throng of the agitated congregation. At the threshold of the church Percy fell off, unceremoniously and hurtfully, and the hog galloped away.

Percy scrambled to his feet, and, feeling somehow personally responsible, and even possessive, he gave chase, running down the side of North Carolina Highway 50, after that great boar hog, who had just disrupted the services of St. Thomas Aquinas Presbyterian Church beyond conceivable imagination. Running, Percy didn't even give a second thought to the fact that they were running, unmistakably, inevitably, to his own home.

Though Percy's house was less than a mile from the church, he stood in the doorway breathless, his heart pounding dangerously, sweat pouring copiously down his face, for he had not run this far, or this fast, in years; not to mention the nausea he had been battling all morning. He tugged off his tie and doffed his coat to the floor, and stalked to his study. His mind was a red place, a hot place, a place of brimstone and vengeance; he was not simply angry with a thing, but with an intangible yet tangible circumstance, a situation, a tangle of happenstance and botheration. He knew there was one way to get rid of it all, a way that had never clearly presented itself before, since the creature had never acted so hatefully.

Percy marched into his study, and, perhaps due to the anger and the urgent need to strike out at something, broke the glass of his gun rack with his elbow and a Rebel yell, rather than waste time looking for the key which was in his pocket. He reached for the old elephant gun he had used once in Africa in 1952, and not since, though he had kept it clean religiously. He loaded the shells, feeling the ungodly size of them in his hands, himself feeling suddenly potent with each insertion, wondering to himself why he had not done this most obvious of things long before.

Percy raised his head to the door, and, as he knew he would be, there stood his hog, his hog, insolent, inquisitive, mocking. Percy sneered at the beast, thinking and then saying out loud, for none could appreciate this outsized drama more than he, like some celluloid cowboy show in his brain: "End of the line, fella."

Percy had the hog in his sights, right between the eyes. They both stood there, stock-still for a period of time Percy could not easily name.

Percy and the hog. The hog and Percy. The hog did not move, and by and by, Percy thought, What a magnificent creature. Unaccountably he began to tremble and inadvertently he peered into the hog's eyes, into the depth of them, perhaps toward the soul of it; and to Percy it seemed the hog did the same to him. Percy's trembling increased and a feeling began to wash over him and into him, and Percy began to feel puny. Naked. Ashamed. Just as he had at that moment when he discovered that his penis was not the largest in creation and that the juice of his testicles would neither save nor solve humanity; neither save nor solve himself; that all he had he and his father had stolen and robbed for, and that he had no right to any of it; that he was next to nothing, and that the mask of his flesh, once glorious, now wrinkling and withering, would in time be dust and ash, and that he was really not very, very much at all, not even as valuable as a hog.

Percy began to cry. He could not shoot. He would not shoot. He should not shoot. He understood in this moment of pregnant possibility, this showdown, this climax of it all, what the hog was. And in a moment of quiescence and acquiescence, Percival Malcolm Terrell let it all go, let the gun slip from his hands, and slumped to the floor of his study, a feeling like exhaustion settling into his bones. The great boar hog, on scuffling hooves, came rushing, and leapt, springing impossibly up, into the air, and Percy, in chilled fright, watched as the mammoth creature sailed, like a gargantuan football, toward him; and he could only shield his face with his hands, and quake.

A few instants later he heard Rose run into the house, calling, "Percy, are you all right? My God, Percy!" He slowly uncovered his face to see only the open window, a breeze gently troubling the sheer curtains inward, barely a billow. Percy continued to sob, though the sob had altered in its tenor and meaning: Now the sob was a sweet, deep wonderful and profound sob, his body shaking, snot running down his nose. Rose walked into the room, but Percy did not really see her or hear her, so intent was he upon this newfound and peaceful feeling. He felt just like that bird in the old Hank Williams song, the one too blue to fly, and tried to mouth that line about the lonesome whippoorwill, but only the mumblings of a child emerged. Lonesome, O so Lonesome.

TAHORAH

He was in the CCU and sick of all the barbaric grunts and cries coming from next door and out in the hallway. What name to pin them with he wasn't sure, something foreign because the lingo they were speaking made no sense and got on his nerves almost as much as the crying and sobbing and all that, but he couldn't do anything about it because he was soaking in morphine and wasn't concerned about *the details;* the details he gave up on during the second heart attack, all that pain, big walls of it, like in the movies, groaning and trying to guide the truck over to the side; where was this? A hundred and fifty miles outside of Altoona? Almost home? Somewhere in Jersey? No one on the medical staff seemed to know, or care. The crunch of gravel on the breakdown lane, the smooth, low scrape as he hit the guardrail, the scream of plastic bumper stuff peeling off—and then skidding like that, rolling partway over, up on the side, his cab, deep crimson red, while the trailer ripped loose and flipped and tumbled down the hill. The babble of prayer—that's what was coming from next door, he knew, at least some little part of him knew. Some of them were jawing away at it right outside his door. And here's the guy Angela sent saying *our prayers are with you* and talking, his lips close, Listerine breath, one of those mango brows—a real caveman, this preacher from the Bethel First Christ down in Rutherford, or near there. It's Angela's idea of a bad joke, a last hurrah, knowing damn well he wouldn't want it, probably making up a long story about her ex-husband and guilt and how she felt he needed consolation and affirmation in what were sure to be his final hours. Now along with the carrying on in the hall there was the mumbling pious tones of this guy's voice to contend with, too, talking something about the narrow way of Christ; funny that it was the only thing he knew, or felt like knowing, about his heart, the narrow closing of that artery clogged with too many doughnuts and too much coffee and long hours on the road popping crank, mixing vodka with whatever the hell he got his hands on the last few years doing transcon runs of whatever freight he could land. Hitch your cab to the trailer and ask no questions.

When they tried to get the shunt in, the artery collapsed on itself, final and for good, and he had a second coronary right on the table. Nothing to do now, the doctor said, except wait out the twenty-four-hour grace or lack of grace period, the rough time, and hope for the best, because no matter what, part of his heart was permanent dead matter. If you're gonna die, the doc said, it's most likely gonna be in the next twenty-four hours.

Now this dwarf priest or whatever lecturing him on Christ's narrow way.

"What do you want, Father?" His lips would barely open, corrugated with dryness. His mouth had been dry all night, dry into the day, and was now dry in the afternoon no matter how many of the little plastic cups of cranberry juice he sucked down.

"Father?" the guy said, softly. Then he cleared his throat. "You don't have to address me that way."

"What are you doing here, Father?"

"I'd prefer Bill, if you don't mind."

"All right, Bill," he said, his lips contorted around the words the way they do in a movie when the sound track is off slightly.

The preacher, or minister, or pastor, seemed uncomfortable standing and went to get a chair, pulling it over with a loud screech, sitting up close to the bed, then leaning his arms on the rail and looking down at his charge.

"I've come to deliver unto you the word of God," the guy said, speaking in what was mostly a mumble, hardly audible over the beeps and sighs of the machines; tubes and wires yanked on his chest and arms and legs. Just then, before the preacher could begin yapping again, there was a sudden, persistent beep. A nurse came in quickly and pulled the white cotton blanket down from his neck and exposed the deep, dark curls of chest hair and prodded it until that sustained beep stopped and only his heart rate was left, and the smooth gulps of the balloon machine, the aortic counterpulsation device. Minister Bill moved his chair back and sat quietly during all this. All for the better. He was wading through the softness of the morphine, or whatever pain reliever he was on. The word of God could wait. But then the nurse left and the preacher pulled his chair back, picking it up this time, and leaned on the rail again and began talking about the *way* of God and Christ, the whole rigmarole, talking about how much Angela loved him even though the scag hadn't been in touch since '76, good old bicentennial: Twenty years, he thought, and then it came to a dwarf priest blabbing about his favorite hymn, something like "O Worship the King, All Glorious Above," and quoting it to him, his medicinal breath up close, taking advantage of his helplessness to get right in there, not even a half foot from his face, and even singing it a little bit—a kind of singsong lullaby—"frail children of dust, and feeble as frail, in thee do we trust, nor find thee to fail"—and then he said to the dwarf priest, having to really dig to talk, "Father, do me a favor. Shut up. Or speak in tongues if you want. But if you sing any more, I'll get out of this frickin' bed and break your neck."

It was down in Tennessee—on a run to Florida with a load of machine parts—that he saw the speaking-in-tongues church. Hooked up with a girl named Lauren, sweet girl, at a truck bar, ended up in her trailer screwing away and then the next day, Sunday, being dragged to her church and watching them blabbing in their snakelike tongues. He left the church, got his rig warmed up, and headed south, pronto. Now in the room, with Father Bill there in the chair sitting silently, he hears that sizzle of voices out in the hall, a whole family grieving over some loss, hacking away in their language, then bits of English, then their language again. Other times blending the two; all melded together into a hiss that seemed like the ones used by those speaking in tongues that morning down in whatever Podunk state he happened to be in—Tennessee or Kentucky.

For a second he wants to ask this preacher about Angela, just how she's doing, but he knows the guy, most likely sworn not to disclose anything, will just say, "Fine, fine," and leave it at that. What else was he going to say? That she was wallowing in shit, dirt poor, missing payments on that piece-of-crap house in Elmwood, or Shorthills. For all he knew she wasn't there anymore, but he thought of it anyhow when he thought of her, with the kids, toiling away over a tub of dirty clothing and a washboard or something—nothing real. When he imagined it, that's how it was, images out of someplace that never existed because he couldn't remember what had existed. The house they owned in Rutherford. A simple clapboard number, a Sears catalog house. A nice weedy yard with one of those clothes-drying trees, and always laundry on it like a blooming white rose of sheets and underwear when he got home from work the one year he was working steady, providing, doing his bit; old Preacher Bill wouldn't admit, if asked, that she was bathing in pain like he was, maybe worse off, cancer of the brain, an invalid, or nuts, bedded full-time in some ward someplace. Of course she was fine, Bill would say. He tried to remember what she looked like and got a vision of her dark red hair, wide oval face, smooth, very white skin, and her lively laugh. He got a vision of her at the cabin they rented upstate, down by the water, toking on hand-rolled smokes and drinking beer until they ended up in the bed, a rattling iron thing, with their clothing off and only that pale summer twilight, half there, half gone, milking their skin smooth as whole milk; such wonderful smoothness, he recalled, especially at the flat of her belly going down, down to the pubis bone, the hard ridge on both sides, and with the breeze like that, not too hot or too cool, coming through the screens.

When he woke it was night, pale green light from the screen overhead and hard orange parking-ramp lights in the window. From the hallway came a pure, downy, neon brilliance. Father Bill had vanished, his chair empty where he left it near the door. The light throb of the pump going; the faint pulse of the device in his chest cavity opening up with air and deflating next to his heart like a little bird nesting between his ribs.

How long he lay he didn't know; hours, minutes. Just the machine and a few cries in the hall—Arabic or something, some little kid making wailing noises, the family still gathered out there but kind of quiet and silent now, maybe it was too late, asleep the lot of them out in the lounge with the others. There had to be plenty; a big hospital, overcrowded, lots of dying going on in the ICU and the CCU.

One of the docs came in looking over the charts and poking around and not talking much because he knew better, knew this old codger who'd been dragged in off the highway had a nasty temperament and didn't care much for small talk. A few pokes and probes, a check of the data on the screen.

"We're going to remove the balloon pump," he said. "We've gone long enough now and it's a pretty pricey hunk of machinery, and there's a patient just coming out of emergency surgery who's going to need it right off. The police might drive another one over from Newark, but I think you're stabilized enough now."

Strapped beneath his leg was a long plank to keep things flat and even, and in his leg, up near his crotch, was a hole about the size of a dime but feeling more like a quarter to him, a hole leading into the femoral artery. A hole in my frickin' leg, he'd thought a few dozen times, and not a bullet hole. He'd thought that if he ever had a real hole in his leg—a genuine hole—it would've been from a bullet from one of the skags at the crappy bars he frequented en route from CA to NY. The nurses came in—a Hispanic girl, a bit on the plump side, but he'd take her anyhow if he had the heart—hardy har, har—and a large older woman with blue-gray hair, and then a male nurse; all three held on to him, gripping different parts while the doc slowly drew the balloon out from against his heart, pulling the wire through the dime-sized hole, drawing it down his femoral artery where it shouldn't have been and sure as fuck couldn't fit because the pain was red hot, explosive, convulsive, and he screwed up his face—all jawbone and sun-weathered crags—and screamed like a stuck pig: "Give me some fricking pain killers, you morons, you mooorrrrons," while the doc jammed something that looked like a wine bottle opener over the hole and gave one last little tug and got it out, not a word, working silently except for a little murmur of directions to one of the nurses.

"Sorry." The doc shrugged.

"I'll bet you are." He could barely speak. The pain was making bursts of sparks on the inside of his eyelids.

The nurses and doc exchanged glances, as if to say: This one's a real nasty bastard, keep your distance; if we could we'd put a muzzle on him, costing the hospital money and the government money and the whole world bits of spirit; but the doc put his hand on the guy's fore-

head and rubbed it there a little bit. He kept his hand there way too
long to be any kind of test for fever or a thump to listen to something.

"What happened to preacher man?" he said.

"Excuse me," Doc said.

"The pastor, the Bible-thumper, what happened to him?"

"Can't help you there."

Then they left him alone with the hard throb of the pain, or the
remains of the pain, because that's how it was, like a swish of chalk
on a board, or an imprint or something—a feeling all the way up his
leg and into his empty chest, now without the little nesting bird, nothing but frickin' air and his own heart bobbing away in there—a feeling
of the pain of that thing being yanked down the inside of his leg by
the moron doctor. A soft, faint beep from the machine indicating his
pulse and him alone and the noise in the hall kind of getting louder
with the babble and all that, more voices, the soft squeak of tennis
sneaker on the waxed floor; another set of steps, more, and more.

In the hall, before he came out and placed his ghostly visage before
them, hanging with tubes and in his flimsy gown, gasping for air, the
family was bunched up to the side, praying, talking, crying—two little
kids allowed on the unit only because it was the last few hours, if not
minutes, of Tara's life. A few days ago the doctors had put her chances
at slim to none—or they laid it out in some numbers, most likely, trying to keep it mathematical, the odds, because whenever you were talking about lost youth—death at an early age—you had to couch things
as much as you could in figures. Tara's father was wearing, and had
been for two days, a dark brown tweed sports coat, penny loafers, a
pair of Docker khakis, and had his head buried in his hands. He was
slouched down against the wall, talking to himself, jouncing his heels
against the floor. Next to him, seated on the floor listening, was Stanley, his brother, who, upon getting the news, had flown in directly from
Israel; he was jet-lagged and exhausted and felt himself floating in the
bedazzling clean space of the hallway. He'd been there all afternoon,
trying to soothe the soul of his poor brother, from whom he'd been
estranged. All because of what?—a bad shipment of goods he'd sent
over, or lined up; nothing really his fault at all; he'd been nothing but
the usual middleman, but the deal somehow wedged in between the

men and, after a while, except for enough small pleasantries meant to keep at least an outward semblance of civility (mainly, it had to be admitted, for the women), the two rarely spoke. The bad deal became large over time—the sum of money lost debated—until everything else that had happened before that, all the way back to petty squabbles over marble games on the dirt tarmac outside their apartment in Israel, each tense moment, seemed prophetic. For Stanley, who was fearful of elevators and tall buildings, flying out had been a grand gesture, a great flourishing of his arms outward over the skies of Tel Aviv (as he saw it); a token of his true, deep love, a love that went beyond that bad deal (five thousand pipe wrenches, all of them forged with a wobbling claw).

Behind them, in the room with Tara, the women were around the bed, resting the tips of their fingers on the bedding, brushing the hair back from her forehead. A car had gone through a stop sign in Hackensack—a Saturday afternoon, light traffic for that corner, an elderly man driving a pale green Buick Skylark with his blood level four times above the legal limit sped right through and broadsided her Toyota at seventy-five miles an hour.

When she got close to the end—and they could tell, or rather the nurses indicated it silently by nods of the head and slight eye movements—there was a quieting. Calls went out from the pay phone in the lounge, where people limp in their anxiety lay sprawled over huge, square-cut maroon chairs. To speak the words that he had to speak— not that she was dead but that she was, as they said (although he thought it was kind of a phony phrase) near death (as if death were an island, a vacation resort)—Stanley found himself listening to his own voice. He was a dummy; some other guy was holding him, composed and serene and bearing terrible news; the ventriloquist; as he spoke, he heard his own voice quiver—dry and husky from the long flight— beneath the weight of the news he had to offer up; at the same time, he was thinking of the old radio show routines he and Howard had loved so much as kids.

With the pump removed from his chest, everything out in the hall became amplified by the silence. He didn't know it, but the prayers were in Hebrew, mainly, although some were in English, and some of what he heard was just talking, and crying, and emotive phrases such as *How can it be?* and *Why why why?* and *If only* . . . and *Oh God!* And a rocking motion verbalized in a kind of cantorial singsong—and even a little actual singing from one of the really little kids who didn't know what was going on, a rapturous little tune with senseless lyrics about a goat and a shoe and the Fourth of July.

Just before he dragged himself up, decided to shut them up out there, he remembered a night right after that night upstate, with the wonderful breeze through the screen, when he and Angela sat on the end of the dock drinking beers and watching the stars clarify and listening to the fish rise, splashing, mostly bluegills but some pretty good large-mouth bass he was sure (he'd spent that afternoon casting a huge spoon, loaded up with worms, to no avail). Up and down the shore the fish were leaping like mad while behind Angela, in the thick darkness under the trees, firefly light was being exchanged in frantic waves up and down the beach.

"What'cha thinking?" he asked her.

"I'm just thinking, you know, about all we're gonna do and how good it's gonna be and all that," she said. It was a song she was singing, her own little hymn to the portents the future held.

"Hummm," he said, taking a huge slug on his beer, a sizzle down his throat.

"And what'cha thinkin' yourself?"

"About nothing, nothing at all except being here and how good it is here, with you, now." And he meant it. His middle brother Gray had died a year before working a roofing job, and shaking the grief of that loss, the recurrent image of the idiot slipping on a loose slate and falling two stories, breaking his neck, had until that very moment, seemed impossible; now something was lifting, or at least that's what he felt, recalling that night on the dock with Angela while he, in turn, lay flat on his back in the hospital with his blood pumped full of morphine; the same bright lifting, like he was flying up over the lake. Some kind of grace, a moment of it, on the end of the dock with the shore webbed in the light of fireflies.

One might hope for some kind of divine justice. An amazing feat how he got himself up and dragged himself into the hall to scream at them, considering the odds, the wires and tubes and warning beeps, the very low flow pressure his heart offered. He spoke his mind out there in the hall, shouting at them. If God had been just, he would've slammed him with an occlusion; a major, major infarct that locked his heart into a knot, a clench of fibers so tight, a fist in the center of his rib cage, a burst of blinding pain that sent him stumbling, gasping for his last. Instead he had a minor event—one he hardly felt at the time.

He did die. He died a few days later, alone, in the middle of the night, when a series of infarctions began and he went into a major arrest and the staff came in and performed heroic measures (because he said hell no to that living will crap. No way. No how am I gonna sign that? You'll put me under for Christ's sake. Why should I trust you morons after the way you jerked that fucking balloon out of my leg?), giving him a zap with the jelled electrodes, pumping him full of anticoagulants, working a sweat up over the guy.

Seven days of mourning without the hard leather of shoes, and during Shiva only once was the crazy guy mentioned; brought up by Stanley—who in his grief had gone downstairs twice, out onto the sidewalk along Riverside Drive to take in the fresh air off the Hudson and to sip single malt from one of those little bottles he'd bought on the flight over; he was on his third bottle. He was back inside the apartment, on the floor, talking softly with Saul, a buyer for the hardware chain, and in passing other subjects, sliding through them in his buzz, he sadly metioned the Gentile who'd stumbled out into the hallway half alive, filling the air with his foul curses; it was the way he leaned into Saul; it was the way he tried to flatten his voice out from his Hebraic to an Ohio twang (and trying to whisper at the same time, too)—*Shut the fuck up for Christ sake you babbling idiots; go back to where you came from.* It was the form, not the content, that got the men laughing, just as Tara's father came down the stairs, arm in arm with his wife.

Out the tall windows the Hudson glinted flecks of white light, and spread before them was a view embracing New Jersey across the river all the way up to the GW Bridge. When Tara died, the word went out via optical fibers, calls made to Israel, making sure everybody who had to mourn knew of her death so that no one would be called upon to begin mourning later; because from the moment the news was heard, those so obligated had to observe the laws and customs as set down in the Talmud. The ritual washing of the body, Tahora, had been performed because none of her injuries, all internal and concussive, had drawn enough blood to soak her clothes, in which case she would have been buried in the bloodied garments. After the funeral they went to the cemetery, pausing the seven times to recite Psalm 91,

> He that dwelleth in the secret place of the most High
> shall abide under the shadow of the Almighty

before spreading the dirt over the coffin.

While Stanley recounted the story of the crazy man in the hospital, upstairs in the bedroom Tara's father had been been ripping up all of his ties, one by one, and piling them aside. He rent each one apart, yanking hard, skinny narrow ones from back in the early eighties, wide ones from the sixties with huge stripes, and semiwide ones from the nineties. He tore them down the middle, if he could, and he tore them apart from the center, opening them up, plying apart the silk backing and ripping down the sides. His hands were dry and cracked and caught the silk. When his wife went up to see where he was, he was nearly finished, seated on the side of the bed next to a jostled pile of twisted fabric spilling over the edge of the poplin bedspread, doing one last tie, a Calvin Klein with deep blue triangles set in a lighter blue background beset with swirls and splats à la Jackson Pollack that Tara had given him for the holidays two years ago. Pollack had been her favorite artist. Maybe once every couple of weeks, for a year, he wore it, and then put it aside in favor of ones he had picked out himself, more conservative patterns. He had performed the standard Qeri'ah at the funeral, rending the tiny strip of ribbon pinned to his left lapel, but apparently that act hadn't been enough. Stop, his wife said. Stop. Stop. Stop. And he did, bowing his head into his palms and heaving out a long cry, kicking his heels into the carpet, cradling what was left of the tie up to his lips.

Come downstairs with me, she said, placing her hand along the curve of his neck.

All right. For you, I'll go downstairs. He cleared his throat and got up and slowly lifted a few strands of neckties onto the bed.

The faces seemed to have answers for him as he walked down the spiral stairs into the Shiva; people hunched down talking softly, moving food up to their mouths; he would remember seeing each face in turn: the tight lips of Erma, his wife's best friend, holding a sob; his business associates looking away, casting glances out over New Jersey; the kids obliviously playing with dolls near the entrance to the kitchen. But what he would remember the most, what he centered on later, was the strange, twisted smile on his brother's face, a blessed smile that seemed to go way back to their childhood secrets; it was the way Stanley smiled when he was trying not to smile, the tightness in the corners of his mouth that led to two half-moon dimples; a wonderful grimace and smirk combined; and seeing it, something lifted slightly; it was only the first bit of weight off of his grief but it was significant in that it was the first; he went over, and the two men held each other, tighter and tighter.

"What are you laughing about?"

"Nothing."

"Come on."

"The foolishness of the world," Stanley said.

Out the windows the afternoon was waning. Beams of orange cut between buildings in Jersey. The elongated shadows of buildings pressed behind the view.

It was never spoken of again, that scene, that moment in the hospital corridor. It didn't go down in family lore. It didn't go anywhere except for that moment into the smile on Stanley's face, the thing Tara's father saw when he entered back into the Shiva.

DEMONOLOGY

They came in twos and threes, dressed in the fashionable Disney costumes of the year, Lion King, Pocahontas, Beauty and the Beast, or in the costumes of televised superheroes, Protean, shape-shifting, thus arrayed, in twos and threes, complaining it was too hot with the mask on, *Hey, I'm really hot!*, lugging those orange plastic buckets, bartering, haggling with one another, *Gimme your Smarties, please?* as their parents tarried behind, grownups following after, grownups bantering about the schools, or about movies, about local sports, about their marriages, about the difficulties of long marriages, kids sprinting up the next driveway, kids decked out as demons or superheroes or dinosaurs or as advertisements for our multinational entertainment-providers, beating back the restless souls of the dead, in search of sweets.

They came in bursts of fertility, my sister's kids, when the bar drinking, or home-grown dope-smoking, or bed-hopping had lost its luster; they came with shrill cries and demands—little gavels, she said, instead of fists—*Feed me! Change me! Pay attention to me!* Now it was Halloween and the mothers in town, my sister among them, trailed after their kids, warned them away from items not fully wrapped, *Just give me that, you don't even like apples,* laughing at the kids hobbling in their bulky costumes—my nephew dressed as a shark, dragging a mildewed gray tail behind him. But what kind of shark? A great white? A blue? A tiger shark? A hammerhead? A nurse shark?

She took pictures of costumed urchins, my sister, as she always took pictures, e.g., my nephew on his first birthday (six years prior), black-faced with cake and ice cream, a dozen relatives attempting in turn to read to him—about a tugboat—from a brand-new rubberized book. *Toot toot!* His desperate, needy expression, in the photo, all out of phase with our excitement. The first nephew! The first grandchild! He was trying to get the cake in his mouth. Or: a later photo of my niece (his younger sister) attempting to push my nephew out of the shot—against a backdrop of autumn foliage; or a photo of my brother wearing my dad's yellow double-knit paisley trousers (with a bit of flair in the cuffs), twenty-five years after the heyday of such stylings; or my father and stepmother on their powerboat, peaceful and happy, the riotous wake behind them; or my sister's virtuosic photos of *dogs*—Mom's irrepressible golden retriever chasing a tennis ball across an overgrown lawn, or my dad's setter on the beach with a perspiring Löwenbräu leaning against his snout. Fifteen or twenty photo albums on the shelves in my sister's living room, a whole range of leathers and faux-leathers, no particular order, and just as many photos loose, floating around the basement, castoffs, and files of negatives in their plastic wrappers.

She drank *the demon rum,* and she taught me how to do it, too, when we were kids; she taught me how to drink. We stole drinks, or we got people to steal them for us; we got reprobates of age to venture into the pristine suburban liquor stores. Later, I drank bourbon. My brother drank beer. My father drank single malt scotches. My grandmother drank half-gallons and then fell ill. My grandfather drank the finest collectibles. My sister's ex-husband drank more reasonably priced fac-similes. My brother drank until a woman lured him out of my mother's house. I drank until I was afraid to go outside. My uncle drank until the last year of his life. And I carried my sister in a blackout from a bar once—she was mumbling to herself, humming melodies, mostly unconscious. I took her arms; Peter Hunter took her legs. She slept the whole next day. On Halloween, my sister had a single gin and tonic before going out with the kids, before ambling around the condos of

Kensington Court, circling from multifamily unit to multifamily unit, until my nephew's shark tail was grass-stained from the freshly mown lawns of the common areas. Then she drove her children across town to her ex-husband's house, released them into his supervision, and there they walked along empty lots, beside a brook, under the stars.

When they arrived home, these monsters, disgorged from their dad's Jeep, there was a fracas between girl and boy about which was superior (in the Aristotelian hierarchies), Milky Way, Whoppers, Slim Jim, Mike 'n Ikes, Sweet Tarts or Pez—this bounty counted, weighed and inventoried (on my niece's bed). Which was the Pez dispenser of greatest value? A Hanna-Barbera Pez dispenser? Or, say, a demonic *totem pole Pez dispenser*? And after this fracas, which my sister refereed wearily (*Look, if he wants to save the Smarties, you can't make him trade!*), they all slept, and this part is routine, my sister was tired as hell; she slept the sleep of the besieged, of the overworked, she fell precipitously into whorls of unconsciousness, of which no snapshot can be taken.

In one photograph, my sister is wearing a Superman outfit. This from a prior Halloween. I think it was a *Supermom* outfit, actually, because she always liked these bad jokes, degraded jokes, things other people would find ridiculous. (She'd take a joke and repeat it until it was leaden, until it was funny only in its awfulness.) Jokes with the fillip of sentimentality. Anyway, in this picture her blond hair—brightened a couple of shades with the current technologies—cascades around her shoulders, disordered and impulsive. *Supermom.* And her expression is skeptical, as if she assumes the mantle of Supermom—raising the kids, accepting wage-slavery, growing old and contented—and thinks it's dopey at the same time.

Never any good without coffee. Never any good in the morning. Never any good until the second cup. Never any good without freshly ground Joe, because of my dad's insistence, despite advantages of class and style, on *instant coffee*. No way. Not for my sister. At my dad's house, where she stayed in the summer, she used to grumble derisively, while staring out the kitchen window, out the expanse of windows that gave onto the meadow there, *Instant coffee!* There would be horses in the meadow and the ocean just over the trees, the sound of the surf and *instant coffee!* Thus the morning after Halloween, with my nephew the shark (who took this opportunity to remind her, in fact, that last year he saved his Halloween candy *all the way till Easter, Mommy*) and my niece, the Little Mermaid, orbiting around her like a fine dream. My sister was making this coffee with the automatic grinder and the automatic drip device, and the dishes were piled in the sink behind her, and the wall calendar was staring her in the face, with its hundred urgent appointments, e.g., *jury duty* (the following Monday) and *R & A to pediatrician;* the kids whirled around the kitchen, demanding to know who got the last of the Lucky Charms, who had to settle for the Kix. My sister's eyes barely open.

Now this portrait of her cat, Pointdexter, twelve years old—he slept on my face when I stayed at her place in 1984—Pointdexter with the brain tumor, Pointdexter with the Phenobarbital habit. That morning—All Saints' Day—he stood entirely motionless before his empty dish. His need was clear. His dignity was immense. Well, except for the seizures. Pointdexter had these seizures. He was possessed. He was a demon. He would bounce off the walls, he would get up *a head of steam*, mouth frothing, and run straight at the wall, smack into it, shake off the ghosts and start again. His screeches were unearthly. Phenobarbital was prescribed. My sister medicated him preemptively, before any other chore, before diplomatic initiatives on matters of cereal allocation. *Hold on, you guys, I'll be with you in a second.* Drugging the cat, slipping him the Mickey Finn in the Science Diet, feeding the kids, then getting out the door, pecking her boyfriend on the cheek (he was stumbling sleepily down the stairs).

She printed snapshots. At this photo lab. She'd sold cameras (mnemonic devices) for years, and then she'd been kicked upstairs to the lab. Once she sold a camera to Pete Townshend, the musician. She told him—in her way both casual and rebellious—that she didn't really like The Who. Later, from her job at the lab, she used to bring home *other people's pictures,* e.g., an envelope of photographs of the Pope. Had she been out to Giants Stadium to use her telephoto lens to photograph John Paul II? No, she'd just printed up an extra batch of, say, Agnes Venditi's or Joey Mueller's photos. *Caveat emptor.* Who knew what else she'd swiped? Those Jerry Garcia pix from the show right before he died? Garcia's eyes squeezed tightly shut, as he sang in the heartbroken, exhausted voice of his? Or: somebody's trip to the Caribbean or to the Liberty Bell in Philly? Or: her neighbor's private documentations of love? Who knew? She'd get on the phone at work and gab, call up her friends, call up my family, printing pictures while gabbing, sheet after sheet of negatives, of memories. Oh, and circa Halloween, she was working in the lab with some new, exotic chemicals. She had a wicked headache.

My sister didn't pay much attention to the church calendar. Too busy. Too busy to concetrate on theologies, too busy to go to the doctor, too busy to deal with her finances, her credit-card debt, etc. Too busy. (And maybe afraid, too.) She was unclear on this day set aside for God's awesome tabernacle, unclear on the feast for departed faithful, didn't know about the church of the Middle Ages, didn't know about the particulars of the Druidic ritual of Halloween—it was a Hallmark thing, a marketing event—or how All Saints' Day emerged as an alternative to Halloween. She was not much preoccupied with, nor attendant to articulations of loss nor interested in how this feast in the church calendar was hewn into two separate holy days, one for the saints, *that great cloud of witnesses,* one for the dearly departed, the regular old believers. She didn't know of any attachments that bound together these constituencies, didn't know, e.g., that God would *wipe away all tears from our eyes and there would be no more death,* according to the evening's reading from the book of Revelation. All this academic stuff was lost on her, though she sang in the church choir, and though on All Saints' Day, a guy from the church choir happened to come into the camera store, just to say hi, a sort of an angel (let's say), and she said, *Hey, Bob, you know, I never asked you what you do.*

To which Bob replied, *I'm a designer.*

My sister: *What do you design?*

Bob: *Steel wool.*

She believed him.

She was really small. She barely held down her clothes. Five feet tall. Tiny hands and feet. Here's a photo from my brother's wedding (two weeks before Halloween); we were dancing on the dance floor, she and I. She liked *to pogo* sometimes. It was the dance we preferred when dancing together. We created mayhem on the dance floor. Scared peo-

ple off. We were demons for dance, for noise and excitement. So at my
brothers's wedding reception I hoisted her up onto my shoulder, and
she was so light, just as I remembered from years before, twenty years
of dances, still tiny, and I wanted to crowd-surf her across the reception, pass her across upraised hands, I wanted to impose her on older
couples, gentlemen in their cummerbunds, old guys with tennis elbow
or arthritis, with red faces and gin-blossoms; they would smile, passing
my sister hither, to the microphone, where the wedding band was playing, where she would suddenly burst into song, into some sort of rec-
onciliatory song, backed by the wedding band, and there would be stills
of this moment, flash bulbs popping, a spotlight on her face, a tiny bit
of reverb on her microphone, she would smile and concentrate and
sing. Unfortunately, the situation around us, on the dance floor, was
more complicated than this. Her boyfriend was about to have back surgery. He wasn't going to do any heavy lifting. And my nephew was too
little to hold her up. And my brother was preoccupied with his duties
as groom. So instead I twirled her once and put her down. We were
laughing, out of breath.

On All Saints' Day she had lunch with Bob the angelic designer of steel
wool (maybe he had a crush on her) or with the younger guys from
the lab (because she was a middle-aged free spirit), and then she
printed more photos of Columbus Day parades across Jersey, or photos
of other people's kids dressed as Pocahontas or as the Lion King, and
then at 5:30 she started home, a commute of forty-five minutes, Mor-
ristown to Hackettstown, on two-laners. She knew every turn. Here's
the local news photo that never was: my sister slumped over the wheel
of her Plymouth Saturn after having run smack into a local deer. All
along those roads the deer were upended, disemboweled, set upon by
crows and hawks, and my sister on the way back from work, or on the
way home from a bar, must have grazed an entire herd of them at one
time or another, missed them narrowly, frozen in the headlights of her
car, on the shoulders of the meandering back roads, pulverized.

Her boy lives on air. Disdains food. My niece, meanwhile, will eat
only candy. By dinnertime, they had probably made a dent in the orange plastic bucket with the Three Musketeers, the Cadbury's, Hot
Tamales, Kit Kats, Jujyfruits, Baby Ruths, Bubble Yum—at least my

niece had. They had insisted on bringing a sampling of this booty to school and from there to their afterschool play group. Neither of them wanted to eat anything; they complained about the whole idea of supper, and thus my sister offered, instead, to take them to the *McDonaldLand play area* on the main drag in Hackettstown, where she would buy them a Happy Meal, or equivalent, a hamburger topped with *American processed cheese food,* and, as an afterthought, she would insist on their each trying a little bit of a salad from the brand new McDonald's salad bar. She had to make a deal to get the kids to accept the salad. She suggested six mouthfuls of lettuce each and drew a hard line there, but then she allowed herself to be talked down to two mouthfuls each. They ate indoors at first, the three of them, and then went out to the playground, where there were slides and jungle gyms in the reds and yellows of Ray Kroc's empire. My sister made the usual conversation, *How did the other kids make out on Halloween? What happened at school?* and she thought of her boyfriend, fresh from spinal surgery, who had limped downstairs in the morning to give her a kiss, and then she thought about *bills, bills, bills,* as she caught my niece at the foot of a slide. It was time to go sing. Home by nine.

My sister as she played the guitar in the late sixties with her hair in braids; she played it before anyone else in my family, wandering around the chords, "House of the Rising Sun" or "Blackbird," on classical guitar, sticking to the open chords of guitar tablature. It never occurred to me to wonder about which instruments were used on those AM songs of the period (the Beatles with their sitars and cornets, Brian Wilson with his theremin), not until my sister started to play the guitar. (All of us sang—we used to sing and dance in the living room when my parents were married, especially to *Abbey Road* and *Bridge over Troubled Water.*) And when she got divorced she started hanging around this bar where they had live music, this Jersey bar, and then she started hanging around at a local record label, an indy operation, and then she started *managing a band* (on top of everything else), and then she started to sing again. She joined the choir at St. James Church of Hackettstown and she started to sing, and after singing she started to pray—prayer and song being, I guess, styles of the same beseechment.

*   *   *

I don't know what songs they rehearsed at choir rehearsal, but Bob was there, as were others, Donna, Frank, Eileen and Tim (I'm making the names up), and I know that the choir was warm and friendly, though perhaps a little bit out of tune. It was one of those Charles Ives small-town choruses that slips in and out of pitch, that misses exits and entrances. But they had a good time rehearsing, with the kids monkeying around in the pews, the kids climbing sacrilegiously over that furniture, dashing up the aisle to the altar and back, as somebody kept half an eye on them (five of the whelps in all) and after the last notes ricocheted around the choir loft, my sister offered her summation of the proceedings, *Totally cool! Totally cool!*, and now the intolerable part of this story begins—with joy and excitement and a church interior. My sister and her kids drove from St. James to her house, her condo, this picturesque drive home, Hackettstown as if lifted from picture postcards of autumn, the park with its streams and ponds and lighted walkways, leaves in the streetlamps, in the headlights, leaves three or four days past their peak, the sound of leaves in the breeze, the construction crane by her place (they were digging up the road), the crane swaying above a fork in the road, a left turn after the fast-food depots, and then into her parking spot in front of the condo. The porch by the front door with the Halloween pumpkins: a cat's face complete with whiskers, a clown, a jack-o'-lantern. My sister closed the front door of her house behind her. Bolted it. Her daughter reminded her to light the pumpkins. Just inside the front door, Pointdexter, on the top step, waiting.

Her keys on the kitchen table. Her coat in the closet. She sent the kids upstairs to get into their pajamas. She called up to her boyfriend, who was in bed reading a textbook, *What are you doing in bed, you total slug!* and then, after checking the messages on the answering machine, looking at the mail, she trudged up to my niece's room to kiss her good night. Endearments passed between them. My sister loved her kids, above all, and in spite of all the work and the hardships, in spite of my niece's reputation as a firecracker, in spite of my nephew's sometimes diabolical smarts. She loved them. There were endearments, therefore, lengthy and repetitive, as there would have been with my nephew, too. And my sister kissed her daughter multiply, because my niece is a little impish redhead, and its hard *not* to kiss her. *Look, it's late, so I can't read to you tonight, okay?* My niece protested temporarily, and then my sister arranged the stuffed animals around her daughter (for the sake of arranging), and plumped a feather pillow, and switched off the bedside lamp on the bedside table, and she made sure the night light underneath the table (a plug-in shaped like a ghost) was illumined, and then on the way out the door she stopped for a second. And looked back. The tableau of domesticity was what she last contemplated. Or maybe she was composing endearments for my nephew. Or maybe she wasn't looking back at my niece at all. Maybe she was lost in this next tempest.

Out of nowhere. All of a sudden. All at once. In an instant. Without warning. In no time. Helter-skelter. *In the twinkling of an eye.* Figurative language isn't up to the task. My sister's legs gave out, and she fell over toward my niece's desk, by the door, dislodging a pile of toys and dolls (a Barbie in evening wear, a poseable Tinkerbell doll), colliding with the desk, sweeping its contents off with her, toppling onto the floor, falling heavily, her head by the door. My niece, startled, rose up from under covers.

More photos: my sister, my brother and I, *back in our single digits,* dressed in matching, or nearly matching outfits (there was a naval flavor to our look), playing with my aunt's basset hound—my sister grinning mischievously; or: my sister, my father, my brother and I, in my dad's Karmann-Ghia, just before she totaled it on the straightaway on Fishers Island (she skidded, she said, *on antifreeze or something slippery)*; or: my sister, with her newborn daughter in her lap, sitting on the floor of her living room—mother and daughter with the same bemused impatience.

My sister started to seize.

The report of her fall was, of course, loud enough to stir her boyfriend from the next room. He was out of bed fast. (Desite physical pain associated with his recent surgery.) I imagine there was a second in which other possibilities occurred to him—hoax, argument, accident, anything—but quickly the worst of these seemed most likely. You know these things somewhere. You know immediately the content of all middle-of-the-night telephone calls. He was out of bed. And my niece called out to her brother, to my nephew, next door. She called my nephew's name, plaintively, like it was a question.

My sister's hands balled up. Her heels drumming on the carpeting. Her muscles all like nautical lines, pulling tight against cleats. Her jaw clenched. Her heart rattling desperately. Fibrillating. If it was a conventional seizure, she was unconscious for this part—maybe even unconscious throughout—because of reduced blood flow to the brain, because of the fibrillation, because of her heart condition; which is to say that my sister's *mitral valve prolapse*—technical feature of her *broken heart*—was here engendering an arrhythmia, and now, if not already, she began to hemorrhage internally. Her son stood in the doorway, in his pajamas, shifting from one foot to the other (there was a draft in the hall). Her daughter knelt at the foot of the bed, staring, and my sister's boyfriend watched, as my poor sister shook, and he held her head, and then changed his mind and bolted for the phone.

After the seizure, she went slack. (Meredith's heart stopped. And her breathing. She was still.) For a second, she was alone in the room, with her children, silent. After he dialed 911, Jimmy appeared again, to try to restart her breathing. Here's how: he pressed his lips against hers. He didn't think to say, *Come on, breathe dammit,* or to make similar imprecations, although he did manage to shout at the kids, *Get the hell out of here, please! Go downstairs!* (It was advice they followed only for a minute.) At last, my sister took a breath. Took a deep breath, a sigh, and there were two more of these. Deep resigned sighs. Five or ten seconds between each. For a few moments more, instants, she looked at Jimmy, as he pounded on her chest with his fists, thoughtless about anything but results, stopping occasionally to press his ear between her breasts. Her eyes were sad and frightened, even in the company of the people she most loved. So it seemed. More likely she was unconscious. The kids sat cross-legged on the floor in the hall, by the top of the stairs, watching. Lots of stuff was left to be accomplished in these last seconds, even if it wasn't anything unusual, people and relationships and small kindnesses, the best way to fry pumpkin seeds, what to pack for Thanksgiving, whether to make turnips or not, snapshots to be culled and arranged, photos to be taken—these possibilities spun out of my sister's grasp, torrential futures, my beloved sister, solitary with pictures taken and untaken, gone.

EMS technicians arrived and carried her body down to the living room where they tried to start her pulse with expensive engines and devices. Her body jumped while they shocked her—she was a revenant in some corridor of simultaneities—but her heart wouldn't start. Then they put her body on the stretcher. To carry her away. Now the moment arrives when they bear her out the front door of her house and she leaves it to us, leaves to us the house and her things and her friends and her memories and the involuntary assemblage of these into language. Grief. The sound of the ambulance. The road is mostly clear on the way to the hospital; my sister's route is clear.

I should fictionalize it more, I should conceal myself. I should consider the responsibilities of characterization, I should conflate her two children into one, or reverse their genders, or otherwise alter them, I should make her boyfriend a husband, I should explicate all the tributaries of my extended family (its remarriages, its internecine politics), I should novelize the whole thing, I should make it multigenerational, I should work in my forefathers (stonemasons and newsapermen), I should let artifice create an elegant surface, I should make the events orderly, I should wait and write about it later, I should wait until I'm not angry, I shouldn't clutter a narrative with fragments, with mere recollections of good times, or with regrets, I should make Meredith's death shapely and persuasive, not blunt and disjunctive, I shouldn't have to think the unthinkable, I shouldn't have to suffer, I should address her here directly (these are the ways I miss you), I should write only of affection, I should make our travels in this earthly landscape safe and secure, I should have a better ending, I shouldn't say her life was short and often sad, I shouldn't say she had her demons, as I do too.

VARIATIONS ON GRIEF

Four years ago my oldest friend died, presenting me with an occasion not to be sad, not to cry, not to tell people and have them not know how to respond. Four years ago I decided to create an ironic occurrence rather than a tragedy, a cautionary tale rather than the wretched injustice it really was. This is a neat trick, this business of utter detachment from everything less than great that goes on, this position of being perched on a cartoon drawing of a crescent moon looking down at all the lonely people, all the stupid ones with their souls so foolishly close to the linings of their coats.

What my friend did was catch a virus from the air. This is true. This is, in fact, the only aspect of the event that remains unequivocal. I now suspect it was hantavirus, the strain that is passed along from even the remotest contact with rodents, but there was never any concrete evidence of this. Like a tuft of dandelion seed, this virus wafted into Brian Peterson's body—the way odors do—as he walked down the street or sat by a window or perhaps even slept in the bed he'd purchased from Jensen Lewis, the bed with the Ralph Lauren sheets for which he'd fastidiously shopped at Bloomingdale's—"fabric for living." Except that he died. All but dropped dead. Unlike an encounter with a dandelion seed, contact with such a virus is a one-in-eight-million chance. Four to six people each year die of this. One stands in greater risk of being abducted by a celebrated criminal, or of being visited by the Publisher's Clearing House Prize Patrol, or of standing on the precise acre of land where a jetliner falls after the failure of a hydraulics system. This is the sort of chance that upon impact transcends itself and becomes something closer to fate.

Brian is someone who accomplished nothing in his life other than his death. This is an ugly admission, a brutal interpretation of facts I have not been able to process any other way. He died at twenty-two. Very few people came to his funeral. There were only a handful of friends to call, vague acquaintances who had faded into the murk of adulthood, who had disappeared down roads of maturity that always appeared to Brian as hazy and not worth the trip. His life had been a string of failures, an unremarkable education in suburban public schools, an abandoned college career, a less than half-witted attempt to become a writer. He was an only child, spoiled by parents who had no friends and furnished him with an expensive car and expensive clothes that he drove and wore no particular place. His audience was himself, a reflexive relationship that resulted in unbearably empty spaces for both parties. This was a life bereft of even tragedy, until he finally fixed that. He let death come to him, although that, of course, is a matter of interpretation, as is every component of the existence and lack of existence of Brian Peterson.

I liked Brian because he liked me, because he laughed at my jokes, let me drive his car and complimented my appearance even when I'd done something atrocious to my hair. I liked him because he didn't hold me in contempt for refusing to reciprocate the romantic aspects of his affection for me. He let me talk about other men. He let me watch whatever I wanted on his TV, even if it was National Geographic specials about the spotted leopard of Ghana. I liked Brian because he had nothing to do with the passage of time. He was immune to maturity, resistant to forward motion. He existed the way childhood homes are supposed to and never do, as a foundation that never shifts, a household that never gets new wallpaper or turns your bedroom into a study or is sold in exchange for a condo in Florida.

When he left this world, he left me and very few others, and if those Christian alternatives to life really exist, then he must know by now that we will never be reunited. If those opposable H's are true, then he is in Heaven for never committing any crime and I'll find myself in Hell one day for the spin that I have put on his death. My spin is this:

I believe that he couldn't do anything other than die. None of us who grew up with him could imagine an alternative. And the fact that he didn't officially kill himself was enough to make anyone believe in the supernatural, or at least some kind of devilish warden hovering over our lives, whispering in our waxy ears, "Do something, or die."

Some specifics: Over New Year's weekend of 1993, Brian came down with the flu. He called in some antibiotics and took a few. Then he left the cigarettes on the kitchen table, lay down in bed, and never got up. Also on the table was the December 22 edition of the *New York Post*, the January issue of *Esquire*, and a copy of *TV Guide* already cracked at the spine. He was a person who planned his television watching as if the programs were activities written in a Filofax, as if they were the contents of his life, which they, in fact, were. They were standing appointments, not even penciled in.

On January 4, Brian's mother called me. I was eating a bagel. I answered on the third ring; somehow I remember this. She told me he was in the hospital, that he had lain in bed in his apartment for six days until she and his father had come in from New Jersey to see what was wrong. She said something about shallow breathing. There were some words to the effect of calling a private ambulance service, of Brian being too weak to move from his bedroom to the elevator, then the intensive care unit, some diagnosis of atypical pneumonia, some negative HIV test, some reversal of the pneumonia diagnosis, some rapid deterioration of lung tissue, doctors "in a quandary," relatives flying up from Florida. Apparently there was a priest involved; things were that bad. Brian's mother spoke in simple, even words. I debated in my mind whether I should call her Mrs. Peterson or Jan, her first name. If I called her Mrs. Peterson, as I probably had in the past, would that mean that things were normal, that I was acting "normal" about it? She told me not to come to the hospital, that Brian didn't want people to see him as he looked very bad. I wrote a card and sent it by messenger from my office the next day. I had one of those jobs that allowed for such things. I worked at a magazine about beauty. I had an office and a computer and a phone with many lines. I had swank health insurance, a gym membership, all the things Brian never got around to acquiring because he never got off the frozen plateau I'd long considered to be nothing more than his pathetic ass.

This is about death. Although for Brian, death seemed to be there from the beginning. It seemed to have settled, seedlike, into his pores from the time he was small. For Brian, there was something about life that he just couldn't do. And what was amazing was the unusual way in which he chose not to do it. Nothing about him was morbid. His world was clean and high in quality. He took hour-long showers. He wore Armani jackets. He drove his very expensive car to New Orleans for the hell of it. He dropped out of two colleges because he wasn't enjoying them. He refused to get a job because he didn't want one. His parents paid his rent on a huge apartment in SoHo, which he decorated with the obvious accessories of one who sees life through fashion magazines and Williams-Sonoma catalogs. On the walls he had the Ansel Adams photograph, the Van Gogh print. Brian was the owner of six separate remote controls. There was the television, the VCR, the cassette player, the compact disc player, the other cassette player, the cable box. As with his magazines, he often spread the remote controls out into a fanlike shape on the chrome coffee table. He dusted and vacuumed every day. He talked about his life as being "very good."

Brian was a firm believer in not spending time doing anything that wasn't enjoyable. The result is that he did very little; there was never much to enjoy. I say this as a person who knew him from the beginning of adolescence to the end of it, a time when pleasure comes in tiny spurts, when happiness presents itself in bursts at the end of long, painful confusion. He had absolutely no concept of work, of the notion of reward following sacrifice, of dark preceding dawn and all of that. It seems unlikely that he really ever knew how to study, that he understood what it meant to make a phone call in order to find a job or make a professional connection or even arrange for anything other than Chinese food delivery or a haircut, the latter of which he obtained at Bergdorf Goodman for eighty-five dollars. I have never in my life witnessed a person like Brian, a person who never witnessed life. I have never in my life allowed a person to cater to my whims the way he did, believing, as he did, that I had a life, albeit a cheap and filthy life, full of low-paying jobs, too much homework, and a college dorm room that smelled, as he declared the one time he visited, "like urine." Maybe this is what I liked about him, that he could easily turn me into a working-class heroine, that even in my saddest moments of friendlessness and directionlessness, I had ten times the life that he had. And I never even had to feel guilty; he still thought his life was great, an empty space of leisure and blank pleasure that I too could obtain if I had fewer of what he termed "hang-ups."

This is about death and it is about blame. I blame Brian's parents for everything. The thing I say to no one is that they killed him. By paying his rent, by not making him study trigonometry or stay in college, by not saying no to the car or the apartment or the gas money for solitary trips to nowhere or the racks and racks of Paul Stuart shirts, Howard and Jan Peterson caused the death of their son.

The moment I declared this in my mind is the moment I became despicable. The emotions that surround my experience of Brian's death are by far the ugliest and most unforgiving sentiments I have bestowed on any event of my life. I chose, perhaps for my own sanity, more likely because I was too afraid to choose anything else, to feel as if his death at twenty-two had been imminent from the day he was born. Because Brian died of no defined cause, because the diagnosis was inconclusive, because his parents allowed no autopsy, because he simply *died,* I chose to believe it happened on purpose. I chose to feel as if death for him was an achievement, a blessing, a trophy honoring all that he never bothered to complete. I chose to take his death as a cautionary tale, a message that if one did not *do* one would die. So I did quite a bit. I worked long hours. I swam at six in the morning. I told myself that I was going places, that I was a "comer." Brian, of course, was a "goner." Like the unearned Armani jackets, death became him. The turns of phrase went on and on.

Brian's death took less than three weeks to complete. He was in the hospital for seventeen days. The day he went in was the day most of our mutual friends from childhood had flown back from Christmas vacation to the homes that were constituting the early part of their adulthoods. This meant California, Ohio, Massachusetts. I lived directly across the park from Mount Sinai Hospital where Brian lay bloated from virus-fighting steroids and motionless from paralytic drugs. Any movement, the doctors said, would have stressed his lungs. When he lost consciousness, his parents asked me to start coming over; they believed he'd hear my voice and "wake up." I took the bus to the hospital every three nights. This was what I had promised myself: that I would go on Sundays, Tuesdays, and Thursdays, that even though his father called me twice a day to give me a "report"—"they still don't know," "things are better," "no they're worse," "the numbers on the machine are up today," "I was thinking about that time on Nantucket, did Brian ever mention it?"—I would not wreck my life by living, as they did, in the visitors lounge of the Intensive Care Unit on the fourth floor of the Guggenheim Pavilion.

This is also about lying.

The Peterson family unit was a tiny thing—mom, dad, kid There were no other siblings, only a handful of relatives, no neighbors, no friends. I believe Howard Peterson received a visit at the hospital from his boss. After a few trips to the fourth-floor lounge, after a few times of seeing these parents who couldn't speak, who couldn't bathe, who had lost all sense of time, after a few times of seeing the faces of the nurses and medical students and even the relatives of patients who had been merely shot in the cranium or shattered on motorcycles, I realized that the only way to handle the situation was to tell lies. Though it was plain that death was something already occurring, that this hospital stay was no longer about healing but about the slow submergence of a doomed ocean liner, the game to play seemed to be a game of denial. Jan and Howard Peterson were interested in everything that was not reality. They were interested in all that their son was not. They wanted to know about his friends and what movies he liked and, as they put it, "his art." They wanted to know who had left the pack of Lucky Strikes on his kitchen table and should that person be called regarding "the situation."

I told them yes, and yes, and yes. I scrounged for morsels of truth and expanded them into benign, purposeful lies. I told them Brian liked Fellini—it was true, I believed, that he had once rented *8½* from the video store. I told them he was devoted to his writing, that he planned to arrive at a masterpiece one day and buy them a house in Nantucket. To their delight, I spoke about him in the present tense. I pontificated about all that I planned to do with him when he, as they kept putting it, "got out." I surmised that Brian would someday write a lovely prose poem about his stay in the hospital. They ate this up: "More, more" they said without speaking, though Howard spoke a lot, "needed to keep talking," he said, whereas his wife lay on the plastic couch in the lounge and looked at the ceiling.

I came to know Howard Peterson better than I'd ever known a friend's parent. Though I hated him for the delusional, sugar-coated approach he had taken to parenting, obsessed as I was at the time with what I defined as *reality*, with the cold, hard truths of the corporate working world, and rent paying, and late-night subway rides taken because a cab would cost too much, I wasn't outwardly cruel enough to express any inkling of opinion. I hated him for denying his son the postmodern rights of passage, for never arguing with Brian, for never hesitating to write the checks, for perpetually neglecting to crack the whip. Even now, it is a mystery to me who Jan and Howard Peterson are. For twenty years they lived in a small and badly decorated house in New Jersey. They drove a 1983 Oldsmobile Cutlass. Howard worked as a bond trader. Jan did nothing. They became rich in the 1980s and spent it all on Brian, invested it all in the enterprise that seemed an experiment in passivity, as if lack of movement was the ultimate freedom, as if people who say "I'm going to win the lottery and spend the rest of my life doing nothing" really know what they're talking about.

But my relationship to Howard during these days in the visitors lounge presented me with an interesting set of rules, a subtle opportunity for mind manipulation. Since Jan wouldn't speak and talking to Howard terrified me in that he broke down in tears after just a few sentences, my decision to "think positively" about the situation, to be optimistic and cheerful and phrase things in precisely the opposite way than I normally do, served the function of putting myself at a remove from the whole thing. As actors say, I made a choice. I made a decision to cross to upstage left, to tell them that Brian was working on a screenplay, to refrain from getting upset because, as I said, "there's nothing to be upset about because he's going to pull through." My best line was this: "Brian will not die because people our age can't conceive of death in relation to ourselves. It's not in his vocabulary; therefore it's impossible."

I was for this sort of language that Howard called me one night to come visit him in his hotel room. He and Jan were staying a few blocks from the hospital at a place called the Hotel Wales. Howard said he wanted to talk about Brian. He said he "wanted to gain a greater insight" into his son. I was sitting in my room drinking wine from a plastic tumbler when he called. My bedroom window was open and flecks of snow were floating in. A news report emitted from the clock radio, something about George Bush, who was technically still in office, although the inauguration was days away. I had been engrossed in the election, smitten by James Carville, newly invigorated by politics, the campaign buses and falling-down balloons of it all. Brian had taken little interest, though he'd appeared bemused by my chattering.

So this is what it was when Howard called, the wine in the tumbler, me still in my work clothes. I took a cab to the hotel, readied myself for more lies, for more of the acting I hadn't done since a high school performance of *The Man Who Came to Dinner*, a performance for which Brian had brought me flowers. I was terrified to meet Howard the way I had feared going on stage, the dread of the audience mixing with a longing for the whole thing to end in triumph, for some crowd to cheer, for a late-night cast party followed by peaceful sleeping in my child-hood bed.

This was a luxurious hotel: green and gold wallpaper, wood mold-ings polished until they were mirrorlike. When Howard opened the door he was wearing the same sweater he'd worn the past four times I'd seen him, only now there was a food stain on it. His hair stuck out on either side like a clown's. He wanted to hear the line again, the line about death not being in Brian's vocabulary. He wanted it repeated over and over, like a child hearing a bedtime story. I was afraid that if I flubbed the word order he'd correct me, that if I slipped into past tense he'd ask why. He said I was his favorite person to talk to these days, that the doctors were "paid to be pessimistic," that relatives were evasive, that his wife had given up and was simply praying.

The room was not a room but a suite—living room, bedroom, kitchen. Howard made himself a glass of water, took some pills out of his pocket and swallowed them. He asked what books Brian read, what programs he watched on television. I said Dostoyevsky, Doctorow, and *Seinfeld*. I said *The Picture of Dorian Gray*; that one, I believed, was true. I said that Brian was a lover of the good life, that unlike the rest of us, he lived for the day, that he'd quit school because he realized it wasn't right for him. I and the rest of Brian's friends, I explained, were just robots for doing our homework, for not trying to beat the system. Brian was a rebel. He was a lover, a fighter, and a hero all in one. He would never die. There was no way it could happen.

This went on for three hours, until Howard went into the bedroom, lay down, and fell asleep. I waited ten minutes and slunk out. He'd left cab money for me on the table, which I took, like a whore. This was four days before the end.

* * *

Brian died around six-thirty in the morning, around the time when I usually returned from my swim at the health club, my thirty laps, my participation in the society in which Brian refused to take part. I arrived home, saw the light blinking on my answering machine, and knew. For a few minutes I avoided replaying the tape because there seemed no reason. Outside it was still dark, still dead, cold, January. My chlorinated hair was frozen on my scalp because I never wore a hat to walk the four blocks from the club. Howard's voice was steady on the machine: "Are you there? Are you screening your calls? . . . Brian didn't make it." He began to say something else but his voice cracked and he hung up. All I could think was that I wouldn't have to go to the hospital anymore. All I could wonder was whether I should go to work. I had no inclination to cry, although I believe I tried, conjuring up sad stories, again like the high schol actress to which this event had partially restored me. I tried to do something appropriate. I made coffee. I took a shower. I turned on the television and watched the news. It was inauguration day. Bush's out, Clinton's in. The two families passed each other on the White House steps like baseball teams shaking hands after a game. Such somber, upright civility.

I had found my metaphor. I had found the moment upon which to seize, the symbol around which to fashion the circumstance of my friend's death. No longer a random occurrence, an inexplicable meeting with a bizarre virus no one else catches, Brian's death became for me a national mandate, an obligatory component of a cultural changing of the guard. Just as I had delighted in the fact that the Clinton campaign's theme song was Fleetwood Mac's "Don't Stop," a message that had prompted me to propel my thoughts vehemently into all that the future would bring—the information superhighway, congressional term limits, corporate subsidized health clubs for hard working, *realistic*, people like me—I rationalized that Brian's refusal to ever think about tomorrow had led to his demise. For the first time since he had become ill three weeks before, I allowed myself to spell the words out: Brian died because he refused to live. He refused to live because he refused to work. It was all out of some Ayn Rand manifesto: One must make profound sacrifices in order to live a life without compromise. Brian had attempted the latter without the former. He had seized the day so intensely that the day finally seized him. More turns of phrase.

I reveled in them. I reclined back and watched my stylistic light show, curled up into my big, derisive comfy chair. In my mind, in the milieu that I had built around this event—the perfunctory hospital visits, the heading for the wine bottle the minute I returned home, the reluctance to tell other friends for fear that it would be awkward—I set up an incident that had more to do with psychology than medicine. Brian was so drugged up, we were told, that he had no idea what was happening. He was a minor player. There was no dying involved, only the dealing with it. There was no body, only Hallmark cards, no last breaths of life but instead cigarettes in the breezeway outside the Guggenheim Pavillion. As far as I was concerned at the time, there would be no grief, only irony.

And the sickest part about the whole thing is that I felt the irony while it was actually going on. There was nothing retrospective about this view, no longing for hindsight as it seemed to have emerged precociously while events were still occurring. The monstrosity that Brian's parents were being asked to wrap their minds around was more, I knew, than I could ever conceive. The singular event of their dying son carried more horror than the worst catastrophes in the combined lives of me and everyone I'd ever known. What could I possibly have compared it to? The breakup of my parents' marriage? Being rejected by Yale? That my milk-fed existence was now being soured by a tragedy that was not my own but someone else's put me in the peculiar position of grieving vicariously, a condition so cynical that the only option was to shut up about it. So I faked it. I threw myself into their needs with a duplicity intense enough to distract me from whatever sadness it did not occur to me to feel for myself.

Gamesmanship is something this is also about. Verbal gamesmanship, *sparring*, though the feeling was more like hitting a tennis ball against a wall.

The words I said to Jan and Howard Peterson after their son was dead were even bigger lies than the ones I'd said when he wasn't. I continued with the present tense. "Brian's probably laughing at us now" and "Brian, though he is sad to leave you, is probably fascinated by whatever he is experiencing now." They loved this, especially Howard, who in the forty-eight hours between inauguration day and the funeral, had become obsessed with the afterlife, "the other side," as he called it. I spoke at the mass, gave a neat little spech because no one else would. I regarded this as an opportunity to do some writing, to "be creative," which was something my job was not allowing. I was a huge hit; people came up to me at the burial and congratulated me on my performance. My parents, though disconcerted at my use of the present tense in my speech, remarked that I was a skilled speaker. For me and the few friends who had returned home for the funeral, seeing our parents was almost worse than seeing Jan and Howard. They wore on their faces the look of having just avoided a fatal car crash. They were like people run off the road, shell-shocked drivers breathing heavily and staring at the steering wheel while the tractor-trailer ambled on ahead. "All I can think is thank God it's them and not us," my mother said to me out loud. I hadn't worn a coat—didn't own a proper one to wear with a dress—and someone else's mother went home between the mass and the burial to fetch me one, which she angrily insisted I wear as we stood by the grave. My father expressed his fear that I would catch Brian's mysterious virus. Like me, he wanted to know the mechanics of the thing, how and where it gained its entry, what Brian had done to contract it, what error in judgment had been made to cause this.

After the burial I returned to my apartment in the city, threw up, and continued on with my life. I came to see grief as something I would simply never have. I attached it to sentiment that dwelled in the hearts of others, tucked neatly underneath a rug I'd never even owned. I became obsessed with movement, with productivity. At the time, this meant doing a good job at work, being the best editorial assistant a slick, insipid beauty magazine ever had. I wrote killer photo captions, answered my phone perkily, filled out invoices until eight at night. I did all the things Brian never did. I didn't mention "the situation" to anyone. My parents called to check on me, thrilled when I didn't mention the event, relieved when I seemed not to have a cold.

After about thee months, Howard called and asked if I wanted to have dinner. He left a message on my machine, leaving Brian's old number as the place to call back. When I did, Brian's voice came on, deep and reticent. "I'm not available, please leave a message." I hated Howard all over again. He picked up when I spoke. He and Jan wanted to have dinner with me "in order to talk about Brian." They wanted me to meet them at Brian's apartment where they were staying. They wanted only to eat in restaurants where Brian had eaten, so could I recommend one?

Brian had only eaten in stylish places with ceiling fans and aspiring models at the bar. I had always hated this about him. I had always been embarrassed to go to establishments I had no business patronizing, establishments Brian had even less business eating at, although he always paid for both of us and ordered many drinks and an expensive entree and usually dessert. Once, while I was in college, he'd taken me to a place he'd read about in a magazine, a small club that had recently opened in SoHo. There we saw a girl from my school, a very rich girl with a famous mother, both of whom had been profiled in *Vanity Fair* a year earlier. This girl, who had never spoken to me on campus, came to our table and kissed me on the cheek. Brian was ecstatic. I was furious. I felt I was dressed terribly, and even if I had been dressed well I would have been merely acting as a poseur, which was worse than merely existing in a state of pathetic delusion, which is what Brian did adamantly, with stubborn, insistent braggadocio. Still, this encounter held him for several weeks. He mentioned it repeatedly, talking about "Meghan's friend Countess X" to whichever of our other friends managed to drag themselves back into town to see him.

Restricting my lies to the big ones—how bad would it have been, after all, to suggest to Brian's parents that we eat at Pizzera Uno because Brian had loved the single deep dish?—I told Howard to make a reservation at Odeon because Brian loved it and often used it as a location in his writing, which was true. When I arrived at Brian's apartment, the Lucky Strikes were still on the kitchen table along with the December 22 edition of the *New York Post,* the January issues of *Esquire* and the copy of *TV Guide* cracked at the spine. "We haven't touched these," said Howard. He was wearing corduroy pants and a polyester sweater. Jan wore wide wales and an L. L. Bean blouse. We went to Odeon. I scanned the room for fear of Countess X. Howard said he only wanted to order dishes that Brian had ordered. I had no recollection but told him the salmon.

It was during this meal that Jan and Howard first began to demonstrate their expertise in "the other side." Howard had read several books on the subject and had brought with him a list of the titles so that I, too, could learn more about "Brian's new life." Howard had had dreams, he explained, where Brian spoke to him and elaborated on the fun he was having. They had been to a psychic on Long Island who claimed to see Brian amid a field of roses and flanked by two other people, an older man—"probably his grandfather," said Jan—and a pretty, young girl whose name began with M. "I thought for a moment that might be you," she said. "But then you're not dead."

Then Jan declared loudly that she was considering killing herself. "I know just how I'd do it," she said. What got to me about this was not that she said it but that she said it so loudly. I looked over at the next table at three impeccably dressed men whose eyes seemed to momentarily shift over to us. It seems bizarre to me now that I didn't ask her how she planned to kill herself for fear that it was an inappropriate question. It seems bizarre that even after this meal, after I turned down their invitation to go to a late movie, after I again took cab fare from them, which I pocketed and instead rode the subway, I met Jan and Howard several more times. This went on for about a year. Howard would call every few months and if I was in a guilty mood, which I almost always was, flagellating myself as I did about every inadequate job performance or overdue phone bill or call I screened for fear it would be them, I said yes. I said yes and continued to lie and say that I had read the afterlife books and that I, too, awaited the day of my death so I could see Brian again and that the world was hardly worth inhabiting when such a vibrant figure was removed from it.

The dynamic was this: The more I saw Jan and Howard, the more evil thoughts I harbored, which caused me guilt, which caused me to dig in my heels and see them again. This was my self-styled redemption, my faux little journey into good samaritanism. If I saw the Petersons on a Saturday, I could be bad for the rest of the week. If I lied to Howard about the salmon, I could call a coworker a bitch behind her back on Monday. What happened was that I began to hate the world. Just as I hated Jan and Howard for being so lax as parents that I believed their son died of inertia, I hated everyone else for existing in a condition that I defined as "fake." Like Holden Caulfield, I became obsessed with "phoniness." I saw everyone as innate liars, as zombified self-deluders who were dangers to themselves as well as the rest of the world. I hated people who walked too slowly down the sidewalk, grocery store clerks who took too long to count the change, days when there was nothing but junk mail. I hated anything that impeded whatever I considered to be progress, whatever I had determined was my ticket to a socialized, productive life. Unlike Brian, I would pursue a career. Unlike him, I would shop at the grocery store efficiently. I would meet friends for lunch and drinks and have people over to my apartment to watch the Oscars. I would walk quickly down the street because I actually had someplace to go. I would do anything necessary to participate in what I considered to be life, which to me meant getting up extremely early and doing things like putting all the apartment's trash into a small plastic bag, which I would throw out on the way to the club to go swimming, after which I would go to work and for lunch go to the gourmet deli on Fourth-sixth Street where I tapped my fingers on the counter if the people in front of me were taking too long to order because *I had somewhere to be,* because I was impressively busy with this thing called life, because I was sternly committed to the pursuit of whatever was the opposite of death.

By the following Christmas, Jan and Howard had stopped calling me. I had expected to hear from them around the anniversary of Brian's death, the one-year mark of the Clinton administration. When they didn't call, I imagined them dead in their poorly decorated house. I imagined empty sleeping pill bottles on the night table or a hose hooked up to the back of the Oldsmobile with Howard's lifeless body five feet away. Since I'd never learned how they planned to kill themselves, it was difficult to put my finger on one particular scenario. Like "the situation" itself, there seemed so many variations on the truth, so many evil interpretations of events upon which to fixate. Through one of the mutual friends, I learned they hadn't killed themselves. Like a normal person, this friend, in town for Christmas, had called Jan and Howard himself and then driven over to the house. Like a good person, he sat in the living room and spoke honestly about this horrible thing that had happened. Unlike me, he saw no reason to lie. Unlike me, he wasn't hung up on some twisted symbolism, on some mean-spirited rationalization employed to keep fear at bay, to keep grief a thing depicted in movies rather than a loss felt in one's own flesh.

Here's another true scene from the movie. It's a flashback, a time I remember with Brian when we were small, playing with other kids. We stood in a circle and called off our teams, the reds versus the blues, something like that. Then we needed an "it," a dreaded tagger who would tap us on the shoulder and freeze us. No one wanted the job, including myself, and I'd watched as Brian just stood there, silent amid the chants, bewildered as the shouting came over him: "Not it!" I yelled. "Not it!" someone else yelled. "Not it!" we all said until there was no one but Brian, a pale and clueless eight-year-old suspended in those moments before realizing he'd lost the game. And so it was him. He was it. We weren't.

Luc Sante

THE UNKNOWN SOLDIER

The last thing I saw was a hallway ceiling, four feet wide, finished along its edges with a plaster molding that looked like a long row of small fish each trying to swallow the one ahead of it. The last thing I saw was a crack of yellow sky between buildings, partly obscured by a line of washing. The last thing I saw was the parapet, and beyond it the trees. The last thing I saw was his badge, but I couldn't tell you the number. The last thing I saw was a full shot glass, slid along by somebody who clapped me on the back. The last thing I saw was the sedan that came barreling straight at me while I thought, It's okay, I'm safely behind the window of the doughnut shop. The last thing I saw was a boot, right foot, with nails protruding from the instep. The last thing I saw was a turd. The last thing I saw was a cobble. The last thing I saw was night.

I lost my balance crossing Broadway and was trampled by a team of brewery horses. I was winching myself up the side of a six-story corner house on a board platform with a load of nails for the cornice when the weak part of the rope hit the pulley sideways and got sheared. I lost my way in snowdrifts half a block from my flat. I drank a bottle of carbolic acid not really knowing whether I meant to or not. I got very cold, coughed, and forgot things. I went out to a yard to try and give birth in secret, but something happened. I met a policeman who mistook me for somebody else. I was drunk on my birthday and I fell off the dock trying to grab a gold piece that looked like it was floating. I was hanged in the courtyard of the Tombs before a cheering crowd and people clogging the rooftops of the buildings all around, but I still say that rascal had it coming to him. I stole a loaf of bread and started eating it as I ran down the street, but there was a wad of raw dough in the middle that got caught in my throat. I was supposed to get up early that morning but I couldn't move. I heard a sort of whistling noise above my head as I was passing by the post office and that's all I know. I was hustling a customer who looked like a real swell but when we got upstairs he pulled out a razor. I owed a lot of rent and got put out and that night curled up in somebody else's doorway and he came home in a bad mood. I was bitten by that black dog that used to hang around and I forgot all about it for six months or so. I ate some oysters I dug up myself. I took a shot at the big guy but the hammer got stuck. I felt very hot and shaky and strange and everybody in the shop was looking at me and I kept trying to tell them that I'd be all right in a minute but I just couldn't get it out.

I never woke up as the fumes snaked into my room. I stood yelling as he stabbed me again and again. I picked up a passenger who braced me in the middle of Broadway and made me turn off. I shot up the bag as soon as I got home but I think it smelled funny when I cooked it. I was asleep in the park when these kids came by. I crawled out the window and felt sick looking down, so I just threw myself out and looked up as I fell. I thought I could get warm by burning some newspaper in a soup pot. I went to pieces very slowly, and was happy when it finally stopped. I thought the train was going way too fast but I kept on reading. I let this guy pick me up at a party and sometime later we went off in his car. I felt real sick but the nurse thought I was kidding. I jumped over to the other fire escape but my foot slipped. I thought I had time to cross the street. I thought the floor would support my weight. I thought nobody could touch me. I never knew what hit me.

They put me in a bag. They nailed me up in a box. They walked me down Mulberry Street followed by altar boys and four priests under a canopy and everybody in the neighborhood singing the Libera Me Domine. They collected me in pieces all through the park. They laid me in state under the rotunda for three days. They engraved my name on the pediment. They drew my collar up to my chin to hide the hole in my neck. They laughed about me over the baked meats and rye whiskey. They didn't know who I was when they fished me out, and still didn't know six months later. They held my body for ransom and collected, but by that time they had burned it. They never found me. They threw me in the cement mixer. They heaped all of us into a trench and stuck a monument on top. They cut me up at the medical school. They weighed down my ankles and tossed me in the drink. They gave speeches claiming I was some kind of tin saint. They hauled me away in the ashman's cart. They put me on a boat and took me to an island. They tried to keep my mother from throwing herself in after me. They bought me my first suit and dressed me up in it. They marched to City Hall holding candles and shouting my name. They forgot all about me and took down my picture.

So give my eyes to the eye bank, give my blood to the blood bank. Make my hair into switches, put my teeth into rattles, sell my heart to the junkman. Give my spleen to the mayor. Hook my lungs to an engine. Stretch my guts down the avenue. Stick my head on a pike, plug my spine to the third rail, throw my liver and lights to the winner. Grind my nails up with sage and camphor and sell it under the counter. Set my hands in the window as a reminder. Take my name from me and make it a verb. Think of me when you run out of money. Remember me when you fall on the sidewalk. Mention me when they ask you what happened. I am everywhere under your feet.

CONTRIBUTORS

Daphne Beal is writing a novel set in South Asia. She earned her M.F.A. from New York University, where she was a *New York Times* Fellow.

Michael Cunningham is the author of *A Home at the End of the World* and *Flesh and Blood,* and is at work on a new novel.

Meghan Daum's essays have appeared in *Self, The New York Times Magazine, The New York Times Book Review,* and other publications.

Lydia Davis is a translator and the author of two collections, *Break It Down* and *Almost No Memory,* and a novel, *The End of the Story.*

Junot Díaz is the author of *Drown.* His stories have appeared in *Story, The New Yorker, The Paris Review,* and elsewhere. He is currently writing a novel.

Jennifer Egan is the author of *The Invisible Circus,* a novel, and *Emerald City,* a collection of stories. Her nonfiction has appeared in *The New York Times Magazine.* She is working on a novel.

Maggie Estep is a poet, performance artist, and musician. She has toured for Lolapalooza and received a fellowship from Yaddo. Her first novel is titled *Diary of an Emotional Idiot,* and she is at work on another novel and a collection of stories, *Soft Maniacs.*

Ken Foster is the recipient of a fellowship from Yaddo and an MFA from Columbia University. He has published fiction in *Bomb* and nonfiction in *Plazm.* He is writing a novel.

Elizabeth Gilbert is the author of *Pilgrims,* a collection of short stories.

Her nonfiction has appeared in *Spin, The New York Times Magazine,* and *GQ.*

Lucy Grealy is the author of *Autobiography of a Face.*

Joanna Greenfield is writing a book about her work in Africa.

Kathryn Harrison is the author of *Thicker Than Water, Exposure, Poison,* and *The Kiss.* She recently completed a new novel.

A. M. Homes is the author of the novels *The End of Alice, In a Country of Mothers,* and *Jack,* and a collection of stories, *The Safety of Objects.*

Randall Kenan is the author of a collection of stories titled *Let the Dead Bury Their Dead,* and a novel, *A Visitation of Spirits.*

Sheila Kohler has published two novels, *The Perfect Place* and *The House on R. Street,* and a collection of stories, *Miracles in America.* "Cracks" is taken from a recently completed novel.

Diane Lefer's short story collection is called *The Circles I Move In.* "A Good German" is taken from her recently completed novel *Hunger.* She lives in Los Angeles.

David Means has published fiction in *Harper's, Bomb,* and his collection, *A Quick Kiss of Redemption.*

Jan Meissner has published in *Story, Fiction, Columbia, Epoch,* and *The Massachusetts Review.* She is currently writing a novel.

Rick Moody's books include *Garden State, The Ice Storm,* and *Purple America*—all novels—as well as *The Ring of Brightest Angels Around Heaven*—stories and a novella. With Darcey Steinke, he edited the anthology *Joyful Noise.*

Tom Paine has published his stories in *The New Yorker, Harper's, Zoetrope Story,* and *Playboy* and his work has been anthologized in *Prize Stories: The O. Henry Awards, The Pushcart Prize XXI* and *XXII.* He teaches creative writing at Middlebury College.

Steven Rinehart has published his short stories in *Harper's, GQ,* and *Story,* among other places.

Luc Sante is the author of *Evidence, Low Life,* and *The Factory of Facts.* He is also the recipient of numerous awards including a Whiting Award and a Grammy.

Elissa Schappell has published fiction and nonfiction in *Vanity Fair, The Paris Review, Witness,* and *Bomb.* A collection of stories is forthcoming from Rob Weisbach Books.

Ben Schrank is a columnist and fiction editor for *Seventeen.* "The Good

Chance Chicken" is excerpted from his novel, *Miracle Man,* to be published by William Morrow.

Helen Schulman is the author of *Not a Free Show, Out of Time,* and most recently *The Revisionist.* She is the editor, with Jill Bialosky, of an anthology titled *Wanting a Child.*

Christine Schutt is the author of *Nightwork.* Her stories have appeared in numerous literary magazines, including *The Quarterly, The Alaska Quarterly,* and *The Mississippi Review* and have been anthologized in *Prize Stories: The O. Henry Awards.*

Matthew Sharpe has published his stories in *Harper's, Zoetrope,* and *Mississippi Mud.* His *Stories from the Tube* will be published by Villard.

Jacqueline Woodson is the author of many award-winning novels for young adults. "Fire" is taken from an adult novel, in progress, titled *Early.*

PERMISSIONS

"Azure." Copyright © 1996 by Daphne Beal. First published in *American Short Fiction*. Reprinted by permission of the author.

"Mister Brother." Copyright © 1998 by Michael Cunningham. All rights reserved. Reprinted by permission of Brandt & Brandt Literary Agents, Inc.

"Variations on Grief." Copyright © 1996 by Meghan Daum. First published in the *Bellingham Review*. Reprinted by permission of International Creative Management, Inc.

"Old Mother and the Grouch." Copyright © 1992 by Lydia Davis. First appeared in the *Partisan Review*. Reprinted by permission of Georges Borchardt, Inc., for the author.

"Ysrael." Copyright © 1996 by Junot Díaz. Reprinted by permission of Riverhead Books, a division of the Putnam Publishing Group, from *Drown* by Junot Díaz.

"XO." Copyright © 1998 by Jennifer Egan. First published in *GQ*. Reprinted by permission of the Virginia Barber Agency.

"The Patient." Copyright © 1998 by Maggie Estep. Reprinted by permission of the author. All rights reserved.

"Indelible." Copyright © 1998 by Ken Foster. Reprinted by permission of the author. All rights reserved.

"Buckle Bunnies." Copyright © 1994 by Elizabeth Gilbert. First published in *Spin* magazine. Reprinted with the permission of the Wylie Agency, Inc.

"Dancing a Sad Thought." Copyright © 1998 by Lucy Grealy. Reprinted by permission of the author. All rights reserved.

"Hyena." Copyright © 1996 by Joanna Greenfield. First published in *The New Yorker*. Reprinted by permission of International Creative Management, Inc.

"Tick." Copyright © 1996 by Kathryn Harrison. First published in *The New Yorker*. Reprinted by permission of International Creative Management, Inc.

"His Confession." Copyright © 1995 by A. M. Homes. First published in *Appendix A*. Reprinted with the permission of the Wylie Agency, Inc.

"Now Why Come That Is?" Copyright © 1997 by Randall Kenan. First read at KGB, February 11, 1996. Reprinted with the permission of the Wylie Agency, Inc.

"Cracks." Copyright © 1998 by Sheila Kohler. First published in the *Paris Review*. Reprinted by permission of the author.

"A Good German." Copyright © 1995 by Diane Lefer. First published in *Columbia: A Journal of Literature and Art*. Reprinted by permission of the author.

"Tahorah." Copyright © 1998 by David R. Means. Reprinted by permission of Georges Borchardt, Inc., for the author.

"Placedo Junction." Copyright © 1995 by Jan Meissner. First published in *Columbia: A Journal of Literature and Art*. Reprinted by permission of the Virginia Barber Agency.

"Demonology." Copyright © 1996 by Rick Moody. First published in *Conjunctions*. Reprinted by permission of the Melanie Jackson Agency.

"Me & Michelangelo." Copyright © 1998 by Tom Paine. Reprinted by permission of the author. All rights reserved.

"Make Me." Copyright © 1995 by Steven Rinehart. First published in *Harper's*. Reprinted by permission of the author.

"The Unknown Soldier." Copyright © 1995 by Luc Sante. Reprinted by permission of the author.

"Novice Bitch." Copyright © 1998 by Elissa Schappell. Reprinted by permission of the author. All rights reserved.

"The Good Chance Chicken." Copyright © 1998 by Ben Schrank. Reprinted by permission of the author. All rights reserved.

"P.S." Copyright © 1997 by Helen Schulman. First published in *GQ*. Reprinted by permission of International Creative Management, Inc.

"Sickish." Copyright © 1998 by Christine Schutt. Reprinted by permission of the author. All rights reserved.

"A Car." Copyright © 1996 by Matthew Sharpe. First published in *Mississippi Mud*. Reprinted by permission of the author.

"Fire." Copyright © 1996 by Jacqueline Woodson. First published in *Story*. Reprinted by permission of the author.